MW00814278

THE
LSATs
DECONSTRUCTED
SERIES

VOLUME 51:
THE DECEMBER 2006 LSAT

POWERSCORE
TEST PREPARATION

Copyright © 2008 by PowerScore Incorporated.

All Rights Reserved. No part of this publication may be reproduced, stored in a retrieval system, or transmitted in any form or by any means electronic, mechanical, photocopying, recording, scanning, or otherwise, without the prior written permission of the Publisher. Parts of this book have been previously published in other PowerScore publications and on the powerscore.com website.

All actual LSAT questions printed within this work are used with the permission of Law School Admission Council, Inc., Box 2000, Newtown, PA 18940, the copyright owner. LSAC does not review or endorse specific test preparation materials or services, and inclusion of licensed LSAT questions within this work does not imply the review or endorsement of Law Services. LSAT is a registered trademark of Law Services.

Law Services and PrepTest are registered trademarks of the Law School Admission Council, Inc.

PowerScore® is a registered trademark. The Logical Reasoning Bible™, The Logic Games Bible™, The Reading Comprehension Bible™, The LSATs Deconstructed™, The Logical Reasoning Primary Objectives™, The Conclusion Identification Method™, The Fact Test™, The Uniqueness Rule of Answer Choices™, The Justify Formula™, The Supporter/Defender Assumption Model™, The Assumption Negation Technique™, The Opposition Construct™, The Logic Ladder™, The Negative Logic Ladder™, The Complete Table of Formal Logic Additive Inferences™, The Elemental Attack™, The Not Law™, The Separation Principle™, The Variance Test™, and The Agree/Disagree Test™ are the exclusive service marked property of PowerScore. Any use of these terms without the express written consent of PowerScore is prohibited.

First Edition published 2008

Published by
PowerScore Publishing, a division of PowerScore Incorporated
37V New Orleans Road
Hilton Head Island, SC 29928

Authors: David M. Killoran
             Steven G. Stein

Published in the United States
Manufactured in the United States
April 2008

ISBN: 978-0-9801782-1-0

Need More Help?
We Offer Live LSAT Courses Nationwide.

Live LSAT Preparation Courses

Our test professionals have designed the PowerScore courses to provide you with the maximum exposure to the concepts that appear on the LSAT, access to the best possible instructors and classroom material, and the best support system to complement your studies. All of our instructors have scored in the 99th percentile on a real LSAT (administered by LSAC), and are LSAT experts. Whether you take our 80-hour Full-Length Course, our 45-hour Virtual Course, or our 16-hour Weekend Course, you will find that we offer the best classes and instruction for your valuable time and money. For more information, please visit www.powerscore.com.

Full-Length LSAT Course————————————————————$1195

This comprehensive course is best if you prefer the energy and motivation of a small group setting, have 8 weeks to prepare, and like a structured study environment.

- 80 hours of class time, including 64 lecture hours and 16 hours of practice tests
- Free LSAT Hotline and Online Student Center
- Over 2,500 pages of materials, including over 20 take-home LSATs

Student Testimonials:

"**PowerScore did an excellent job preparing me for the LSAT**.... I am already recommending the course to many of my friends. Thanks PowerScore and I hope the secret of this company keeps spreading rapidly."
–M. Shah • Cornell University

"**I would recommend this course to anyone who is serious about maximizing their potential on the LSAT**. My instructor and the students in my class made this course fun and helped me to remain focused.... "
–J. Bart • Austin, TX

"I never would have felt as confident on the day of the test if I hadn't taken the PowerScore course.... **Thanks, Powerscore! I couldn't have done it without you!**"
–N. Todman • Baltimore, MD

Weekend LSAT Course————————————————————$350

For some students, time, location, and budget will dictate that they take the Weekend Course. The Weekend course is best if you need a quick jumpstart into your LSAT preparation, need to refine your LSAT techniques and approaches, or don't have much time to prepare.

- 16 hours of live, in-class instruction on one weekend
- Free Email Assistance and Online Student Center
- Over 600 pages of materials, including 8 take-home LSATs
- Repeat the course for free within a year, no strings attached

Student Testimonials:

"... the class showed me how to **attack the LSAT in a way studying on my own never did**. I would recommend this class to anyone!"
–M. Smith • West Texas, A&M University

"**Unbelievable!** That is the only word that describes how informative and productive the weekend course was. The instructor presented the material in a clear, precise manner while also making it interesting and enjoyable...."
–P. Reithmeier, R.N. • Temple University

"**I think that the weekend course is amazing**....The instructor helped break down the questions so that they are so clear to me now. The wrong answers jump off the page and the right ones are easier to find."
–C. Oweis, Atlanta, GA

Prepare for the LSAT from the comfort of your home or office with

PowerScore's Virtual LSAT Course.
Available worldwide!

Our live, online course offers you the structure and group interaction of a classroom course, without any schedule restrictions or travel requirements. And, just like our other courses, you'll have all of the features PowerScore is known for—the best course materials, use of real LSAT questions, 99th percentile instructors, and an unparalleled level of support and customer service. PowerScore's Virtual LSAT course is the perfect solution for people with time constraints, busy schedules, and those who want the benefits of live instruction and support without having to travel to a class location. For more information, please visit www.powerscore.com.

Virtual LSAT Course —————————————————————————— $995

The virtual classroom environment brings the best features of a physical class into the comfort of your home or office. You are able to hear the instructor, see notes and questions on the online whiteboard, ask questions both verbally and by instant messenger, and interact with the instructor and fellow students by using the headset we provide. The course is highly interactive and allows for extensive personal attention.

All virtual classes are archived for later review if needed (which is great if you miss a class), and closed captioning is available. You can attend this course from anywhere in the world and access the course material 24 hours a day, seven days per week.

- 10 live online lessons, each lasting for 3 hours, for a total of 30 hours of live online lessons
- 15 hours of additional instructor-led discussions covering the most advanced concepts, strategies, and techniques necessary for test success - for a total of 45 course hours
- In-depth, written explanation for every homework question and answer choice
- Lessons taught by two of our senior instructors, each of whom has scored in the 99th percentile on a previously administered LSAT
- 4 full-length practice tests plus 10 additional take-home LSATs, each with online scoring and detailed feedback
- Course materials and homework shipped directly to your home or office
- Comprehensive Online Student Center
- Free Two-way headset for use during lessons to communicate with instructor and class members
- Available worldwide

Student Testimonials:

"The course itself is just phenomenal... I am learning so much about the LSAT and the preparation needed to achieve high success on it. Jon is an intelligent, personable guy who really cares for the students and loves the material. The communication between student and instructor is excellent and very prompt. This has been a great investment."

—Robert L.

"This class is the most helpful study tool out there. It was so convenient and practical. I loved the interaction and personal attention. Awesome materials and PLENTY to keep me busy and practicing up to test time!"

—Mariah R.

"The technology as well as the detailed instruction was very intuitive and rewarding. I especially liked the archived classes. It was like having my own transcription service."

—Dan Y.

An Incredible Value!

The total cost of $995 includes 45 hours of total instruction, all of the course materials, and a complimentary headset. You will also have access to the online resources for two test administrations after the course ends!

Also Available...

PowerScore LSAT Logic Games Bible (Revised)

The ultimate guide for attacking the analytical reasoning section of the LSAT. *The LSAT Logic Games Bible* features a detailed methodology for attacking the games section, extensive drills, and 30 real LSAT logic games with detailed analyses.

Available on the PowerScore website for $41.99.
Website: www.powerscore.com/pubs.htm

PowerScore LSAT Logical Reasoning Bible

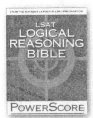

One of the most highly anticipated publications in LSAT history, the *PowerScore LSAT Logical Reasoning Bible™* is a comprehensive how-to manual for solving every type of Logical Reasoning question. Featuring over 100 real Logical Reasoning questions with detailed explanations, the Bible is the ultimate resource for improving your LSAT Logical Reasoning score.

Available on the PowerScore website for $49.99.
Website: www.powerscore.com/pubs.htm

COMING SOON!

PowerScore LSAT Reading Comprehension Bible

The Reading Comprehension Bible provides the complete guide to reading difficult passages, increasing comprehension, understanding argumentation, and effectively attacking different question types. It includes complete explanations of passages and questions drawn from actual LSATs, guides to passage diagramming, and multiple practice drills.

Available soon on the PowerScore website.
Website: www.powerscore.com/pubs.htm

PowerScore Logic Games Ultimate Setups Guide

The Ultimate Setups Guide features setups for every game in each released LSAT PrepTest from 1995 to 2002. Each setup includes a diagram of the rules and the variables, as well an identification of key inferences. A number of questions are explained, and additional game notes are included. *The Ultimate Setups Guide* also includes the setup for every single game in the *10 More Actual, Official LSAT PrepTests*.

Available on the PowerScore website for $29.99.
Website: www.powerscore.com/pubs.htm

PowerScore 2004 LSATs Deconstructed

The *PowerScore 2004 LSATs Deconstructed™* is a comprehensive, question-by-question analysis of the June, October, and December LSATs from 2004. This book will provide you with a detailed explanation for every question and answer choice for the Logical Reasoning, Reading Comprehension, and Analytical Reasoning sections from each of the three released LSATs from 2004 – over 300 questions in all! The concepts presented in the *PowerScore 2004 LSATs Deconstructed* are representative of the techniques covered in PowerScore's live courses and have consistently been proven effective for thousands of our students.

Available on the PowerScore website for $29.99.
Website: www.powerscore.com/pubs.htm

Also Available...

PowerScore Logic Games Bible Flashcards

The Games Bible Flashcards relay and test foundational concepts such as games terminology, game-type recognition, and rule language, as well as advanced conceptual approaches including conditional reasoning, formal logic, and numerical distribution. Mini-challenges allow test takers to develop the skills necessary to create effective diagrams and draw sound logical inferences. Each set includes 140 cards that test the concepts and approaches to logic games taught in the LGB and in PowerScore LSAT courses.

Available on the PowerScore website only for $24.99.
Website: www.powerscore.com/pubs.htm

COMING SOON!

PowerScore Logical Reasoning Bible Flashcards

The Logical Reasoning Bible Flashcards introduce and test concepts taught in our courses and in PowerScore's LSAT Logical Reasoning Bible. The flashcards cover everything from foundational definitions and question type recognition to more advanced Logical Reasoning skills, including causal reasoning, conditional reasoning, and understanding formal logic. The LRB Flashcards can be used as a stand-alone study aid, or as an ideal complement to the renowned Logical Reasoning Bible.

Available on the PowerScore website only for $29.99.
Website: www.powerscore.com/pubs.htm

PowerScore LSAT Private and Telephone Tutoring

Tutoring is ideal for students unable to enroll in one of our preparation courses, or who need assistance with a specific area. Whether you need personalized lesson plans designed for you, or you just need to work on a few concepts, we can create a tutoring experience that will address all of your LSAT difficulties. Since both you and the instructor work off the same materials, describing the correct approach and appropriate diagramming is easy.

Our tutors are the same people that teach our classes, and every tutor has scored in the 99th percentile on a LSAC-administered LSAT. We offer in-person tutoring or telephone tutoring, with multiple price points and package rates. Please visit www.powerscore.com, or call 1-800-545-1750 for more information.

PowerScore Law School Admissions Counseling

While your LSAT score and GPA will undeniably be major factors in admissions, you can separate yourself from the rest of the applicant pool by assembling the most powerful application folder possible. To do this you must have a perfect personal statement, top-notch letters of recommendation, and flawless overall presentation. PowerScore has gathered a team of admissions experts—including former law school admissions board members, top lawyers, and students from top-ten law schools—to address your admissions counseling and personal statement needs. Please visit www.powerscore.com, or call 1-800-545-1750 for more information.

CHAPTER ONE: INTRODUCTION

Introduction

Welcome to *The LSATs Deconstructed Series, Volume 51* by PowerScore. The purpose of this book is to help you better understand the methods and procedures of the test makers by deconstructing every question in three actual Law School Admission Tests (LSATs). We strongly believe that by studying the logic behind each question you will increase your ability to perform well on the LSAT.

The use of real questions while preparing is essential to your success on the LSAT, and no question in this book has been modified from its original form.

How to Use this Book

We strongly suggest that you take the test in this book as a timed practice test. Accordingly, prior to the test we have provided a Timing Notes page that explains how to properly time yourself.

After you complete the test, we suggest that you carefully read the explanation of each problem, including the explanation of the correct answer choice and the explanations of the incorrect answer choices. Closely examine each problem and determine which elements led to the correct answer, and then study the analyses provided in the book and check them against your own work. By doing so you will greatly increase your chances of recognizing the patterns present within the LSAT.

The remainder of this chapter provides a brief overview of the sections of the LSAT, how the LSAT is scored, the uses of the LSAT in law school admissions, and how to approach each section of the test. The next chapter contains the LSAT followed by complete explanations. The final chapter provides a glossary of terms used in this book and a brief overview of the concepts that appear on the LSAT.

If you are looking to further improve your LSAT score, we recommend that you pick up a copy of the renowned *PowerScore LSAT Logic Games Bible* and *PowerScore LSAT Logical Reasoning Bible*. The *Logic Games Bible* contains our system for attacking the Analytical Reasoning section of the LSAT. The *Logical Reasoning Bible* details the PowerScore approach to the Logical Reasoning sections of the LSAT. When the two are combined, they provide a formidable methodology for attacking the test. The *LSAT Bibles* are available through our website at www.powerscore.com and at fine retailers everywhere.

Because access to accurate and up-to-date information is critical, we have devoted a section of our website to *Deconstructed Series* students. This free online resource area offers supplements to the book material, answers questions posed by students, and provides updates as needed. There is also an official book evaluation form that we strongly encourage you to use. The exclusive *Deconstructed Series* online area can be accessed at:

www.powerscore.com/deconseries

If we can assist you in your LSAT preparation in any way, or if you have any questions or comments, please do not hesitate to contact us via email at lsat@powerscore.com. Additional contact information is provided at the end of this book. We look forward to hearing from you!

A Brief Overview of the LSAT

The Law School Admission Test is administered four times a year: in February, June, September/October, and December. This standardized test is required for admission to any American Bar Association-approved law school. According to Law Services, the producers of the test, the LSAT is designed "to measure skills that are considered essential for success in law school: the reading and comprehension of complete texts with accuracy and insight; the organization and management of information and the ability to draw reasonable inferences from it; the ability to reason critically; and the analysis and evaluation of the reasoning and argument of others." The LSAT consists of the following five sections:

- 2 Sections of Logical Reasoning (short arguments, 24-26 total questions)
- 1 Section of Reading Comprehension (3 long reading passages, 2 short comparative reading passages, 26-28 total questions)
- 1 Section of Analytical Reasoning (4 logic games, 22-24 total questions)
- 1 Experimental Section of one of the above three section types.

You are given 35 minutes to complete each section. The experimental section is unscored and is not returned to the test taker. A break of 10 to 15 minutes is given between the 3rd and 4th sections.

The five-section test is followed by a 35 minute writing sample.

The Logical Reasoning Section

Each Logical Reasoning Section is composed of approximately 24 to 26 short arguments. Every short argument is followed by a question such as: "Which one of the following weakens the argument?" "Which one of the following parallels the argument?" or "Which one of the following must be true according to the argument?" The key to this section is time management and an understanding of the reasoning types and question types that frequently appear.

Since there are two scored sections of Logical Reasoning on every LSAT, this section accounts for approximately 50% of your score.

The Analytical Reasoning Section

This section, also known as Logic Games, is probably the most difficult for students taking the LSAT for the first time. The section consists of four games or puzzles, each followed by a series of five to eight questions. The questions are designed to test your ability to evaluate a set of relationships and to make inferences about those relationships. To perform well on this section you must understand the major types of games that frequently appear and develop the ability to properly diagram the rules and make inferences.

When you take an actual LSAT, they take your thumbprint at the testing site. This is done in case of test security problems.

At the conclusion of the LSAT, and for five business days after the LSAT, you have the option to cancel your score. Unfortunately, there is no way to determine exactly what your score would be before cancelling.

The Reading Comprehension Section

This section is composed of three long reading passages, each approximately 450 words in length, and two shorter comparative reading passages. The passage topics are drawn from a variety of subjects, and each passage is followed by a series of five to eight questions that ask you to determine viewpoints in the passage, analyze organizational traits, evaluate specific sections of the passage, or compare facets of two different passages. The key to this section is to read quickly with understanding and to carefully analyze the passage structure.

The Experimental Section

Each LSAT contains one experimental section, which does not count towards your score. The experimental can be any of the three section types described above, and the purpose of the section is to test and evaluate questions that will be used on *future* LSATs. By pretesting questions before their use in a scored section, the experimental helps the makers of the test determine the test scale. To learn more about the experimental section, we suggest you visit the PowerScore website, where you can find an extensive discussion of the experimental section, including how to identify the section and how to approach the section.

The Writing Sample

A 35-minute Writing Sample is given at the conclusion of the LSAT. The Writing Sample is not scored, but a copy is sent to each of the law schools to which you apply.

The format of the Writing Sample is called the Decision Prompt: you are asked to consider two possible courses of action, decide which one is superior, and then write a short essay supporting your choice. Each course of action is described in a short paragraph and you are given two primary criteria to consider in making your decision. Typically the two courses of action each have different strengths and weaknesses, and there is no clearly correct decision.

You must attempt the Writing Sample! If you do not, Law Services reserves the right not to score your test.

Do not agonize over the Writing Sample; in law school admissions, the Writing Sample is usually not a determining element for three reasons: the admissions committee is aware that the essay is given after a grueling three hour test and is about a subject you have no personal interest in; they already have a better sample of your writing ability in the personal statement; and the committee has a limited amount of time to evaluate applications.

The LSAT Scoring Scale

Each administered LSAT contains approximately 101 questions, and your LSAT score is based on the total number of questions you answer correctly, a total known as the raw score. After the raw score is determined, a unique Score Conversion Chart is used for each LSAT to convert the raw score into a scaled LSAT score. Since June 1991, the LSAT has utilized a 120 to 180 scoring scale, with 120 being the lowest possible score and 180 being the highest possible score. Notably, this 120 to 180 scale is just a renumbered version of the 200 to 800 scale most test takers are familiar with from such tests as the SAT and GMAT. Just drop the "1" and add a "0" to the 120 and 180.

Although the number of questions per test has remained relatively constant over the last eight years, the overall logical difficulty of each test has varied. This is not surprising since the test is made by humans and there is no precise way to completely predetermine logical difficulty. To account for these variances in test "toughness," the test makers adjust the Scoring Conversion Chart for each LSAT in order to make similar LSAT scores from different tests mean the same thing. For example, the LSAT given in June may be logically more difficult than the LSAT given in December, but by making the June LSAT scale "looser" than the December scale, a 160 on each test would represent the same level of performance. This scale adjustment, known as equating, is extremely important to law school admissions offices around the country. Imagine the difficulties that would be posed by unequated tests: admissions officers would have to not only examine individual LSAT scores, but also take into account which LSAT each score came from. This would present an information nightmare.

The LSAT Percentile Table

It is important not to lose sight of what LSAT scaled scores actually represent. The 120 to 180 test scale contains 61 different possible scores. Each score places a student in a certain relative position compared to other test takers. These relative positions are represented through a percentile that correlates to each score. The percentile indicates where the test taker ranks in the overall pool of test takers. For example, a score of 165 represents the 93rd percentile, meaning a student with a score of 165 scored better than 93 percent of the people who have taken the test in the last three years. The percentile is critical since it is a true indicator of your positioning relative to other test takers, and thus law school applicants.

Charting out the entire percentage table yields a rough "bell curve." The number of test takers in the 120s and 170s is very low (only 1.9% of all test takers receive a score in the 170s), and most test takers are bunched in the middle, comprising the "top" of the bell. In fact, approximately 40% of all test takers score between 145 and 155 inclusive, and about 70% of all test takers score between 140 and 160 inclusive.

Since the LSAT has 61 possible scores, why didn't the test makers change the scale to 0 to 60? Probably for merciful reasons. How would you tell your friends that you scored a 3 on the LSAT? 123 sounds so much better.

There is no penalty for answering incorrectly on the LSAT. Therefore, you should guess on any questions you cannot complete.

The median score on the LSAT scale is approximately 151. The median, or middle, score is the score at which approximately 50% of test takers have a lower score and 50% of test takers have a higher score. Typically, to achieve a score of 151, you must answer between 56 and 61 questions correctly from a total of 101 questions. In other words, to achieve a score that is perfectly average, you can miss between 40 and 45 questions. Thus, it is important to remember that you do not have to answer every question correctly in order to receive an excellent LSAT score. There is room for error, and accordingly you should never let any single question occupy an inordinate amount of your time.

The Use of the LSAT

The use of the LSAT in law school admissions is not without controversy. Experts agree that your LSAT score is one of the most important determinants of the type of school you can attend. At many law schools an admissions index consisting of your LSAT score and your undergraduate grade point average is used to help determine the relative standing of applicants, and at some schools a sufficiently high admissions index guarantees your admission.

For all the importance of the LSAT, the exam is not without flaws. As a standardized test currently given in the paper-and-pencil format, there are a number of skills that the LSAT cannot measure, including listening skills, note-taking ability, perseverance, etc. Law Services is aware of these limitations and on an annual basis they warn all law school admission offices about overemphasizing LSAT results. Still, because the test ultimately returns a number for each student, the tendency to rank applicants is strong. Fortunately, once you get to law school the LSAT is forgotten. For the time being, consider the test a temporary hurdle you must leap in order to reach the ultimate goal.

For more information on the LSAT or to register for the test, contact Law Services at (215) 968-1001 or at their website at www.lsac.org.

Basic Approaches for Each Section of the LSAT █████████

The Logic Games Section

There are three parts to every Logic Game: the scenario, the rules, and the questions. The scenario describes the game—what players are involved in the game and what situation those players are involved in; the rules provide the parameters those players must act under. Always read the scenario and rules before you begin diagramming.

After reading the scenario and the rules, make a main diagram at the bottom of the page. Your diagram should include the following:

- A list of the variables and their exact total number
- An identification of any variable that is random (that is, a variable that does not appear in any of the rules)
- A diagram of the variable sets
- A diagram of each rule
- A listing of each inference

Logic Games Question Types

Games questions are either Global or Local. Global questions ask about information derived only from the initial rules, such as "Who can finish first?" or "Which one of the following must be true?" Use your main diagram to answer global questions. Local questions occur when the question imposes a new condition in addition to the initial rules, such as "If Laura sits in the third chair, which one of the following must be true?" The additional conditions imposed by local questions apply to that question only and do not apply to any of the other questions. It is essential that you focus on the implications of the new conditions. Ask yourself how this condition affects the variables and the existing rules. For local questions, do your work next to the question; do not use your main diagram except as a reference.

Local questions almost always require you to produce a "mini-setup" next to the question.

Within the global/local designation, all questions ultimately ask for one of four things: what must be true, what is not necessarily true, what could be true, and what cannot be true. All questions are a variation of one of these four basic ideas. At all times, you must be aware of the exact nature of the question you are being asked, especially when "except" questions appear. If you find that you are missing questions because you miss words such as "false" or "except" when reading, then take a moment at the beginning of the game to circle the key words in each question, words such as "must," "could," etc.

If you frequently misread games questions, circle the key part of each question before you begin the game. You will not forget about a word like "except" if you have it underlined!

Logic Games General Notes

The key to optimal performance on Logic Games is to be focused and organized. This involves a number of factors:

1. Play to your strengths and away from your weaknesses

You are not required to do the games in the order presented on the test, and you should not expect that the test makers will present the games in the best order for you. Students who expect to have difficulty on the games section should attack the games in order of their personal preferences and strengths and weaknesses.

2. Create a strong setup for the game

The key to powerful games performance is often to create a good setup. At least 80% of the games on the LSAT are "setup games" wherein the quality of your setup dictates whether or not you are successful in answering the questions.

3. Look to make inferences

There are always inferences in a game, and the test makers expect you to make at least a few of them. Always check the rules and your setup with an eye towards finding inferences, and then always look to use your inferences when answering questions.

4. Be smart during the game

If necessary, skip over time consuming questions and return to them later. Remember that it is sometimes advisable to do the questions out of order. For example, if the first question in a game asks you for a complete and accurate list of the positions "C" could occupy, because of time considerations it would be advisable to skip that question and complete the remaining questions. Then you could return to the first question and use the knowledge you gained from the other questions to quickly and easily answer the first question.

5. Do not be intimidated by size

A lengthy game scenario and a large number of initial rules do not necessarily equal greater difficulty. Some of the longest games are easy because they contain so many restrictions and limitations.

6. Keep an awareness of time

With four games and 35 minutes to complete the section, you have approximately eight minutes and forty-five seconds to complete each game

PowerScore offers a selection of silent timers on our website, powerscore.com.

and bubble in your answers. Use an analog watch during the LSAT so you always know how much time remains, and avoid spending too much time on any one game or question.

If you do only three games, you have 11 minutes and 40 seconds to complete each game. If you do just two games, you have 17 minutes and 30 seconds to complete each game.

7. Maintain a positive attitude and concentrate

Above all, you must attack each game with a positive and energetic attitude. The games themselves are often challenging yet fun, and students who actively involve themselves in the games generally perform better overall.

The Logical Reasoning Section

As outlined in the *Logical Reasoning Bible*, to attack Logical Reasoning questions we use a general approach that systematically breaks down the stimulus and the answer choices. This approach is organized in steps called the Primary Objectives™:

Primary Objective #1: Determine whether the stimulus contains an argument or if it is only a set of factual statements.

Primary Objective #2: If the stimulus contains an argument, identify the conclusion of the argument. If the stimulus contains a fact set, examine each fact.

Primary Objective #3: If the stimulus contains an argument, determine if the argument is strong or weak.

Primary Objective #4: Read closely and know precisely what the author said. Do not generalize!

Primary Objective #5: Carefully read and identify the question stem. Do not assume that certain words are automatically associated with certain question types.

Primary Objective #6: Prephrase: after reading the question stem, take a moment to mentally formulate your answer to the question stem.

Primary Objective #7: Always read each of the five answer choices.

Primary Objective #8: Separate the answer choices into Contenders and Losers. After you complete this process, review the Contenders and decide which answer is the correct one.

Primary Objective #9: If all five answer choices appear to be Losers, return to the stimulus and re-evaluate the argument.

By consistently applying the points above, you give yourself the best opportunity to succeed on each question.

The Thirteen Logical Reasoning Question Types

Each question stem that appears in the Logical Reasoning section of the LSAT can be classified into one of thirteen different types:

1. Must Be True/Most Supported
2. Main Point
3. Point at Issue
4. Assumption
5. Justify the Conclusion
6. Strengthen/Support
7. Resolve the Paradox
8. Weaken
9. Method of Reasoning
10. Flaw in the Reasoning
11. Parallel Reasoning
12. Evaluate the Argument
13. Cannot Be True

Occasionally, students ask if we refer to the question types by number or by name. We always refer to the questions by name as that is an easier and more efficient approach. Numerical question type classification systems force you to add two unnecessary levels of abstraction to your thinking process. For example, consider a question that asks you to "weaken" the argument. In a numerical question classification system, you must first recognize that the question asks you to weaken the argument, then you must classify that question into a numerical category (say, Type 10), and then you must translate Type 10 to mean "Weaken." Literally, numerical classification systems force you to perform an abstract, circular translation of the meaning of the question, and the translation process is both time-consuming and valueless.

In the following pages we will discuss each question type in brief. Later we will examine the various question types as they appear on the test.

1. Must Be True/Most Supported

    This category is simply known as "Must Be True." Must Be True questions ask you to identify the answer choice that is best proven by the information in the stimulus. Question stem examples:

    "If the statements above are true, which one of the following must also be true?"

    "Which one of the following can be properly inferred from the passage?"

2. Main Point

Main Point questions are a variant of Must Be True questions. As you might expect, a Main Point question asks you to find the primary conclusion made by the author. Question stem example:

"The main point of the argument is that"

3. Point at Issue

Point at Issue questions require you to identify a point of contention between two speakers, and thus these questions appear almost exclusively with two-speaker stimuli. Question stem example:

"Larew and Mendota disagree about whether"

4. Assumption

These questions ask you to identify an assumption of the author's argument. Question stem example:

"Which one of the following is an assumption required by the argument above?"

5. Justify the Conclusion

Justify the Conclusion questions ask you to supply a piece of information that, when added to the premises, proves the conclusion. Question stem example:

"Which one of the following, if assumed, allows the conclusion above to be properly drawn?"

6. Strengthen/Support

These questions ask you to select the answer choice that provides support for the author's argument or strengthens it in some way. Question stem examples:

"Which one of the following, if true, most strengthens the argument?"

"Which one of the following, if true, most strongly supports the statement above?"

7. Resolve the Paradox

Every Resolve the Paradox stimulus contains a discrepancy or seeming contradiction. You must find the answer choice that best resolves the situation. Question stem example:

"Which one of the following, if true, would most effectively resolve the apparent paradox above?"

8. Weaken

Weaken questions ask you to attack or undermine the author's argument. Question stem example:

"Which one of the following, if true, most seriously weakens the argument?"

9. Method of Reasoning

Method of Reasoning questions ask you to describe, in abstract terms, the way in which the author made his or her argument. Question stem example:

"Which one of the following describes the technique of reasoning used above?"

10. Flaw in the Reasoning

Flaw in the Reasoning questions ask you to describe, in abstract terms, the error of reasoning committed by the author. Question stem example:

"The reasoning in the astronomer's argument is flawed because this argument"

11. Parallel Reasoning

Parallel Reasoning questions ask you to identify the answer choice that contains reasoning most similar in structure to the reasoning presented in the stimulus. Question stem example:

"Which one of the following arguments is most similar in its pattern of reasoning to the argument above?"

12.   Evaluate the Argument

With Evaluate the Argument questions you must decide which answer choice will allow you to determine the logical validity of the argument. Question stem example:

"The answer to which one of the following questions would contribute most to an evaluation of the argument?"

13.   Cannot Be True

Cannot Be True questions ask you to identify the answer choice that cannot be true or is most weakened based on the information in the stimulus. Question stem example:

"If the statements above are true, which one of the following CANNOT be true?"

As you attack each problem, remember that each question stem falls into one of four Families that governs the flow of information within the problem:

- The First Family uses the stimulus to prove that one of the answer choices must be true. No information outside the sphere of the stimulus is allowed in the correct answer choice. Example question types include Must Be True, Main Point, Point at Issue, Method of Reasoning, Flaw in the Reasoning, and Parallel Reasoning.

- The Second Family takes the answer choices as true and uses them to help the stimulus. Information outside the sphere of the stimulus is allowed in the correct answer choice. Example question types include Strengthen, Justify the Conclusion, Assumption, and Resolve the Paradox.

- The Third Family takes the answer choices as true and uses them to hurt the stimulus. Information outside the sphere of the stimulus is allowed in the correct answer choice. The primary question type is Weaken.

- The Fourth Family uses the stimulus to prove that one of the answer choices cannot occur. No information outside the sphere of the stimulus is allowed in the answer choices. The primary question type is Cannot Be True.

Within the stimulus, there are different types of reasoning used, such as Conditional Reasoning and Causal Reasoning, and we will address these as they appear in each question.

The Reading Comprehension Section

As you begin the Reading Comprehension section, search for passages with interesting or appealing subject matter. If all else is equal, choose the passage with the greatest number of questions. Also keep in mind that on a number of occasions the last passage has been the easiest passage.

Be sure to read each passage at your normal reading speed. Reading too slowly will prevent you from having adequate time to answer all of the questions. Reading too quickly will cause you to miss much of the detailed information presented in the passage and will force you to reread most of the passage, something that will also prevent you from answering all the questions. Do not skim the paragraphs. Skimming will not effectively prepare you to answer all the questions.

Your primary goal while reading is to find the main point of the passage. Although in the majority of passages the main point is stated in the first paragraph, it is not always the case that the main point appears in the first or second sentence. The main point of many passages has appeared in the final sentence of the first paragraph or in the first sentence of the second paragraph. On average, about 30% of the questions deal directly with the main idea.

As you read, attempt to identify the underlying logical structure of the passage. This will help you quickly find information once you begin to answer the questions. For example, many passages open by stating the background of a thesis that will be challenged later in the passage. In the following paragraphs the author will present an alternative viewpoint to the thesis and perhaps specific counterexamples which provide support for the alternative view. Awareness of this general structure will allow you to reduce the time you spend searching for information when you need to refer back to the passage.

Keep in mind that it is neither possible nor necessary for you to know every detail of a passage. For many questions you should return to the passage to confirm what you remember from your first reading of the passage.

Once you have finished reading the passage, take a moment to focus on the main point and the arguments that support the main point. Many students get so caught up in absorbing the information presented in a passage that they fail to take the time to mentally organize that information. If you are having difficulty remembering the main point of the passage, take a moment after reading the passage to write down the main point in a short, simple sentence.

Refrain from heavily underlining or marking up the passage. This will waste entirely too much time. Limit what you write to noting where the author makes a major point or changes the course of his or her argument.

Pay attention to the language the author uses in the passage. The following basic word lists can help identify the direction the author is taking with his or her argument:

Continuing the same idea	Introducing a new idea
furthermore	however
moreover	but
additionally	still
similarly	yet
in fact	although
indeed	in contrast
for example	nevertheless

Your state of mind when approaching these passages is extremely important. Make sure that you take a positive, energetic attitude to the passages. Many passages in the Reading Comprehension section discuss conflicts between different viewpoints and this makes the reading inherently more interesting. Getting involved in the argument will make the passage more enjoyable for you and will also allow you to focus more clearly on the material.

Always remember what the author is trying to achieve. In almost every case, he or she is discussing a body of information and trying to draw new points about that information. Rarely will the writer simply restate known situations without bringing in a new view of the situation. As is the case with any person trying to sound perceptive, the author will often use intellectual and complex language. Don't be intimidated by this—although the terminology may be difficult, the main point seldom is.

Reading Comprehension Question Types

Over 70% of the questions in the Reading Comprehension section are exactly the same as Must Be True Logical Reasoning questions. Whether the question asks for the main point or for details from the passage, the answer must be true according to what you have read. The following question types appear within the Must Be True designation:

■ Main Point/Primary Purpose (MP)

As in the Logical Reasoning section, main point questions ask you to select the statement which best sums up the author's core ideas. Primary purpose questions ask you to describe why the author wrote the passage.

■ Passage Organization (PO)

These questions ask you to describe a characteristic of the overall structure of the passage.

For example, "The second paragraph serves primarily to....," and "Which one of the following best describes the organization of the passage." These questions are similar to the Method of Reasoning questions in the Logical Reasoning section, but they are generally broader.

- Author's Perspective and Tone (AP)

  Author's perspective questions ask you to select the answer choice that best reflects the author's views, such as "The author of the passage would most likely agree with which one of the following statements?" Tone questions ask you to identify the author's attitude toward a subject.

- Function (F)

  Function questions ask why the author referred to a particular word, phrase, or idea. This is essentially an extended Method of Reasoning question, requiring you to go beyond simply identifying the argument structure, and asking you the reasons behind the author's use of words or ideas.

- Specific Reference (SR)

  These questions provide you with a specific line reference or a reference to an easily found word or phrase within the passage. To attack these questions, refer to the reference in the question and then begin reading about 5 lines above the reference.

The following question types appear outside of the Must Be True designation:

- Strengthen and Weaken Questions

  These questions are the same in both the Logical Reasoning section and Reading Comprehension section.

- Parallel Reasoning Questions

  In Reading Comprehension, Parallel Reasoning questions are usually broader in scope, asking you to find the scenario most analogous to an action in the passage. There is less of a focus on identifying premises and conclusions than in the Logical Reasoning section

As always, if you have difficulty answering one of the questions in a passage, continue on and complete the other questions in the passage first. Many students have a tendency to stop when confronted with a difficult question and reread the answer choices over and over. If you cannot choose an answer within a reasonable amount of time, go on and return to the question later.

Reading Comprehension Passage Features

Reading Comprehension passages tend to possess many of the same general characteristics. The most common are:

- **Strong purpose or main point:** Always remember that your primary goal while reading is to find the main point. There will almost always be at least one question on this idea.

- **Difficult words, phrases, or concepts:** The test makers use these words and ideas to distract you. Try to look past the word or phrase; instead, focus on the underlying meaning in order to understand the big picture.

- **Enumerations/Lists:** If a decision was made in the passage and several reasons are given to explain that decision, expect to be questioned on your knowledge of those reasons. This is a very common question indicator!

- **Authoritative references:** When authorities are cited by the text, be prepared to be asked about the function and application of the citation. Sometimes different groups will be associated with conflicting ideas— be sure that you are careful not to confuse the groups being referenced.

- **Dates and Numbers:** These are useful because they help mark the chronology of the passage. If there are many dates, they can also be confusing, so make sure you are careful to match the dates given to the correct event.

- **Mixed References:** If a phrase or topic is mentioned in one area of the passage and then again in an entirely different area, be prepared for a specific reference question which will refer to only one of the two citings. Although you will be referred to a specific line in the passage, the relevant information for answering the question is usually found elsewhere in the passage where that same topic or phrase was discussed.

- **Competing perspectives:** If several alternative viewpoints are offered on a particular subject, make certain you know the details of each view as well as who is supporting each view. Several of the questions will probably test your knowledge of the different viewpoints.

  Further, when explaining arguments, many authors bring up counterpoints or drawbacks to that argument in an effort to show their awareness of other viewpoints. These counterpoints are often introduced by terms such as "however," "although," and "yet," and test takers are sometimes questioned on their understanding of these counterpoints, however brief they might have been.

- **Definitions:** If a definition is given during the course of a passage, make a notation and expect to be questioned on your understanding of that definition.

- **Initial Information:** Many questions are asked about information that is presented in the first five lines of a passage. The test makers have found that students often forget what was initially stated in the passage and instead concentrate on the information presented in the main body of the passage, so these questions could be hard to answer if you were not reading carefully from the very beginning.

As you read through each passage, you must keep track of each of these elements as they appear, as you are likely to be tested on each idea if it is present.

Comparative Reading Passages

In addition to the three single passages, the LSAT also contains one pair of dual passages, for total of four question sets. Dual passages are quite similar to the single passages, but rather than just one selection from a single author, two passages are given on a similar or related subject (by two separate authors, generally with different points of view). Comparative reading passages are followed by five to eight questions, and, like the single passage sets, these questions should be answered only on the basis of the information provided in their accompanying passages.

As you read the passages for their respective main points, remember that the passages will relate to each other in various ways. As the test makers recently stated, "In some cases, the authors of the passages will be in general agreement with each other, while in others their views will be directly opposed. Passage pairs may also exhibit more complex types of relationships: for example, one passage might articulate a set of principles, while the other passage applies those or similar principles to a particular situation."

The primary goal for comparative reading is clearly to identify the main point of each passage and then to relate those ideas to each other, focusing on the passages' similarities and differences. Questions in comparative reading tend to focus less on the detailed common question indicators observed in single passages—specific examples, new terms or phrases, lists—and more on broader, holistic ideas—main point, author's tone and opinion, and function. Many students find it useful to pause briefly after reading Passage A to organize their thoughts about what they have just read. Once you have taken a moment to ensure that you are comfortable with the information from the first passage, move on to Passage B and read with the intention of establishing the relationship between the approach and attitude of both authors.

Finally, as with all Reading Comprehension, remember that maintaining a positive attitude is critical. Do not be intimidated by the dual format; you should find the comparative reading to be extremely similar to (and possibly easier than) the other three passages in your Reading Comprehension section.

CHAPTER TWO: THE DECEMBER 2006 LSAT

Taking the December 2006 LSAT

This chapter contains the complete text of the December 2006 LSAT, including an answer key and scoring scale. For the closest possible re-creation of the conditions of the LSAT, take this exam as a timed exercise. The exam will take just less than three hours, and there is an answer sheet included so that you can record your answers. Per Law Services protocol, here are the directions for taking the test under timed conditions:

Section 1 = allow yourself exactly 35 minutes
Section 2 = allow yourself exactly 35 minutes
Section 3 = allow yourself exactly 35 minutes
Section 4 = allow yourself exactly 35 minutes

Writing Sample = allow yourself exactly 35 minutes

The rules for the test are as follows:

During the test you are allowed to work only on the section being timed. You cannot go back or forward to work on any other section of the test.

Do not take a break between any of the sections (on the actual LSAT, an unscored experimental section will be included, and a 10-15 minute break will be given after section 3; because this test has no experimental section, you should not take a break between any of the sections).

You may not use any scratch paper while working on the test; only the test pages themselves are available for your use.

After completing the test, refer to the answer key and the "Computing Your Score" section at the end of the test to find your LSAT score.

Your answer sheet is on the next page, and complete explanations are in the following chapters.

SECTION I
Time—35 minutes
25 Questions

Directions: The questions in this section are based on the reasoning contained in brief statements or passages. For some questions, more than one of the choices could conceivably answer the question. However, you are to choose the best answer; that is, the response that most accurately and completely answers the question. You should not make assumptions that are by commonsense standards implausible, superfluous, or incompatible with the passage. After you have chosen the best answer, blacken the corresponding space on your answer sheet.

1.   Editorial: Almost every year the Smithfield River floods the coastal fishing community of Redhook, which annually spends $3 million on the cleanup. Some residents have proposed damming the river, which would cost $5 million but would prevent the flooding. However, their position is misguided. A dam would prevent nutrients in the river from flowing into the ocean. Fish that now feed on those nutrients would start feeding elsewhere. The loss of these fish would cost Redhook $10 million annually.

Which one of the following most accurately expresses the main conclusion of the editorial's argument?

(A)   The Smithfield River should be dammed to prevent flooding.
(B)   Nutrients from the Smithfield River are essential to the local fish population.
(C)   Damming the Smithfield River is not worth the high construction costs for such a project.
(D)   For Redhook to build a dam on the Smithfield River would be a mistake.
(E)   The Smithfield River floods cost Redhook $3 million every year.

2.   We already knew from thorough investigation that immediately prior to the accident, either the driver of the first vehicle changed lanes without signaling or the driver of the second vehicle was driving with excessive speed. Either of these actions would make a driver liable for the resulting accident. But further evidence has proved that the first vehicle's turn signal was not on, though the driver of that vehicle admits to having changed lanes. So the driver of the second vehicle is not liable for the accident.

Which one of the following would be most important to know in evaluating the conclusion drawn above?

(A)   whether the second vehicle was being driven at excessive speed
(B)   whether the driver of the first vehicle knew that the turn signal was not on
(C)   whether any other vehicles were involved in the accident
(D)   whether the driver of the first vehicle was a reliable witness
(E)   whether the driver of the second vehicle would have seen the turn signal flashing had it been on

3.   In some places, iceberg lilies are the mainstay of grizzly bears' summer diets. The bears forage meadows for the lilies, uprooting them and eating their bulbs. Although the bears annually destroy a large percentage of the lilies, scientists have determined that the bears' feeding habits actually promote the survival of iceberg lilies.

Which one of the following, if true, most helps to resolve the apparent discrepancy in the statements above?

(A)   When grizzly bears forage for iceberg lilies, they generally kill many more lilies than they eat.
(B)   Iceberg lilies produce so many offspring that, when undisturbed, they quickly deplete the resources necessary for their own survival.
(C)   A significantly smaller number of iceberg lily flowers are produced in fields where grizzly bears forage than in fields of undisturbed iceberg lilies.
(D)   The geographic regions in which iceberg lilies are most prevalent are those regions populated by grizzly bears.
(E)   Iceberg lilies contain plentiful amounts of some nutrients that are necessary for grizzly bears' survival.

GO ON TO THE NEXT PAGE.

4. Advertisement: Seventy-five percent of dermatologists surveyed prefer Dermactin to all other brands of skin cream. Why? We consulted dermatologists during the development of Dermactin to ensure that you have the best skin cream on the market. So if you need a skin cream, use Dermactin.

The reasoning in the advertisement is questionable because the advertisement

(A) overlooks the possibility that other types of doctors have cause to use Dermactin, which would render the sample unrepresentative
(B) fails to state the number of dermatologists surveyed, which leaves open the possibility that the sample of doctors is too small to be reliable
(C) presumes, without providing justification, that some dermatologists are less qualified than others to evaluate skin cream
(D) relies on an inappropriate appeal to the opinions of consumers with no special knowledge of skin care
(E) overlooks the possibility that for a few people, using no skin cream is preferable to using even the best skin cream

5. Landscape architect: If the screen between these two areas is to be a hedge, that hedge must be of either hemlocks or Leyland cypress trees. However, Leyland cypress trees cannot be grown this far north. So if the screen is to be a hedge, it will be a hemlock hedge.

In which one of the following is the pattern of reasoning most similar to that in the landscape architect's argument?

(A) If there is to be an entrance on the north side of the building, it will have to be approached by a ramp. However, a ramp would become impossibly slippery in winter, so there will be no entrance on the north side.
(B) If visitors are to travel to this part of the site by automobile, there will be a need for parking spaces. However, no parking spaces are allowed for in the design. So if visitors are likely to come by automobile, the design will be changed.
(C) The subsoil in these five acres either consists entirely of clay or consists entirely of shale. Therefore, if one test hole in the area reveals shale, it will be clear that the entire five acres has a shale subsoil.
(D) Any path along this embankment must be either concrete or stone. But a concrete path cannot be built in this location. So if there is to be a path on the embankment, it will be a stone path.
(E) A space the size of this meadow would be suitable for a playground or a picnic area. However, a playground would be noisy and a picnic area would create litter. So it will be best for the area to remain a meadow.

6. Deirdre: Many philosophers have argued that the goal of every individual is to achieve happiness-that is, the satisfaction derived from fully living up to one's potential. They have also claimed that happiness is elusive and can be achieved only after years of sustained effort. But these philosophers have been unduly pessimistic, since they have clearly exaggerated the difficulty of being happy. Simply walking along the seashore on a sunny afternoon causes many people to experience feelings of happiness.

Which one of the following most accurately describes a reasoning flaw in Deirdre's argument?

(A) It dismisses a claim because of its source rather than because of its content.
(B) It fails to take into account that what brings someone happiness at one moment may not bring that person happiness at another time.
(C) It allows the key term "happiness" to shift in meaning illicitly in the course of the argument.
(D) It presumes, without providing justification, that happiness is, in fact, the goal of life.
(E) It makes a generalization based on the testimony of a group whose views have not been shown to be representative.

7. Global ecological problems reduce to the problem of balancing supply and demand. Supply is strictly confined by the earth's limitations. Demand, however, is essentially unlimited, as there are no limits on the potential demands made by humans. The natural tendency for there to be an imbalance between demand and sustainable supply is the source of these global problems. Therefore, any solutions require reducing current human demand.

Which one of the following is an assumption on which the argument depends?

(A) Supply and demand tend to balance themselves in the long run.
(B) It is possible to determine the limitations of the earth's sustainable supply.
(C) Actual human demand exceeds the earth's sustainable supply.
(D) It is never possible to achieve a balance between the environmental supply and human demand.
(E) Human consumption does not decrease the environmental supply.

GO ON TO THE NEXT PAGE.

8. We can now dismiss the widely held suspicion that
    sugar consumption often exacerbates hyperactivity in
    children with attention deficit disorder. A scientific
    study of the effects of three common sugars—sucrose,
    fructose, and glucose—on children who have attention
    deficit disorder, with experimental groups each
    receiving a type of sugar in their diets and a control
    group receiving a sugar substitute instead of sugar,
    showed no statistically significant difference between
    the groups in thinking or behavior.

    Which one of the following, if true, would most weaken
    the argument above?

    (A) Only one of the three types of sugar used in the
         study was ever widely suspected of exacerbating
         hyperactivity.
    (B) The consumption of sugar actually has a calming
         effect on some children.
    (C) The consumption of some sugar substitutes
         exacerbates the symptoms of hyperactivity.
    (D) The study included some observations of each
         group in contexts that generally tend to make
         children excited and active.
    (E) Some children believe that they can tell the
         difference between the taste of sugar and that of
         sugar substitutes.

9. Philosopher: An action is morally good if it both
                   achieves the agent's intended goal and benefits
                   someone other than the agent.

    Which one of the following judgments most closely
    conforms to the principle cited by the philosopher?

    (A) Colin chose to lie to the authorities questioning
         him, in an attempt to protect his friends.
         The authorities discovered his deception and
         punished Colin and his friends severely. But
         because he acted out of love for his friends,
         Colin's action was morally good.
    (B) Derek prepared a steak dinner to welcome his
         new neighbors to the neighborhood. When they
         arrived for dinner, Derek found out that the
         newcomers were strict vegetarians. Though the
         new neighbors were still grateful for Derek's
         efforts to welcome them, Derek's action was not
         morally good.
    (C) Ellen worked overtime hoping to get a
         promotion. The extra money she earned
         allowed her family to take a longer vacation
         that year, but she failed to get the promotion.
         Nevertheless, Ellen's action was morally good.
    (D) Louisa tried to get Henry into serious trouble by
         making it appear that he stole some expensive
         clothes from a store. But the store's detective
         realized what Louisa did, and so Louisa was
         punished rather than Henry. Since she intended
         to harm Henry, Louisa's action was not morally
         good.
    (E) Yolanda took her children to visit their
         grandfather because she wanted her children to
         enjoy their vacation and she knew they adored
         their grandfather. The grandfather and the
         children all enjoyed the visit. Though Yolanda
         greatly enjoyed the visit, her action was morally
         good.

GO ON TO THE NEXT PAGE.

10. Columnist: A recent research report suggests that by exercising vigorously, one significantly lowers one's chances of developing certain cardio-respiratory illnesses. But exercise has this effect, the report concludes, only if the exercise is vigorous. Thus, one should not heed older studies purporting to show that nonstrenuous walking yields the same benefits.

The reasoning in the columnist's argument is most vulnerable to criticism on the grounds that this argument

(A) fails to consider the possibility that the risk of developing certain cardio-respiratory illnesses can be reduced by means other than exercise

(B) fails to consider that those who exercise vigorously are at increased risk of physical injury caused by exercise

(C) overlooks the possibility that vigorous exercise may prevent life-endangering diseases that have little to do with the cardio-respiratory system

(D) fails to consider the possibility that those who engage in vigorous physical exercise are more likely than others to perceive themselves as healthy

(E) fails to show that a certain conclusion of the recent report is better justified than an opposing conclusion reached in older studies

11. Some statisticians believe that the method called extreme value theory (EVT) is a powerful analytical tool. The curves generated by traditional statistical methods to analyze empirical data on human longevity predict that some humans would live beyond 130 years. According to the curves EVT generates, however, the limit on human life spans is probably between 113 and 124 years. To date, no one has lived beyond the upper limits indicated by EVT analysis.

Which one of the following can be properly inferred from the statements above?

(A) EVT is, in general, a more reliable method for projecting future trends based on past observations than are traditional statistical methods.

(B) EVT fits the data about the highest observed human life spans more closely than do traditional statistical methods.

(C) According to the findings derived through the use of EVT, it is physically impossible for any human being to live longer than 124 years.

(D) Given the results generated by EVT, there is no point in conducting research aimed at greatly extending the upper limit on human life spans.

(E) Traditional statistical methods of empirical data analysis should eventually be replaced by some version of EVT.

12. The number of different synthetic chemical compounds that are known to be carcinogenic but are nonetheless used as pesticides, preservatives, or food additives is tiny compared to the number of nonsynthetic carcinogenic compounds widely found in plants and animals. It is therefore absurd to suppose that the rise in the cancer rate in recent decades is due to synthetic carcinogens.

The reasoning above is most vulnerable to criticism on the grounds that it overlooks the possibility that

(A) the rise in the cancer rate in recent decades is due to increased exposure to nonsynthetic pollutants

(B) the rise in the cancer rate in recent decades is due to something other than increased exposure to carcinogens

(C) some synthetic chemical compounds that are not known to be carcinogenic are in other respects toxic

(D) people undergo significantly less exposure to carcinogens that are not synthetic than to those that are synthetic

(E) people can vary greatly in their susceptibility to cancers caused by nonsynthetic carcinogens

13. It is a mistake to think, as ecologists once did, that natural selection will eventually result in organisms that will be perfectly adapted to their environments. After all, perfect adaptation of an individual to its environment is impossible, for an individual's environment can vary tremendously; no single set of attributes could possibly prepare an organism to cope with all the conditions that it could face.

Which one of the following most accurately expresses the main conclusion of the argument?

(A) It is not possible for an individual to be perfectly adapted to its environment.

(B) Natural selection will never result in individuals that will be perfectly adapted to their environments.

(C) No single set of attributes could enable an individual organism to cope with all of the conditions that it might face.

(D) Because an individual's environment can vary tremendously, no individual can be perfectly adapted to its environment.

(E) Ecologists once believed that natural selection would eventually result in individuals that will be perfectly adapted to their environments.

GO ON TO THE NEXT PAGE.

14. It would not be surprising to discover that the trade routes between China and the West were opened many centuries, even millennia, earlier than 200 B.C. contrary to what is currently believed. After all, what made the Great Silk Road so attractive as a trade route linking China and the West-level terrain, easily traversable mountain passes, and desert oases-would also have made it an attractive route for the original emigrants to China from Africa and the Middle East, and this early migration began at least one million years ago.

That a migration from Africa and the Middle East to China occurred at least one million years ago figures in the above reasoning in which one of the following ways?

(A) It is cited as conclusive evidence for the claim that trade links between China and the Middle East were established long before 200 B.C.

(B) It is an intermediate conclusion made plausible by the description of the terrain along which the migration supposedly took place.

(C) It is offered as evidence in support of the claim that trade routes between China and the West could easily have been established much earlier than is currently believed.

(D) It is offered as evidence against the claim that trade routes between China and Africa preceded those eventually established between China and the Middle East.

(E) It is the main conclusion that the argument attempts to establish about intercourse between China and the West.

15. The typological theory of species classification, which has few adherents today, distinguishes species solely on the basis of observable physical characteristics, such as plumage color, adult size, or dental structure. However, there are many so-called "sibling species," which are indistinguishable on the basis of their appearance but cannot interbreed and thus, according to the mainstream biological theory of species classification, are separate species. Since the typological theory does not count sibling species as separate species, it is unacceptable.

The reasoning in the argument is most vulnerable to criticism on the grounds that

(A) the argument does not evaluate all aspects of the typological theory

(B) the argument confuses a necessary condition for species distinction with a sufficient condition for species distinction

(C) the argument, in its attempt to refute one theory of species classification, presupposes the truth of an opposing theory

(D) the argument takes a single fact that is incompatible with a theory as enough to show that theory to be false

(E) the argument does not explain why sibling species cannot interbreed

16. Chiu: The belief that a person is always morally blameworthy for feeling certain emotions, such as unjustifiable anger, jealousy, or resentment, is misguided. Individuals are responsible for only what is under their control, and whether one feels such an emotion is not always under one's control.

Chiu's conclusion follows logically if which one of the following is assumed?

(A) Individuals do not have control over their actions when they feel certain emotions.

(B) If a person is morally blameworthy for something, then that person is responsible for it.

(C) Although a person may sometimes be unjustifiably angry, jealous, or resentful, there are occasions when these emotions are appropriate.

(D) If an emotion is under a person's control, then that person cannot hold others responsible for it.

(E) The emotions for which a person is most commonly blamed are those that are under that person's control.

GO ON TO THE NEXT PAGE.

17. Industrial adviser: If two new processes under
    consideration are not substantially different in
    cost, then the less environmentally damaging
    process should be chosen. If, however, a company
    already employs an environmentally damaging
    process and retooling for a less damaging process
    would involve substantial cost, then that company
    should retool only if retooling is either legally
    required or likely to bring long-term savings
    substantially greater than the cost.

    Which one of the following judgments conforms most
    closely to the principles described by the industrial
    adviser?

    (A)   A new law offering companies tax credits for
           reducing pollution would enable a company to
           realize a slight long-term savings by changing
           to a more environmentally sound process for
           manufacturing dye, despite the substantial
           cost of retooling. In light of the new law, the
           company should change its process.
    (B)   In manufacturing pincushions, a company uses
           a process that, though legal, has come under
           heavy public criticism for the environmental
           damage it causes. The company should change
           its process to preserve its public image, despite
           some expected long-term losses from doing so.
    (C)   A company is considering two new processes for
           the manufacture of staples. Process A is more
           expensive than process B but not substantially
           so. However, process A is substantially less
           environmentally damaging than process B. The
           company should implement process A.
    (D)   Two new processes are being considered for the
           manufacture of ball bearings. The processes
           are similar, except that the chemicals used in
           process A will pollute a nearby river slightly
           more than will the chemicals for process B.
           Process A is also slightly cheaper than process
           B. The company should use process A.
    (E)   A company is considering changing its process
           for manufacturing shoelaces. The new process
           is cheaper and less environmentally damaging
           than the old. Both are legal. Changing processes
           would be costly, but the cost would be almost
           entirely recovered in long-term savings. The
           company should switch processes.

18. In a poll of a representative sample of a province's
    residents, the provincial capital was the city most
    often selected as the best place to live in that province.
    Since the capital is also the largest of that province's
    many cities, the poll shows that most residents of that
    province generally prefer life in large cities to life in
    small cities.

    The argument is most vulnerable to the criticism that it

    (A)   overlooks the possibility that what is true of the
           residents of the province may not be true of
           other people
    (B)   does not indicate whether most residents of other
           provinces also prefer life in large cities to life in
           small cities
    (C)   takes for granted that when people are polled for
           their preferences among cities, they tend to vote
           for the city that they think is the best place to
           live
    (D)   overlooks the possibility that the people who
           preferred small cities over the provincial capital
           did so not because of their general feelings
           about the sizes of cities, but because of their
           general feelings about capital cities
    (E)   overlooks the possibility that most people may
           have voted for small cities even though a large
           city received more votes than any other single
           city

19. Geneticist: Genes, like viruses, have a strong tendency
    to self-replicate; this has led some biologists to
    call genes "selfish." This term is, in this instance,
    intended to be defined behaviorally: it describes
    what genes do without ascribing intentions to
    them. But even given that genes are ascribed no
    intentions, the label "selfish" as applied to genes
    is a misnomer. Selfishness only concerns bringing
    about the best conditions for oneself; creating
    replicas of oneself is not selfish.

    Which one of the following, if assumed, allows the
    geneticist's conclusion to be properly drawn?

    (A)   Bringing about the best conditions for oneself is
           less important than doing this for others.
    (B)   Creating replicas of oneself does not help bring
           about the best conditions for oneself.
    (C)   The behavioral definition of "selfish" is
           incompatible with its everyday definition.
    (D)   To ignore the fact that self-replication is not
           limited to genes is to misunderstand genetic
           behavior.
    (E)   Biologists have insufficient evidence about
           genetic behavior to determine whether it is best
           described as selfish.

GO ON TO THE NEXT PAGE.

20. Only experienced salespeople will be able to meet the company's selling quota. Thus, I must not count as an experienced salesperson, since I will be able to sell only half the quota.

The pattern of flawed reasoning exhibited by the argument above is most similar to that exhibited by which one of the following?

(A) Only on Fridays are employees allowed to dress casually. Today is Friday but Hector is dressed formally. So he must not be going to work.

(B) Only music lovers take this class. Thus, since Hillary is not taking this class, she apparently does not love music.

(C) Only oceanographers enjoy the Atlantic in midwinter. Thus, we may expect that Gerald does not enjoy the Atlantic in midwinter, since he is not an oceanographer.

(D) As this tree before us is a giant redwood, it follows that we must be in a northern latitude, since it is only in northern latitudes that one finds giant redwoods.

(E) Only accomplished mountain climbers can scale El Capitan. Thus, Michelle must be able to scale El Capitan, since she is an accomplished mountain climber.

21. Designer: Any garden and adjoining living room that are separated from one another by sliding glass doors can visually merge into a single space. If the sliding doors are open, as may happen in summer, this effect will be created if it does not already exist and intensified if it does. The effect remains quite strong during colder months if the garden is well coordinated with the room and contributes strong visual interest of its own.

The designer's statements, if true, most strongly support which one of the following?

(A) A garden separated from an adjoining living room by closed sliding glass doors cannot be well coordinated with the room unless the garden contributes strong visual interest.

(B) In cold weather, a garden and an adjoining living room separated from one another by sliding glass doors will not visually merge into a single space unless the garden is well coordinated with the room.

(C) A garden and an adjoining living room separated by sliding glass doors cannot visually merge in summer unless the doors are open.

(D) A garden can visually merge with an adjoining living room into a single space even if the garden does not contribute strong visual interest of its own.

(E) Except in summer, opening the sliding glass doors that separate a garden from an adjoining living room does not intensify the effect of the garden and room visually merging into a single space.

22. Last summer, after a number of people got sick from eating locally caught anchovies, the coastal city of San Martin advised against eating such anchovies. The anchovies were apparently tainted with domoic acid, a harmful neurotoxin. However, a dramatic drop in the population of *P australis* plankton to numbers more normal for local coastal waters indicates that it is once again safe to eat locally caught anchovies.

Which one of the following, if true, would most help to explain why it is now safe to lift the advisory?

(A) *P australis* is one of several varieties of plankton common to the region that, when ingested by anchovies, cause the latter to secrete small amounts of domoic acid.

(B) *P australis* naturally produces domoic acid, though anchovies consume enough to become toxic only when the population of *P australis* is extraordinarily large.

(C) Scientists have used *P australis* plankton to obtain domoic acid in the laboratory.

(D) A sharp decline in the population of *P australis* is typically mirrored by a corresponding drop in the local anchovy population.

(E) *P australis* cannot survive in large numbers in seawater that does not contain significant quantities of domoic acid along with numerous other compounds.

23. Constance: The traditional definition of full employment as a 5 percent unemployment rate is correct, because at levels below 5 percent, inflation rises.

Brigita: That traditional definition of full employment was developed before the rise of temporary and part-time work and the fall in benefit levels. When people are juggling several part-time jobs with no benefits, or working in a series of temporary assignments, as is now the case, 5 percent unemployment is not full employment.

The dialogue most strongly supports the claim that Constance and Brigita disagree with each other about which one of the following?

(A) what definition of full employment is applicable under contemporary economic conditions

(B) whether it is a good idea, all things considered, to allow the unemployment level to drop below 5 percent

(C) whether a person with a part-time job should count as fully employed

(D) whether the number of part-time and temporary workers has increased since the traditional definition of full employment was developed

(E) whether unemployment levels above 5 percent can cause inflation levels to rise

GO ON TO THE NEXT PAGE.

24. The supernova event of 1987 is interesting in that there is still no evidence of the neutron star that current theory says should have remained after a supernova of that size. This is in spite of the fact that many of the most sensitive instruments ever developed have searched for the tell-tale pulse of radiation that neutron stars emit. Thus, current theory is wrong in claiming that supernovas of a certain size always produce neutron stars.

Which one of the following, if true, most strengthens the argument?

(A) Most supernova remnants that astronomers have detected have a neutron star nearby.

(B) Sensitive astronomical instruments have detected neutron stars much farther away than the location of the 1987 supernova.

(C) The supernova of 1987 was the first that scientists were able to observe in progress.

(D) Several important features of the 1987 supernova are correctly predicted by the current theory.

(E) Some neutron stars are known to have come into existence by a cause other than a supernova explosion.

25. On average, corporations that encourage frequent social events in the workplace show higher profits than those that rarely do. This suggests that the EZ Corporation could boost its profits by having more staff parties during business hours.

Which one of the following, if true, most weakens the argument above?

(A) The great majority of corporations that encourage frequent social events in the workplace do so at least in part because they are already earning above-average profits.

(B) Corporations that have frequent staff parties after business hours sometimes have higher profits than do corporations that have frequent staff parties during business hours.

(C) The EZ Corporation already earns above-average profits, and it almost never brings play into the workplace.

(D) Frequent social events in a corporate workplace leave employees with less time to perform their assigned duties than they would otherwise have.

(E) At one time the EZ Corporation encouraged social events in the workplace more frequently than it currently does, but it has not always been one of the most profitable corporations of its size.

S T O P

IF YOU FINISH BEFORE TIME IS CALLED, YOU MAY CHECK YOUR WORK ON THIS SECTION ONLY.
DO NOT WORK ON ANY OTHER SECTION IN THE TEST.

SECTION II
Time—35 minutes
28 Questions

Directions: Each passage in this section is followed by a group of questions to be answered on the basis of what is <u>stated</u> or <u>implied</u> in the passage. For some of the questions, more than one of the choices could conceivably answer the question. However, you are to choose the <u>best</u> answer; that is, the response that most accurately and completely answers the question, and blacken the corresponding space on your answer sheet.

The work of South African writer Ezekiel Mphahlele has confounded literary critics, especially those who feel compelled to draw a sharp distinction between autobiography and fiction. These critics point
(5) to Mphahlele's best-known works—his 1959 autobiography *Down Second Avenue* and his 1971 novel *The Wanderers*—to illustrate the problem of categorizing his work. While his autobiography traces his life from age five until the beginning of his
(10) self-imposed 20-year exile at age thirty-eight, *The Wanderers* appears to pick up at the beginning of his exile and go on from there. Critics have variously decried the former as too fictionalized and the latter as too autobiographical, but those who focus on
(15) traditional labels inevitably miss the fact that Mphahlele manipulates different prose forms purely in the service of the social message he advances.
　　Even where critics give him a favorable reading, all too often their reviews carry a negative subtext.
(20) For example, one critic said of *The Wanderers* that if anger, firsthand experiences, compassion, and topicality were the sole requirements for great literature, the novel might well be one of the masterpieces of this declining part of the twentieth
(25) century. And although this critic may not have meant to question the literary contribution of the novel, there are those who are outright dismissive of *The Wanderers* because it contains an autobiographical framework and is populated with real-world
(30) characters. Mphahlele briefly defends against such charges by pointing out the importance of the fictional father-son relationship that opens and closes the novel. But his greater concern is the social vision that pervades his work, though it too is prone to
(35) misunderstandings and underappreciation. Mphahlele is a humanist and an integrationist, and his writings wonderfully articulate his vision of the future; but critics often balk at this vision because Mphahlele provides no road maps for bringing such a future
(40) about.
　　Mphahlele himself shows little interest in establishing guidelines to distinguish autobiography from fiction. Though he does refer to *Down Second Avenue* as an autobiography and *The Wanderers* as a
(45) novel, he asserts that no novelist can write complete fiction or absolute fact. It is the nature of writing, at least the writing he cares about, that the details must be drawn from the writer's experiences, and thus are in some sense fact, but conveyed in such a way as to
(50) maximize the effectiveness of the social message

contained in the work, and thus inevitably fiction. As he claims, the whole point of the exercise of writing has nothing to do with classification; in all forms writing is the transmission of ideas, and important
(55) ideas at that: "Whenever you write prose or poetry or drama you are writing a social criticism of one kind or another. If you don't, you are completely irrelevant—you don't count."

1. Based on the passage, with which one of the following statements would Mphahlele be most likely to agree?

   (A) All works of literature should articulate a vision of the future.
   (B) It is not necessary for a writer to write works to fit predetermined categories.
   (C) Literary categories are worth addressing only when literary works are being unjustifiably dismissed.
   (D) Most works of literature that resemble novels could accurately be classified as autobiographies.
   (E) The most useful categories in literature are those that distinguish prose from poetry and poetry from drama.

2. The passage states that Mphahlele believes which one of the following?

   (A) Writing should provide a guide for achieving social change.
   (B) Writing should have as its goal the transmission of ideas.
   (C) Writing is most effective when it minimizes the use of real people and events to embellish a story.
   (D) Good writing is generally more autobiographical than fictional.
   (E) Fiction and autobiography are clearly identifiable literary forms if the work is composed properly.

GO ON TO THE NEXT PAGE.

3. In lines 18-25, the author uses the phrase "negative subtext" in reference to the critic's comment to claim that

  (A) the critic believes that Mphahlele himself shows little interest in establishing guidelines that distinguish fact from fiction in literature
  (B) the comment is unfairly one-sided and gives no voice to perspectives that Mphahlele might embrace
  (C) the requirement of firsthand experiences mentioned in the comment is in direct contradiction to the requirements of fiction
  (D) the requirements for great literature mentioned in the comment are ill conceived, thus the requirements have little bearing on what great literature really is
  (E) the requirements for great literature mentioned in the comment are not the sole requirements, thus Mphahlele's work is implied by the critic not to be great literature

4. According to the passage, critics offer which one of the following reasons for their dismissal of *The Wanderers*?

  (A) It should not have been populated with real-world characters.
  (B) It should have been presented as an autobiography.
  (C) It does not clearly display Mphahlele's vision.
  (D) It intends to deliver controversial social criticisms.
  (E) It places too much emphasis on relationships.

5. The author quotes Mphahlele (lines 55-58) primarily in order to

  (A) demonstrate Mphahlele's eloquence as a writer
  (B) provide a common goal of writing among novelists
  (C) further elaborate the kind of writing Mphahlele values
  (D) introduce the three literary forms Mphahlele uses to write social criticism
  (E) show that Mphahlele makes no distinction among prose, poetry, and drama

6. Which one of the following aspects of Mphahlele's work does the author of the passage appear to value most highly?

  (A) his commitment to communicating social messages
  (B) his blending of the categories of fiction and autobiography
  (C) his ability to redefine established literary categories
  (D) his emphasis on the importance of details
  (E) his plan for bringing about the future he envisions

7. Which one of the following is most strongly suggested by the information in the passage?

  (A) Mphahlele's stance as a humanist and an integrationist derives from an outlook on writing that recognizes a sharp distinction between fiction and autobiography.
  (B) The social vision contained in a work is irrelevant to critics who feel compelled to find distinct categories in which to place literary works.
  (C) Critics are concerned with categorizing the works they read not as a means to judge the quality of the works but as a way of discovering tendencies within literary traditions.
  (D) If Mphahlele were to provide direction as to how his vision of the future might be realized, more critics might find this vision acceptable.
  (E) For a work to be classified as a novel, it must not contain any autobiographical elements.

GO ON TO THE NEXT PAGE.

A vigorous debate in astronomy centers on an epoch in planetary history that was first identified by analysis of rock samples obtained in lunar missions. Scientists discovered that the major craters on the
(5) Moon were created by a vigorous bombardment of debris approximately four billion years ago—the so-called late heavy bombardment (LHB). Projectiles from this bombardment that affected the Moon should also have struck Earth, a likelihood with profound
(10) consequences for the history of Earth since, until the LHB ended, life could not have survived here.

Various theoretical approaches have been developed to account for both the evidence gleaned from samples of Moon rock collected during lunar
(15) explorations and the size and distribution of craters on the Moon. Since the sizes of LHB craters suggest they were formed by large bodies, some astronomers believe that the LHB was linked to the disintegration of an asteroid or comet orbiting the Sun. In this view,
(20) a large body broke apart and peppered the inner solar system with debris. Other scientists disagree and believe that the label "LHB" is in itself a misnomer. These researchers claim that a cataclysm is not necessary to explain the LHB evidence. They claim
(25) that the Moon's evidence merely provides a view of the period concluding billions of years of a continuous, declining heavy bombardment throughout the inner solar system. According to them, the impacts from the latter part of the bombardment were
(30) so intense that they obliterated evidence of earlier impacts. A third group contends that the Moon's evidence supports the view that the LHB was a sharply defined cataclysmic cratering period, but these scientists believe that because of its relatively brief
(35) duration, this cataclysm did not extend throughout the inner solar system. They hold that the LHB involved only the disintegration of a body within the Earth-Moon system, because the debris from such an event would have been swept up relatively quickly.
(40) New support for the hypothesis that a late bombardment extended throughout the inner solar system has been found in evidence from the textural features and chemical makeup of a meteorite that has been found on Earth. It seems to be a rare example of
(45) a Mars rock that made its way to Earth after being knocked from the surface of Mars. The rock has recently been experimentally dated at about four billion years old, which means that, if the rock is indeed from Mars, it was knocked from the planet at
(50) about the same time that the Moon was experiencing the LHB. This tiny piece of evidence suggests that at least two planetary systems in the inner solar system experienced bombardment at the same time. However, to determine the pervasiveness of the LHB, scientists
(55) will need to locate many more such rocks and perhaps obtain surface samples from other planets in the inner solar system.

8. Which one of the following most accurately expresses the main point of the passage?

(A) The LHB is an intense meteorite bombardment that occurred about four billion years ago and is responsible for the cratering on the Moon and perhaps on other members of the inner solar system as well.

(B) Astronomers now believe that they may never collect enough evidence to determine the true nature of the LHB.

(C) If scientists continue to collect new clues at their current rate, the various LHB hypotheses can soon be evaluated and a clear picture will emerge.

(D) The Moon's evidence shows that the LHB was linked to a small body that disintegrated while in solar orbit and sprayed the inner solar system with debris.

(E) New evidence has been found that favors the view that the LHB was widespread, but before competing theories of the LHB can be excluded, more evidence needs to be gathered.

9. The author's attitude toward arguments that might be based on the evidence of the rock mentioned in the passage as being from Mars (lines 44-46) can most accurately be described as

(A) ambivalence because the theory of the rock's migration to Earth is at once both appealing and difficult to believe

(B) caution because even if the claims concerning the rock's origins can be proven, it is unwise to draw general conclusions without copious evidence

(C) skepticism because it seems unlikely that a rock could somehow make its way from Mars to Earth after being dislodged

(D) curiosity because many details of the rock's interplanetary travel, its chemical analysis, and its dating analysis have not yet been published

(E) outright acceptance because the origins of the rock have been sufficiently corroborated

10. The author mentions that the LHB "should also have struck Earth" (lines 8-9) primarily to

(A) support a particular theory of the extent of the LHB

(B) question the lack of LHB evidence found on Earth

(C) advocate certain scientific models for the origins of life on Earth

(D) provide a reason why scientists are interested in studying the LHB

(E) introduce additional support for the dating of the LHB

GO ON TO THE NEXT PAGE.

11. The author implies that all theoretical approaches to the LHB would agree on which one of the following?

    (A)   the approximate duration of the LHB
    (B)   the origin of the debris involved in the LHB
    (C)   the idea that cratering decreased significantly after the LHB
    (D)   the idea that the LHB destroyed the life that existed on Earth four billion years ago
    (E)   the approximate amount of debris involved in the LHB

12. According to the passage, the third group of scientists (line 31) believes that the LHB

    (A)   affected only the Moon
    (B)   was so brief that its extent had to be fairly localized
    (C)   consisted of so little debris that it was absorbed quickly by the planets in the inner solar system
    (D)   occurred more recently than four billion years ago
    (E)   may have lasted a long time, but all its debris remained within the Earth-Moon system

13. Which one of the following, if true, would lend the most support to the view that the LHB was limited to Earth and the Moon?

    (A)   An extensive survey of craters on Mars shows very little evidence for an increase in the intensity of projectiles striking Mars during the period from three billion to five billion years ago.
    (B)   Scientists discover another meteorite on Earth that they conclude had been knocked from the surface of the Moon during the LHB.
    (C)   A re-analysis of Moon rocks reveals that several originated on Earth during the LHB.
    (D)   Based on further testing, scientists conclude that the rock believed to have originated on Mars actually originated on the Moon.
    (E)   Excavations on both Earth and the Moon yield evidence that the LHB concluded billions of years of heavy bombardment.

GO ON TO THE NEXT PAGE.

Specialists in international communications almost unanimously assert that the broadcasting in developing nations of television programs produced by industrialized countries amounts to cultural
(5) imperialism: the phenomenon of one culture's productions overwhelming another's, to the detriment of the flourishing of the latter. This assertion assumes the automatic dominance of the imported productions and their negative effect on the domestic culture. But
(10) the assertion is polemical and abstract, based on little or no research into the place held by imported programs in the economies of importing countries or in the lives of viewers. This is not to deny that dominance is sometimes a risk in relationships
(15) between cultures, but rather to say that the assertion lacks empirical foundation and in some cases goes against fact. For one example, imported programs rarely threaten the economic viability of the importing country's own television industry. For
(20) another, imported programs do not uniformly attract larger audiences than domestically produced programs; viewers are not part of a passive, undifferentiated mass but are individuals with personal tastes, and most of them tend to prefer domestically
(25) produced television over imported television.

The role of television in developing nations is far removed from what the specialists assert. An anthropological study of one community that deals in part with residents' viewing habits where imported
(30) programs are available cites the popularity of domestically produced serial dramas and points out that, because viewers enjoy following the dramas from day to day, television in the community can serve an analogous function to that of oral poetry,
(35) which the residents often use at public gatherings as a daily journal of events of interest.

An empirical approach not unlike that of anthropologists is needed if communications specialists are to understand the impact of external
(40) cultural influences on the lives of people in a society. The first question they must investigate is: Given the evidence suggesting that the primary relationship of imported cultural productions to domestic ones is not dominance, then what model best represents the true
(45) relationship? One possibility is that, rather than one culture's productions dominating another's, the domestic culture absorbs the imported productions and becomes enriched. Another is that the imported productions fuse with domestic culture only where
(50) the two share common aspects, such as the use of themes, situations, or character types that are relevant and interesting to both cultures.

Communications researchers will also need to consider how to assess the position of the individual
(55) viewer in their model of cultural relationships. This model must emphasize the diversity of human responses, and will require engaging with the actual experiences of viewers, taking into account the variable contexts in which productions are
(60) experienced, and the complex manner in which individuals ascribe meanings to those productions.

14. The primary purpose of the passage is to

(A) determine which of two hypotheses considered by a certain discipline is correct
(B) discredit the evidence offered for a claim made by a particular discipline
(C) argue that a certain discipline should adopt a particular methodology
(D) examine similar methodological weaknesses in two different disciplines
(E) compare the views of two different disciplines on an issue

15. Which one of the following most accurately describes the organization of the passage?

(A) The author takes issue with an assertion, suggests reasons why the assertion is supported by its proponents, introduces a new view that runs counter to the assertion, and presents examples to support the new view.
(B) The author takes issue with an assertion, presents examples that run counter to the assertion, suggests that a particular approach be taken by the proponents of the assertion, and discusses two questions that should be addressed in the new approach.
(C) The author takes issue with an assertion, introduces a new view that runs counter to the assertion, presents examples that support the new view, and gives reasons why proponents of the assertion should abandon it and adopt the new view.
(D) The author takes issue with an assertion, presents examples that run counter to the assertion, suggests a change in the approach taken by the proponents of the assertion, and discusses two ways in which the new approach will benefit the proponents.
(E) The author takes issue with an assertion, presents examples that run counter to the assertion, introduces a new view that runs counter to the assertion, and suggests ways in which a compromise may be found between the view and the assertion.

GO ON TO THE NEXT PAGE.

16. Which one of the following is the most logical continuation of the last paragraph of the passage?

   (A) Lacking such an emphasis, we cannot judge conclusively the degree to which cultural relationships can be described by an abstract model.

   (B) Without such an emphasis, we can be confident that the dominance view asserted by communications specialists will survive the criticisms leveled against it.

   (C) Unless they do so, we cannot know for certain whether the model developed describes accurately the impact of external cultural influences on the lives of people.

   (D) Until they agree to do so, we can remain secure in the knowledge that communications specialists will never fully gain the scientific credibility they so passionately crave.

   (E) But even with such an emphasis, it will be the extent to which the model accurately describes the economic relationship between cultures that determines its usefulness.

17. The author most likely discusses an anthropological study in the second paragraph primarily in order to

   (A) provide to international communications specialists a model of cultural relationships

   (B) describe to international communications specialists new ways of conducting their research

   (C) highlight the flaws in a similar study conducted by international communications specialists

   (D) cite evidence that contradicts claims made by international communications specialists

   (E) support the claim that international communications specialists need to take the diversity of individual viewing habits into account

18. Which one of the following can most reasonably be concluded about the television viewers who were the subject of the study discussed in the second paragraph?

   (A) They will gradually come to prefer imported television programs over domestic ones.

   (B) They are likely someday to give up oral poetry in favor of watching television exclusively.

   (C) They would likely watch more television if they did not have oral poetry.

   (D) They enjoy domestic television programs mainly because they have little access to imported ones.

   (E) They watch television for some of the same reasons that they enjoy oral poetry.

19. According to the author, an empirical study of the effect of external cultural influences on the lives of people in a society must begin by identifying

   (A) the viewing habits and tastes of the people in the society

   (B) an accurate model of how imported cultural productions influence domestic ones

   (C) the role of the external cultural influences in the daily life of the people in the society

   (D) shared aspects of domestic and imported productions popular with mass audiences

   (E) social factors that affect how external cultural productions are given meaning by viewers

20. Suppose a study is conducted that measures the amount of airtime allotted to imported television programming in the daily broadcasting schedules of several developing nations. Given the information in the passage, the results of that study would be most directly relevant to answering which one of the following questions?

   (A) How does the access to imported cultural productions differ among these nations?

   (B) What are the individual viewing habits of citizens in these nations?

   (C) How influential are the domestic television industries in these nations?

   (D) Do imported programs attract larger audiences than domestic ones in these nations?

   (E) What model best describes the relationship between imported cultural influences and domestic culture in these nations?

GO ON TO THE NEXT PAGE.

Computers have long been utilized in the sphere of law in the form of word processors, spreadsheets, legal research systems, and practice management systems. Most exciting, however, has been the
(5) prospect of using artificial intelligence techniques to create so-called legal reasoning systems—computer programs that can help to resolve legal disputes by reasoning from and applying the law. But the practical benefits of such automated reasoning
(10) systems have fallen short of optimistic early predictions and have not resulted in computer systems that can independently provide expert advice about substantive law. This is not surprising in light of the difficulty in resolving problems involving the
(15) meaning and applicability of rules set out in a legal text.

Early attempts at automated legal reasoning focused on the doctrinal nature of law. They viewed law as a set of rules, and the resulting computer
(20) systems were engineered to make legal decisions by determining the consequences that followed when its stored set of legal rules was applied to a collection of evidentiary data. Such systems underestimated the problems of interpretation that can arise at every
(25) stage of a legal argument. Examples abound of situations that are open to differing interpretations: whether a mobile home in a trailer park is a house or a motor vehicle, whether a couple can be regarded as married in the absence of a formal legal ceremony,
(30) and so on. Indeed, many notions invoked in the text of a statute may be deliberately left undefined so as to allow the law to be adapted to unforeseen circumstances. But in order to be able to apply legal rules to novel situations, systems have to be equipped
(35) with a kind of comprehensive knowledge of the world that is far beyond their capabilities at present or in the foreseeable future.

Proponents of legal reasoning systems now argue that accommodating reference to, and reasoning from,
(40) cases improves the chances of producing a successful system. By focusing on the practice of reasoning from precedents, researchers have designed systems called case-based reasoners, which store individual example cases in their knowledge bases. In contrast
(45) to a system that models legal knowledge based on a set of rules, a case-based reasoner, when given a concrete problem, manipulates the cases in its knowledge base to reach a conclusion based on a similar case. Unfortunately, in the case-based systems
(50) currently in development, the criteria for similarity among cases are system dependent and fixed by the designer, so that similarity is found only by testing for the presence or absence of predefined factors. This simply postpones the apparently intractable
(55) problem of developing a system that can discover for itself the factors that make cases similar in relevant ways.

21. Which one of the following most accurately expresses the main point of the passage?

(A) Attempts to model legal reasoning through computer programs have not been successful because of problems of interpreting legal discourse and identifying appropriate precedents.
(B) Despite signs of early promise, it is now apparent that computer programs have little value for legal professionals in their work.
(C) Case-based computer systems are vastly superior to those computer systems based upon the doctrinal nature of the law.
(D) Computers applying artificial intelligence techniques show promise for revolutionizing the process of legal interpretation in the relatively near future.
(E) Using computers can expedite legal research, facilitate the matching of a particular case to a specific legal principle, and even provide insights into possible flaws involving legal reasoning.

22. The logical relationship of lines 8-13 of the passage to lines 23-25 and 49-53 of the passage is most accurately described as

(A) a general assertion supported by two specific observations
(B) a general assertion followed by two arguments, one of which supports and one of which refutes the general assertion
(C) a general assertion that entails two more specific assertions
(D) a theoretical assumption refuted by two specific observations
(E) a specific observation that suggests two incompatible generalizations

23. In the passage as a whole, the author is primarily concerned with

(A) arguing that computers can fundamentally change how the processes of legal interpretation and reasoning are conducted in the future
(B) indicating that the law has subtle nuances that are not readily dealt with by computerized legal reasoning programs
(C) demonstrating that computers are approaching the point where they can apply legal precedents to current cases
(D) suggesting that, because the law is made by humans, computer programmers must also apply their human intuition when designing legal reasoning systems
(E) defending the use of computers as essential and indispensable components of the modern legal profession

GO ON TO THE NEXT PAGE.

24. The passage suggests that the author would be most likely to agree with which one of the following statements about computerized automated legal reasoning systems?

   (A) These systems have met the original expectations of computer specialists but have fallen short of the needs of legal practitioners.
   (B) Progress in research on these systems has been hindered, more because not enough legal documents are accessible by computer than because theoretical problems remain unsolved.
   (C) These systems will most likely be used as legal research tools rather than as aids in legal analysis.
   (D) Rule systems will likely replace case-based systems over time.
   (E) Developing adequate legal reasoning systems would require research breakthroughs by computer specialists.

25. It can be most reasonably inferred from the passage's discussion of requirements for developing effective automated legal reasoning systems that the author would agree with which one of the following statements?

   (A) Focusing on the doctrinal nature of law is the fundamental error made by developers of automated legal systems.
   (B) Contemporary computers do not have the required memory capability to store enough data to be effective legal reasoning systems.
   (C) Questions of interpretation in rule-based legal reasoning systems must be settled by programming more legal rules into the systems.
   (D) Legal statutes and reasoning may involve innovative applications that cannot be modeled by a fixed set of rules, cases, or criteria.
   (E) As professionals continue to use computers in the sphere of law they will develop the competence to use legal reasoning systems effectively.

26. Based on the passage, which one of the following can be most reasonably inferred concerning case-based reasoners?

   (A) The major problem in the development of these systems is how to store enough cases in their knowledge bases.
   (B) These systems are more useful than rule systems because case-based reasoners are based on a simpler view of legal reasoning.
   (C) Adding specific criteria for similarity among cases to existing systems would not overcome an important shortcoming of these systems.
   (D) These systems can independently provide expert advice about legal rights and duties in a wide range of cases.
   (E) These systems are being designed to attain a much more ambitious goal than had been set for rule systems.

27. Which one of the following is mentioned in the passage as an important characteristic of many statutes that frustrates the application of computerized legal reasoning systems?

   (A) complexity of syntax
   (B) unavailability of relevant precedents
   (C) intentional vagueness and adaptability
   (D) overly narrow intent
   (E) incompatibility with previous statutes

28. The examples of situations that are open to differing interpretations (lines 25-30) function in the passage to

   (A) substantiate the usefulness of computers in the sphere of law
   (B) illustrate a vulnerability of rule systems in computerized legal reasoning
   (C) isolate issues that computer systems are in principle incapable of handling
   (D) explain how legal rules have been adapted to novel situations
   (E) question the value of reasoning from precedents in interpreting legal rules

S T O P

IF YOU FINISH BEFORE TIME IS CALLED, YOU MAY CHECK YOUR WORK ON THIS SECTION ONLY.
DO NOT WORK ON ANY OTHER SECTION IN THE TEST.

SECTION III
Time—35 minutes
25 Questions

Directions: The questions in this section are based on the reasoning contained in brief statements or passages. For some questions, more than one of the choices could conceivably answer the question. However, you are to choose the best answer; that is, the response that most accurately and completely answers the question. You should not make assumptions that are by commonsense standards implausible, superfluous, or incompatible with the passage. After you have chosen the best answer, blacken the corresponding space on your answer sheet.

1. Studies have shown that treating certain illnesses with treatment X produces the same beneficial changes in patients' conditions as treating the same illnesses with treatment Y. Furthermore, treatment X is quicker and less expensive than treatment Y. Thus, in treating these illnesses, treatment X should be preferred to treatment Y.

Which one of the following, if true, would most weaken the argument above?

(A)   Unlike treatment Y, treatment X has produced harmful side effects in laboratory animals.
(B)   There are other illnesses for which treatment Y is more effective than treatment X.
(C)   Until recently, treatment X was more expensive than treatment Y.
(D)   Treatment Y is prescribed more often by physicians than treatment X.
(E)   A third treatment, treatment Z, is even quicker and less expensive than treatment X.

2. Some political thinkers hope to devise a form of government in which every citizen's rights are respected. But such a form of government is impossible. For any government must be defined and controlled by laws that determine its powers and limits; and it is inevitable that some individuals will learn how to interpret these laws to gain a greater share of political power than others have.

Which one of the following is an assumption required by the argument?

(A)   In any form of government that leads to unequal distribution of political power, the rights of the majority of people will be violated.
(B)   A government can ensure that every citizen's rights are respected by keeping the citizens ignorant of the laws.
(C)   Not all the laws that define a government's power and limits can be misinterpreted.
(D)   In any form of government, if anybody gains a greater share of political power than others have, then somebody's rights will be violated.
(E)   People who have more political power than others have tend to use it to acquire an even greater share of political power.

3. Safety considerations aside, nuclear power plants are not economically feasible. While the cost of fuel for nuclear plants is significantly lower than the cost of conventional fuels, such as coal and oil, nuclear plants are far more expensive to build than are conventional power plants.

Which one of the following, if true, most strengthens the argument?

(A)   Safety regulations can increase the costs of running both conventional and nuclear power plants.
(B)   Conventional power plants spend more time out of service than do nuclear power plants.
(C)   The average life expectancy of a nuclear power plant is shorter than that of a conventional one.
(D)   Nuclear power plants cost less to build today than they cost to build when their technology was newly developed.
(E)   As conventional fuels become scarcer their cost will increase dramatically, which will increase the cost of running a conventional power plant.

4. Pundit: The average salary for teachers in our society is lower than the average salary for athletes. Obviously, our society values sports more than it values education.

The reasoning in the pundit's argument is questionable because the argument

(A)   presumes, without providing justification, that sports have some educational value
(B)   fails to consider that the total amount of money spent on education may be much greater than the total spent on sports
(C)   fails to consider both that most teachers are not in the classroom during the summer and that most professional athletes do not play all year
(D)   compares teachers' salaries only to those of professional athletes rather than also to the salaries of other professionals
(E)   fails to compare salaries for teachers in the pundit's society to salaries for teachers in other societies

GO ON TO THE NEXT PAGE.

5. The area of mathematics called "gauge field theory," though investigated in the nineteenth century, has only relatively recently been applied to problems in contemporary quantum mechanics. Differential geometry, another area of mathematics, was investigated by Gauss in the early nineteenth century, long before Einstein determined that one of its offspring, tensor analysis, was the appropriate mathematics for exploring general relativity.

Which one of the following is best illustrated by the examples presented above?

(A) Applications of some new theories or techniques in mathematics are unrecognized until long after the discovery of those theories or techniques.

(B) Mathematicians are sometimes able to anticipate which branches of their subject will prove useful to future scientists.

(C) The discoveries of modem physics would not have been possible without major mathematical advances made in the nineteenth century.

(D) The nineteenth century stands out among other times as a period of great mathematical achievement.

(E) Mathematics tends to advance more quickly than any of the physical sciences.

6. Recently discovered bird fossils are about 20 million years older than the fossils of the birdlike dinosaurs from which the birds are generally claimed to have descended. So these newly discovered fossils show, contrary to the account espoused by most paleontologists, that no bird descended from any dinosaur.

The reasoning in the argument is flawed in that the argument

(A) draws a generalization that is broader than is warranted by the findings cited

(B) rejects the consensus view of experts in the field without providing any counterevidence

(C) attacks the adherents of the opposing view personally instead of addressing any reason for their view

(D) fails to consider the possibility that dinosaurs descended from birds

(E) ignores the possibility that dinosaurs and birds descended from a common ancestor

7. Whether one is buying men's or women's clothing, it pays to consider fashion trends. A classic suit may stay in style for as long as five years, so it is worthwhile to pay more to get a well-constructed one. A trendy hat that will go out of style in a year or two should be purchased as cheaply as possible.

Which one of the following most accurately expresses the principle underlying the reasoning above?

(A) Formal attire tends to be designed and constructed to last longer than casual attire.

(B) The amount of money one spends on a garment should be roughly proportionate to the length of time one plans to keep wearing it.

(C) One should not buy a cheaply made garment when a well-constructed garment is available.

(D) The amount of money one spends on clothing should be roughly the same whether one is purchasing men's or women's attire.

(E) It is more appropriate to spend money on office attire than on casual attire.

8. Engineers are investigating the suitability of Wantastiquet Pass as the site of a new bridge. Because one concern is whether erosion could eventually weaken the bridge's foundations, they contracted for two reports on erosion in the region. Although both reports are accurate, one claims that the region suffers relatively little erosion, while the other claims that regional erosion is heavy and a cause for concern.

Which one of the following, if true, most helps to explain how both reports could be accurate?

(A) Neither report presents an extensive chemical analysis of the soil in the region.

(B) Both reports include computer-enhanced satellite photographs.

(C) One report was prepared by scientists from a university, while the other report was prepared by scientists from a private consulting firm.

(D) One report focuses on regional topsoil erosion, while the other report focuses on riverbank erosion resulting from seasonal floods.

(E) One report cost nearly twice as much to prepare as did the other report.

GO ON TO THE NEXT PAGE.

---

9. Letter to the editor: I have never seen such flawed reasoning and distorted evidence as that which you tried to pass off as a balanced study in the article "Speed Limits, Fatalities, and Public Policy." The article states that areas with lower speed limits had lower vehicle-related fatality rates than other areas. However, that will not be true for long, since vehicle-related fatality rates are rising in the areas with lower speed limits. So the evidence actually supports the view that speed limits should be increased.

The reasoning in the letter writer's argument is flawed because the argument

(A) bases its conclusion on findings from the same article that it is criticizing
(B) fails to consider the possibility that automobile accidents that occur at high speeds often result in fatalities
(C) fails to consider the possibility that not everyone wants to drive faster
(D) fails to consider the possibility that the vehicle-related fatality rates in other areas are also rising
(E) does not present any claims as evidence against the opposing viewpoint

10. Human settlement of previously uninhabited areas tends to endanger species of wildlife. However, the Mississippi kite, a bird found on the prairies of North America, flourishes in areas that people have settled. In fact, during the five years since 1985 its population has risen far more rapidly in towns than in rural areas.

Which one of the following, if true, most helps to explain why the Mississippi kite population does not follow the usual pattern?

(A) Residents of prairie towns have been setting off loud firecrackers near kites' roosting spots because of the birds' habit of diving at people and frightening them.
(B) Towns on the prairies tend to be small, with a low density of human population and large numbers of wild birds and animals.
(C) Since the international migratory bird protection treaty of 1972, it has been illegal to shoot kites, and the treaty has been effectively enforced.
(D) Wildlife such as pigeons and raccoons had already adapted successfully to towns and cities long before there were towns on the North American prairies.
(E) Trees are denser in towns than elsewhere on the prairie, and these denser trees provide greater protection from hail and windstorms for kites' nests and eggs.

11. When a major record label signs a contract with a band, the label assumes considerable financial risk. It pays for videos, album art, management, and promotions. Hence, the band does not need to assume nearly as much risk as it would if it produced its own records independently. For this reason, it is only fair for a major label to take a large portion of the profits from the record sales of any band signed with it.

Which one of the following most accurately describes the role played in the argument by the claim that a band signed with a major label does not need to assume nearly as much risk as it would if it produced its own records independently?

(A) It is the only conclusion that the argument attempts to establish.
(B) It is one of two unrelated conclusions, each of which the same premises are used to support.
(C) It is a general principle from which the argument's conclusion follows as a specific instance.
(D) It describes a phenomenon for which the rest of the argument offers an explanation.
(E) Premises are used to support it, and it is used to support the main conclusion.

12. Commentator: Recently, articles criticizing the environmental movement have been appearing regularly in newspapers. According to Winslow, this is due not so much to an anti environmental bias among the media as to a preference on the part of newspaper editors for articles that seem "daring" in that they seem to challenge prevailing political positions. It is true that editors like to run anti environmental pieces mainly because they seem to challenge the political orthodoxy. But serious environmentalism is by no means politically orthodox, and anti environmentalists can hardly claim to be dissidents, however much they may have succeeded in selling themselves as renegades.

The commentator's statements, if true, most strongly support which one of the following?

(A) Winslow is correct about the preference of newspaper editors for controversial articles.
(B) Critics of environmentalism have not successfully promoted themselves as renegades.
(C) Winslow's explanation is not consonant with the frequency with which critiques of environmentalism are published.
(D) The position attacked by critics of environmentalism is actually the prevailing political position.
(E) Serious environmentalism will eventually become a prevailing political position.

GO ON TO THE NEXT PAGE.

3

13. Philosopher: Some of the most ardent philosophical opponents of democracy have rightly noted that both the inherently best and the inherently worst possible forms of government are those that concentrate political power in the hands of a few. Thus, since democracy is a consistently mediocre form of government, it is a better choice than rule by the few.

Which one of the following principles, if valid, most helps to justify the philosopher's argument?

(A) A society should adopt a democratic form of government if and only if most members of the society prefer a democratic form of government.

(B) In choosing a form of government, it is better for a society to avoid the inherently worst than to seek to attain the best.

(C) The best form of government is the one that is most likely to produce an outcome that is on the whole good.

(D) Democratic governments are not truly equitable unless they are designed to prevent interest groups from exerting undue influence on the political process.

(E) It is better to choose a form of government on the basis of sound philosophical reasons than on the basis of popular preference.

14. Expert: What criteria distinguish addictive substances from nonaddictive ones? Some have suggested that any substance that at least some habitual users can cease to use is nonaddictive. However, if this is taken to be the sole criterion of nonaddictiveness, some substances that most medical experts classify as prime examples of addictive substances would be properly deemed nonaddictive. Any adequate set of criteria for determining a substance's addictiveness must embody the view, held by these medical experts, that a substance is addictive only if withdrawal from its habitual use causes most users extreme psychological and physiological difficulty.

Which one of the following can be properly inferred from the expert's statements?

(A) If a person experiences extreme psychological and physiological difficulty in ceasing to use a substance habitually, that substance is addictive.

(B) Fewer substances would be deemed addictive than are deemed so at present if an adequate definition of "addictive" were employed.

(C) A substance that some habitual users can cease to use with little or no psychological or physiological difficulty is addictive only if that is not true for most habitual users.

(D) A chemical substance habitually used by a person throughout life without significant psychological or physiological difficulty is nonaddictive.

(E) "Addiction" is a term that is impossible to define with precision.

GO ON TO THE NEXT PAGE.

15. Sociologist: A contention of many of my colleagues—
that the large difference between the wages of the
highest- and lowest-paid workers will inevitably
become a source of social friction—is unfounded.
Indeed, the high differential should have an
opposite effect, for it means that companies will
be able to hire freely in response to changing
conditions. Social friction arises not from large
wage differences, but from wage levels that are
static or slow changing.

Which one of the following is an assumption required
by the sociologist's argument?

(A) When companies can hire freely in response to
changing conditions, wage levels do not tend to
be static or slow changing.
(B) People who expect their wages to rise react
differently than do others to obvious disparities
in income.
(C) A lack of financial caution causes companies to
expand their operations.
(D) A company's ability to respond swiftly to
changing conditions always benefits its workers.
(E) Even relatively well-paid workers may become
dissatisfied with their jobs if their wages never
change.

16. Publisher: The new year is approaching, and with it
the seasonal demand for books on exercise and
fitness. We must do whatever it takes to ship
books in that category on time; our competitors
have demonstrated a high level of organization,
and we cannot afford to be outsold.

Which one of the following most accurately expresses
the main conclusion drawn in the publisher's argument?

(A) The company should make shipping books its
highest priority.
(B) By increasing its efficiency, the company can
maintain its competitive edge.
(C) The company will be outsold if it does not
maintain its competitors' high level of
organization.
(D) It is imperative that the company ship fitness and
exercise books on time.
(E) The company should do whatever is required
in order to adopt its competitors' shipping
practices.

17. Advertiser: There's nothing wrong with a tool that
has ten functions until you need a tool that can
perform an eleventh function! The VersaTool can
perform more functions than any other tool. If
you use the VersaTool, therefore, you will need
additional tools less often than you would using
any other multiple-function tool.

The reasoning in the advertiser's argument is most
vulnerable to criticism on the grounds that the
VersaTool might

(A) include some functions that are infrequently or
never needed
(B) include a number of functions that are difficult to
perform with any tool
(C) cost more than the combined cost of two other
multiple-function tools that together perform
more functions than the VersaTool
(D) be able to perform fewer often-needed functions
than some other multiple-function tool
(E) not be able to perform individual functions as
well as single-function tools

18. The flagellum, which bacteria use to swim, requires
many parts before it can propel a bacterium at all.
Therefore, an evolutionary ancestor of bacteria that
had only a few of these parts would gain no survival
advantage from them.

Which one of the following is an assumption on which
the argument depends?

(A) Any of bacteria's evolutionary ancestors that
had only a few of the parts of the flagellum
would be at a disadvantage relative to similar
organisms that had none of these parts.
(B) For parts now incorporated into the flagellum to
have aided an organism's survival, they would
have had to help it swim.
(C) All parts of the flagellum are vital to each of its
functions.
(D) No evolutionary ancestor of bacteria had only a
few of the parts of the flagellum.
(E) Any of bacteria's evolutionary ancestors that
lacked a flagellum also lacked the capacity to
swim.

GO ON TO THE NEXT PAGE.

19. Style manual: Archaic spellings and styles of punctuation in direct quotations from older works are to be preserved if they occur infrequently and do not interfere with a reader's comprehension. However, if they occur frequently, the editor may modernize them, inserting a note with an explanation to this effect in the text, or if similar modernizing has been done in more than one quotation, inserting a general statement in the preface. On the other hand, obvious typographical errors in quotations from modern works may be corrected without explanation.

Which one of the following follows logically from the statements above?

(A) If an editor corrects the spelling of a quoted word and the word occurs only once in the text, then an explanation should appear in a note or in the text.

(B) An editor may modernize an archaic spelling of a word found in a modern work without providing an explanation.

(C) An editor should modernize an archaic spelling of a word that is quoted from an older work if the spelling interferes with reader comprehension.

(D) An editor may modernize punctuation directly quoted from an older work if that punctuation occurs frequently and interferes with reader comprehension.

(E) If an editor modernizes only one of several similar instances of quoted archaic punctuation, an explanation should appear in the preface of the work.

20. Whoever murdered Jansen was undoubtedly in Jansen's office on the day of the murder, and both Samantha and Herbert were in Jansen's office on that day. If Herbert had committed the murder, the police would have found either his fingerprints or his footprints at the scene of the crime. But if Samantha was the murderer, she would have avoided leaving behind footprints or fingerprints. The police found fingerprints but no footprints at the scene of the crime. Since the fingerprints were not Herbert's, he is not the murderer. Thus Samantha must be the killer.

Which one of the following, if assumed, allows the conclusion that Samantha was the killer to be properly inferred?

(A) If there had been footprints at the scene of the crime, the police would have found them.

(B) Jansen's office was the scene of the crime.

(C) No one but Herbert and Samantha was in Jansen's office on the day of the murder.

(D) The fingerprints found at the scene of the crime were not Jansen's.

(E) The fingerprints found at the scene of the crime were not Samantha's.

21. Most opera singers who add demanding roles to their repertoires at a young age lose their voices early. It has been said that this is because their voices have not yet matured and hence lack the power for such roles. But young singers with great vocal power are the most likely to ruin their voices. The real problem is that most young singers lack the technical training necessary to avoid straining their vocal cords—especially when using their full vocal strength. Such misuse of the cords inevitably leads to a truncated singing career.

Which one of the following does the information above most strongly support?

(A) Young opera singers without great vocal power are unlikely to ruin their voices by singing demanding roles.

(B) Some young opera singers ruin their voices while singing demanding roles because their vocal cords have not yet matured.

(C) Only opera singers with many years of technical training should try to sing demanding roles.

(D) Only mature opera singers can sing demanding roles without undue strain on their vocal cords.

(E) Most young opera singers who sing demanding roles strain their vocal cords.

GO ON TO THE NEXT PAGE.

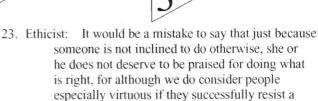

22. Food that is very high in fat tends to be unhealthy. These brownies are fat-free, while those cookies contain a high percentage of fat. Therefore, these fat-free brownies are healthier than those cookies are.

Which one of the following exhibits flawed reasoning most similar to the flawed reasoning exhibited by the argument above?

(A) Canned foods always contain more salt than frozen foods do. Therefore, these canned peas contain more salt than those frozen peas do.

(B) Vegetables that are overcooked generally have few vitamins. Therefore, these carrots, which are overcooked, contain fewer vitamins than those peas, which are uncooked.

(C) The human body needs certain amounts of many minerals to remain healthy. Therefore, this distilled water, which has no minerals, is unhealthy.

(D) Some types of nuts make Roy's throat itch. These cookies contain a greater percentage of nuts than that pie contains. Therefore, these cookies are more likely to make Roy's throat itch.

(E) Eating at a restaurant costs more than eating food prepared at home. Therefore, this home-cooked meal is less expensive than a restaurant meal of the same dishes would be.

23. Ethicist: It would be a mistake to say that just because someone is not inclined to do otherwise, she or he does not deserve to be praised for doing what is right, for although we do consider people especially virtuous if they successfully resist a desire to do what is wrong, they are certainly no less virtuous if they have succeeded in extinguishing all such desires.

The assertion that people are considered especially virtuous if they successfully resist a desire to do what is wrong plays which one of the following roles in the ethicist's argument?

(A) It is a claim for which the argument attempts to provide justification.

(B) It makes an observation that, according to the argument, is insufficient to justify the claim that the argument concludes is false.

(C) It is a claim, acceptance of which, the argument contends, is a primary obstacle to some people's having an adequate conception of virtue.

(D) It is, according to the argument, a commonly held opinion that is nevertheless false.

(E) It reports an observation that, according to the argument, serves as evidence for the truth of its conclusion.

GO ON TO THE NEXT PAGE.

24. Ecologists predict that the incidence of malaria will increase if global warming continues or if the use of pesticides is not expanded. But the use of pesticides is known to contribute to global warming, so it is inevitable that we will see an increase in malaria in the years to come.

The pattern of reasoning in which one of the following is most similar to that in the argument above?

(A) The crime rate will increase if the economy does not improve or if we do not increase the number of police officers. But we will be able to hire more police officers if the economy does improve. Therefore, the crime rate will not increase.

(B) If educational funds remain at their current level or if we fail to recruit qualified teachers, student performance will worsen. But we will fail to recruit qualified teachers. Therefore, student performance will worsen.

(C) If interest rates increase or demand for consumer goods does not decline, inflation will rise. But if there is a decline in the demand for consumer goods, that will lead to higher interest rates. Therefore, inflation will rise.

(D) If global warming continues or if the rate of ozone depletion is not reduced, there will be an increase in the incidence of skin cancer. But reduced use of aerosols ensures both that global warming will not continue and that ozone depletion will be reduced. Thus, the incidence of skin cancer will not increase.

(E) If deforestation continues at the current rate and the use of chemicals is not curtailed, wildlife species will continue to become extinct. But because of increasing population worldwide, it is inevitable that the current rate of deforestation will continue and that the use of chemicals will not be curtailed. Thus, wildlife species will continue to become extinct.

25. In ancient Greece, court witnesses were not cross-examined and the jury, selected from the citizenry, received no guidance on points of law; thus, it was extremely important for litigants to make a good impression on the jurors. For this reason, courtroom oratory by litigants is a good source of data on the common conceptions of morality held by the citizens of ancient Greece.

Which one of the following, if true, would most strengthen the argument?

(A) Litigants believed jurors were more likely to be impressed by litigants whose personality they preferred.

(B) Litigants believed jurors were more likely to subject the litigants' personal moral codes to close critical scrutiny than were people who did not sit on juries.

(C) Litigants believed jurors were likely to be impressed by litigants whose professed moral code most resembled their own.

(D) Litigants believed jurors to be more impressed by litigants who were of the same economic class as the jurors.

(E) Litigants believed jurors were likely to render their decisions based on a good understanding of the law.

S T O P

IF YOU FINISH BEFORE TIME IS CALLED, YOU MAY CHECK YOUR WORK ON THIS SECTION ONLY.
DO NOT WORK ON ANY OTHER SECTION IN THE TEST.

SECTION IV
Time—35 minutes
22 Questions

Directions: Each group of questions in this section is based on a set of conditions. In answering some of the questions, it may be useful to draw a rough diagram. Choose the response that most accurately and completely answers each question and blacken the corresponding space on your answer sheet.

A clown will select a costume consisting of two pieces and no others: a jacket and overalls. One piece of the costume will be entirely one color, and the other piece will be plaid. Selection is subject to the following restrictions:

If the jacket is plaid, then there must be exactly three colors in it.

If the overalls are plaid, then there must be exactly two colors in them.

The jacket and overalls must have exactly one color in common.

Green, red, and violet are the only colors that can be in the jacket.

Red, violet, and yellow are the only colors that can be in the overalls.

1. Which one of the following could be a complete and accurate list of the colors in the costume?

	Jacket	Overalls
(A)	red	red
(B)	red	violet, yellow
(C)	violet	green, violet
(D)	violet	red, violet
(E)	violet	red, violet, yellow

2. If there are exactly two colors in the costume, then which one of the following must be false?

(A)   At least part of the jacket is green.
(B)   At least part of the jacket is red.
(C)   The overalls are red and violet.
(D)   The overalls are red and yellow.
(E)   The overalls are violet and yellow.

3. If at least part of the jacket is green, then which one of the following could be true?

(A)   The overalls are plaid.
(B)   No part of the jacket is red.
(C)   No part of the jacket is violet.
(D)   At least part of the overalls are yellow.
(E)   At least part of the overalls are violet.

4. Which one of the following must be false?

(A)   Both green and red are colors used in the costume.
(B)   Both green and violet are colors used in the costume.
(C)   Both green and yellow are colors used in the costume.
(D)   Both red and violet are colors used in the costume.
(E)   Both violet and yellow are colors used in the costume.

5. If there are exactly three colors in the costume, the overalls must be

(A)   entirely red or else red and violet plaid
(B)   entirely yellow or else violet and yellow plaid
(C)   entirely violet or else red and violet plaid
(D)   entirely red or else entirely yellow
(E)   entirely red or else entirely violet

GO ON TO THE NEXT PAGE.

Questions 6-10

Six hotel suites—F, G, H, J, K, L—are ranked from most expensive (first) to least expensive (sixth). There are no ties. The ranking must be consistent with the following conditions:

    H is more expensive than L.

    If G is more expensive than H, then neither K nor L is more expensive than J.

    If H is more expensive than G, then neither J nor L is more expensive than K.

    F is more expensive than G, or else F is more expensive than H, but not both.

6.   Which one of the following could be the ranking of the suites, from most expensive to least expensive?

    (A)   G, F, H, L, J, K
    (B)   H, K, F, J, G, L
    (C)   J, H, F, K, G, L
    (D)   J, K, G, H, L, F
    (E)   K, J, L, H, F, G

7.   If G is the second most expensive suite, then which one of the following could be true?

    (A)   H is more expensive than F.
    (B)   H is more expensive than G.
    (C)   K is more expensive than F.
    (D)   K is more expensive than J.
    (E)   L is more expensive than F.

8.   Which one of the following CANNOT be the most expensive suite?

    (A)   F
    (B)   G
    (C)   H
    (D)   J
    (E)   K

9.   If L is more expensive than F, then which one of the following could be true?

    (A)   F is more expensive than H.
    (B)   F is more expensive than K.
    (C)   G is more expensive than H.
    (D)   G is more expensive than J.
    (E)   G is more expensive than L.

10.   If H is more expensive than J and less expensive than K, then which one of the following could be true?

    (A)   F is more expensive than H.
    (B)   G is more expensive than F.
    (C)   G is more expensive than H.
    (D)   J is more expensive than L.
    (E)   L is more expensive than K.

GO ON TO THE NEXT PAGE.

Questions 11-15

A locally known guitarist's demo CD contains exactly seven
different songs-S, T, V, W, X, Y, and Z. Each song occupies
exactly one of the CD's seven tracks. Some of the songs
are rock classics; the others are new compositions. The
following conditions must hold:

S occupies the fourth track of the CD. Both W and Y
  precede S on the CD. T precedes W on the CD.
A rock classic occupies the sixth track of the CD.
Each rock classic is immediately preceded on the CD
  by a new composition.
Z is a rock classic.

11. Which one of the following could be the order of
the songs on the CD, from the first track through the
seventh?

(A)   T, W, V, S, Y, X, Z
(B)   V, Y, T, S, W, Z, X
(C)   X, Y, W, S, T, Z, S
(D)   Y, T, W, S, X, Z, V
(E)   Z, T, X, W, V, Y, S

12. Which one of the following is a pair of songs that must
occupy consecutive tracks on the CD?

(A)   S and V
(B)   S and W
(C)   T and Z
(D)   T and Y
(E)   V and Z

13. Which one of the following songs must be a new
composition?

(A)   S
(B)   T
(C)   W
(D)   X
(E)   Y

14. If W precedes Y on the CD, then which one of the
following must be true?

(A)   S is a rock classic.
(B)   V is a rock classic.
(C)   Y is a rock classic.
(D)   T is a new composition.
(E)   W is a new composition.

15. If there are exactly two songs on the CD that both
precede V and are preceded by Y, then which one of the
following could be true?

(A)   V occupies the seventh track of the CD.
(B)   X occupies the fifth track of the CD.
(C)   Y occupies the third track of the CD.
(D)   T is a rock classic.
(E)   W is a rock classic.

GO ON TO THE NEXT PAGE.

Questions 16-22

A courier delivers exactly eight parcels-G, H, J, K, L, M, N, and O. No two parcels are delivered at the same time, nor is any parcel delivered more than once. The following conditions must apply:

L is delivered later than H.
K is delivered earlier than O.
H is delivered earlier than M.
O is delivered later than G.
M is delivered earlier than G.
Both N and J are delivered earlier than M.

16. Which one of the following could be the order of deliveries from first to last?

    (A)   N, H, K, M, J, G, O, L
    (B)   H, N, J, K, G, O, L, M
    (C)   J, H, N, M, K, O, G, L
    (D)   N, J, H, L, M, K, G, O
    (E)   K, N, J, M, G, H, O, L

17. Which one of the following must be true?

    (A)   At least one parcel is delivered earlier than K is delivered.
    (B)   At least two parcels are delivered later than G is delivered.
    (C)   At least four parcels are delivered later than H is delivered.
    (D)   At least four parcels are delivered later than J is delivered.
    (E)   At least four parcels are delivered earlier than M is delivered.

18. If M is the fourth parcel delivered, then which one of the following must be true?

    (A)   G is the fifth parcel delivered.
    (B)   O is the seventh parcel delivered.
    (C)   J is delivered later than H.
    (D)   K is delivered later than N.
    (E)   G is delivered later than L.

19. If H is the fourth parcel delivered, then each of the following could be true EXCEPT:

    (A)   K is the fifth parcel delivered.
    (B)   L is the sixth parcel delivered.
    (C)   M is the sixth parcel delivered.
    (D)   G is the seventh parcel delivered.
    (E)   O is the seventh parcel delivered.

20. Each of the following could be true EXCEPT:

    (A)   H is delivered later than K.
    (B)   J is delivered later than G.
    (C)   L is delivered later than O.
    (D)   M is delivered later than L.
    (E)   N is delivered later than H.

21. If K is the seventh parcel delivered, then each of the following could be true EXCEPT:

    (A)   G is the fifth parcel delivered.
    (B)   M is the fifth parcel delivered.
    (C)   H is the fourth parcel delivered.
    (D)   L is the fourth parcel delivered.
    (E)   J is the third parcel delivered.

22. If L is delivered earlier than K, then which one of the following must be false?

    (A)   N is the second parcel delivered.
    (B)   L is the third parcel delivered.
    (C)   H is the fourth parcel delivered.
    (D)   K is the fifth parcel delivered.
    (E)   M is the sixth parcel delivered.

S T O P

IF YOU FINISH BEFORE TIME IS CALLED, YOU MAY CHECK YOUR WORK ON THIS SECTION ONLY.
DO NOT WORK ON ANY OTHER SECTION IN THE TEST.

LSAT® Writing Sample Topic

© 2006 by Law School Admission Council, Inc. All rights reserved.

Directions: The scenario presented below describes two choices, either one of which can be supported on the basis of the information given. Your essay should consider both choices and argue for one and against the other, based on the two specified criteria and the facts provided. There is no "right" or "wrong" choice: a reasonable argument can be made for either.

The charitable grants manager of Highland Electricity has received funding requests for two worthy programs—*Market Your Art,* a business program for artists, and *Get Certified,* a technical skills program for adults seeking to change careers—but can grant only one. Write an essay in which you argue for one program over the other, keeping in mind the following two criteria:

• Highland wants to help as many people as possible through its charitable giving.
• Grants should enhance the company's corporate stature within its service area.

The first funding request is to provide a grant to an arts center that serves several communities in the utility's defined service territory. The grant money would be used to establish a year-long entrepreneurship program called *Market Your Art,* designed for artists who are new to the business of selling their art. Participants will learn about pricing their work, running a small business, working with art galleries, soliciting corporate work, and bidding for public contracts. Business professionals will work closely with individual artists, and enrollment is limited to around a dozen or so participants. Highland is well known for its financial support of local community projects, yet the utility has in the past turned down numerous funding requests from arts and cultural organizations because the proposed programs did not directly further its economic development objectives.

The second request is for a grant to a nonprofit jobs training program called *Get Certified.* Participants are generally those looking for a career change, and the focus is on needed technical skills. *Get Certified* is now in the final phase of a one-time multi-year grant and is in need of new funding. Although several hundred participants have successfully completed the program, it is not heavily represented inside the utility's service area. Nonetheless, *Get Certified* is well established, increasingly in demand, and may eventually expand to locations in Highland's service area. The utility's involvement at this early stage may provide opportunities for building additional relationships and good will.

Scratch Paper
Do not write your essay in this space.

Directions:

1. Use the Answer Key on the next page to check your answers.

2. Use the Scoring Worksheet below to compute your raw score.

3. Use the Score Conversion Chart to convert your raw score into the 120-180 scale.

Scoring Worksheet

1. Enter the number of questions you answered correctly in each section.

Number Correct

SECTION I. . . . . _____
SECTION II . . . . _____
SECTION III. . . . _____
SECTION IV. . . . _____

2. Enter the sum here: _____
This is your Raw Score.

Conversion Chart:
For Converting Raw Score to the 120-180 LSAT Scaled Score
LSAT Form 6LSN69

Reported Score	Raw Score Lowest	Raw Score Highest
180	98	101
179	97	97
178	96	96
177	95	95
176	94	94
175	_*	_*
174	93	93
173	92	92
172	91	91
171	90	90
170	89	89
169	87	88
168	86	86
167	85	85
166	83	84
165	82	82
164	80	81
163	79	79
162	77	78
161	75	76
160	74	74
159	72	73
158	70	71
157	68	69
156	67	67
155	65	66
154	63	64
153	61	62
152	60	60
151	58	59
150	56	57
149	54	55
148	53	53
147	51	52
146	49	50
145	47	48
144	46	46
143	44	45
142	42	43
141	41	41
140	39	40
139	38	38
138	36	37
137	35	35
136	33	34
135	32	32
134	30	31
133	29	29
132	28	28
131	26	27
130	25	25
129	24	24
128	22	23
127	21	21
126	20	20
125	19	19
124	18	18
123	16	17
122	15	15
121	14	14
120	0	13

SECTION I

1.	D	8.	C	15.	C	22.	B
2.	A	9.	E	16.	B	23.	A
3.	B	10.	E	17.	C	24.	B
4.	B	11.	B	18.	E	25.	A
5.	D	12.	D	19.	B		
6.	C	13.	B	20.	B		
7.	C	14.	C	21.	D		

SECTION II

1.	B	8.	E	15.	B	22.	A
2.	B	9.	B	16.	C	23.	B
3.	E	10.	D	17.	D	24.	E
4.	A	11.	C	18.	E	25.	D
5.	C	12.	B	19.	B	26.	C
6.	A	13.	A	20.	A	27.	C
7.	D	14.	C	21.	A	28.	B

SECTION III

1.	A	8.	D	15.	A	22.	B
2.	D	9.	D	16.	D	23.	B
3.	C	10.	E	17.	D	24.	C
4.	B	11.	E	18.	B	25.	C
5.	A	12.	A	19.	D		
6.	A	13.	B	20.	C		
7.	B	14.	C	21.	E		

SECTION IV

1.	D	8.	A	15.	E	22.	C
2.	A	9.	D	16.	D		
3.	E	10.	D	17.	C		
4.	C	11.	D	18.	D		
5.	E	12.	E	19.	A		
6.	B	13.	D	20.	B		
7.	C	14.	D	21.	C		

CHAPTER THREE: THE DECEMBER 2006 LSAT DECONSTRUCTED

The explanations below are presented in the same order that the questions are given on the exam. Page headers are provided to help you identify which questions are explained on each page, and if you encounter any unknown terms, a glossary is provided at the end of the book. Also, please keep in mind that all explanations draw on methods discussed in *The PowerScore LSAT Logic Games Bible* and *The PowerScore LSAT Logical Reasoning Bible*. Please refer to those texts if you desire a more detailed discussion of a particular concept or approach.

DECEMBER 2006 SECTION 1: LOGICAL REASONING

Overview: Between the two logical reasoning sections on this test, this one was the less challenging, unless you have difficulty with Flaw in the Reasoning questions, which were disproportionately represented (there were six such questions in this section). Other question types were represented roughly equally, with two examples each of the Must Be True, Main Point, Strengthen, Justify, Weaken, Parallel, and Principle question types, and one question each for the Method of Reasoning, Resolve the Paradox, Point at Issue, and Assumption question types. As is typical of logical reasoning on the LSAT, questions tended to get more difficult toward the end of this section.

Question #1: Main Point. The correct answer choice is (D)

This stimulus contains an editorial about the fishing town of Redhook, and a dam on the Smithfield River proposed by the residents of this coastal community. The editorialist notes that the annual flood costs Redhook $3 million, and that the proposed dam would cost $5 million. The editorialist argues against the dam, noting that it would prevent nutrients from flowing from the river into the ocean, which would lead local fish to feed elsewhere. This loss of these fish, the editorialist argues, would cost Redhook $10 million, so damming the river would be misguided:

Premise:	The annual flood costs the community $3 million annually.
Premise:	The dam would cost $5 million
Premise:	The dam-caused lack of local fish would cost the community an additional $10 million.
Conclusion:	Damming the river would be a misguided course of action.

The question stem asks for the main conclusion of the editorial's argument. This answer can be prephrased:

> "*This position* (that it is advisable to dam the river) *is misguided.*"

Answer choice (A): This answer choice advocates the dam, so it cannot reflect the editorialist's conclusion referenced above.

Answer choice (B): If the fish have the option of feeding elsewhere, as asserted in the stimulus, then the Smithfield's nutrients must not be absolutely essential to their population. Further, the main conclusion concerns the dam, which is not even mentioned in this answer choice. This information would only serve as a premise to support the main conclusion of the stimulus, which is that the dam should not be built.

Answer choice (C): While this answer choice ultimately reaches the same conclusion as the editorial writer (that the dam should not be built), it does so based on a different premise. The editorial cites the impact on the local fish population, while this answer choice cites the high construction cost.

Answer choice (D): This is the correct answer choice. This choice states that building the dam would be a mistake, reflecting the conclusion as prephrased above.

Answer choice (E): The cost of the annual flood is uncontested, so this answer choice is accurate according to the stimulus, but it is a premise, rather than the conclusion, of the editorialist's argument.

Question #2: Evaluate the Argument. The correct answer choice is (A)

This stimulus presents information about a traffic accident. From prior investigation, it is known that at least one of the following factors was in play: The driver of the first vehicle did not signal prior to changing lanes, and/or the driver of the second vehicle was speeding. Either of these two would make a driver liable for the resulting accident, as follows:

Driver One signaled ⟶ Driver Two speeding ⟶ Driver Two Liable
Driver Two speeding ⟶ Driver One signaled ⟶ Driver One Liable

It is known that the driver of the first vehicle was changing lanes without signaling. Based on this premise, the author of the stimulus *improperly* concludes that the driver of the second vehicle must not be liable, based on the following **flawed** reasoning:

Driver One signal ⟶ Driver One Liable ⟶ Driver Two Liable

This is a mistaken negation of the first conditional rule diagrammed above. We do know that if Driver Two wasn't speeding, then Driver One must have been at fault, but we cannot logically conclude that if Driver One was at fault, that Driver Two must not have been speeding.

The conclusion that Driver Two is liable is flawed, because the conditional reasoning in the stimulus would allow for shared liability—that is, we know that if one driver isn't liable, the other one must be, but we cannot conclude the reverse: that if one driver is liable, the other one isn't. The question stem asks which answer choice provides the most important information for evaluating the author's conclusion. As we can see from the original conditional statements offered in the stimulus, the only provided method to determine Driver Two's liability concerns that driver's speed.

Answer choice (A): This is the correct answer choice. If the driver of the second vehicle was driving at an excessive speed, then we could properly conclude that the second driver shares in the liability:

Driver Two speeding ⟶ Driver Two Liable

This is the only information, based on the conditional reasoning in the stimulus, that would allow us to draw such a conclusion.

Answer choice (B): The first driver's knowledge of the infraction is immaterial to the question of causality. Unwitting or not, it is the failure to signal that would attach liability for the resulting accident.

Answer choice (C): The involvement of other drivers is also immaterial to the question of liability on the part of the two drivers that we know were involved. The stimulus tells us that "it is known" that either the driver of the first vehicle did not properly signal a lane change or that the driver of the second vehicle was speeding, and that either of these would result in a driver's liability for the resulting accident. The involvement of other vehicles is not relevant to the conditional reasoning provided in the stimulus.

Answer choice (D): If a witness is unreliable, then any conclusions based on premises this witness establishes might also be unreliable. But the stimulus states that "further evidence has *proved* that the turn signal was not on, though the driver of that vehicle admits to having changed lanes." The reliability of the first driver is therefore not at issue, and knowledge of the information from this answer choice would lend no insight into the evaluation of the author's conclusion.

Answer choice (E): The stimulus specifically states that, absent excessive speed by the second driver, failure to signal would be the sole cause of the resulting accident. Thus, whether the second driver would have seen the signal is irrelevant.

Question #3: Resolve the Paradox. The correct answer choice is (B)

This stimulus provides that in some places, iceberg lilies are the mainstay of the summer diet of grizzly bears, who uproot the plants and eat their bulbs. While the bears destroy a large percentage of the iceberg lilies, it has been determined that the survival of the lily is actually promoted by the bears:

<u>Cause</u>   <u>Effect</u>
Bears eat lilies ⟶ Lilies benefit

The question stem asks the test-taker to "resolve the apparent discrepancy" in the stimulus. In prephrasing the answer, one must look for a premise consistent with the two apparently paradoxical premises. In this case, how can the bears' foraging and eating a large percentage of these lilies actually aid in the plant's survival? We need to look for an answer choice that explains how reduction of the lilies' numbers would somehow promote the plant's survival.

Answer choice (A): This answer choice would appear to widen the apparent discrepancy:

Bears eat lilies ⟶ Bears kill more lilies than they eat

Even with this new information, it remains unclear how the bears' actions promote plant growth.

Answer choice (B): This is the correct answer choice, as it shows how "thinning the herd" can actually help the iceberg lily survive. If a *lack* of disturbance leads to depletion of necessary resources, then the bears' disturbance actually provides a valuable service.

Answer choice (C): This choice would seem to widen the apparent discrepancy:

Bears forage ⟶ smaller number of lilies produced

Since this information points to an apparent detriment associated with the bears' foraging, so this answer choice is incorrect.

Answer choice (D): This choice helps explain why it is convenient for the bears to eat the lilies, but it does not explain how this might promote the lilies' survival.

Answer choice (E): This answer choice would explain why the bears would *benefit* from eating the lilies, but it does nothing to explain how the bears *promote* the plant's survival.

Question #4: Flaw in the Reasoning. The correct answer choice is (B)

When an advertisement is presented in a stimulus, we should generally view its claims with some degree of initial skepticism. This stimulus states that 75% of dermatologists surveyed prefer Dermactin to all other forms of skin cream. According to the ad, this is because the makers of Dermactin consulted with dermatologists during the product's development "to ensure…the best skin cream on the market." This assertion incorrectly presumes that the following flawed reasoning is valid:

Consult with dermatologists ⟶ Ensure best skin cream

The question stem asks how the reasoning in the ad is flawed. In prephrasing this answer, we might quickly consider the flaws in the author's reasoning:

First of all, does a consultation with dermatologists really *ensure* the best skin cream on the market?

Second, the argument assumes that the cited dermatologists' preferences were based primarily on the quality of the product (for example, if the surveyed dermatologists owned stock in the company which produces Dermactin, their preferences might have been based on financial considerations).

Finally, we are not told much about the survey methods. We know nothing about how many dermatologists were surveyed, nothing about the questions asked, and nothing about the comparisons made by the survey (perhaps the respondents were given only two poor options from which to choose).

Answer choice (A): The possibility that other types of physicians might have cause to use Dermactin would not necessarily render the sample unrepresentative. Since Dermactin is a skin cream, relevant opinions in this case come from dermatologists, and these are the only opinions on which the advertisement's claims are based.

Answer choice (B): This is the correct answer choice. Without information on the number of dermatologists surveyed, there is no way to determine the validity of the claim of 75% preference among dermatologists. We would need to know the sample size in order to determine the value of the survey results. For example, if only four dermatologists were surveyed during the development of Dermactin, then a 75% preference would only represent three opinions—hardly sufficient to draw any strong conclusions.

Answer choice (C): Since the stimulus doesn't discuss this issue, and no presumptions are suggested regarding the relative qualifications of the various dermatologists polled, this answer choice should be eliminated.

Answer choice (D): The reasoning in the stimlulus does not rely on an appeal to the opinions of consumers with no special knowledge of skin care. While the author of the stimulus does appeal to the expertise of the consulted dermatologists, there is no appeal whatsoever to the opinions of consumers, so this choice is incorrect.

Answer choice (E): The advertisement specifically suggests "*if* you need a skin cream, use Dermactin." Those people who use no skin cream have been explicitly excluded, not overlooked.

Question #5: Parallel Reasoning. The correct answer choice is (D)

This stimulus provides a landscape architect's conditional reasoning regarding a screen: If the screen is a hedge, then that hedge must be made of either hemlocks or Leyland cypress trees:

$$\text{Screen is hedge} \longrightarrow \begin{array}{c} \text{hemlocks} \\ or \\ \text{Leyland cypress trees} \end{array}$$

Location, however, precludes the use of Leyland cypress trees. Therefore, since the use of Leyland trees has been ruled out, if the screen must be a hedge, it must be hemlocks:

$$\text{Screen is hedge} \longrightarrow \text{hemlocks}$$

The question stem asks which pattern of reasoning in the answer choices is most similar to that in the stimulus. In this case, the author presents a conditional statement that allows for two possibilities, and then rules out one of the two. When the second necessary condition is ruled out, it can be concluded that when the sufficient condition is present, the necessary condition that has not been ruled out must also take place.

Answer choice (A): This answer choice presents a conditional statement, and then rules out the sole necessary variable, allowing the author to draw a valid conclusion based on the contrapositive of the conditional statement:

$$\text{North side entrance} \longrightarrow \text{ramp}$$

$$\text{R\o amp} \longrightarrow \text{north si\o de entrance.}$$

Since this choice does not involve two alternative necessary conditions, it does not parallel the reasoning in the stimulus, and this answer choice should be eliminated.

Answer choice (B): In this answer choice, the sole necessary condition is ruled out, and a new outcome is introduced:

$$\text{Visitors allowed} \longrightarrow \text{parking needed}$$

$$\text{Par\o king} \longrightarrow \text{design change}$$

This answer choice does not parallel the reasoning found in the stimulus.

Answer choice (C): Here there are two alternatives. In this scenario, however, the two alternatives are mutually exclusive – clay must exclude shale and vice versa:

$$\text{Clay} \longrightarrow \text{Sh\o ale}$$

$$\text{Shale} \longrightarrow \text{C\o lay}$$

It is then concluded, based on a test sample of shale, that the entire subsoil is made of shale (that is, there is no clay). In the stimulus, on the other hand, the "impossibility" is caused by another factor. Both Leyland cypress trees and hemlocks are legitimate choices for the hedge; only the *location* renders the use of Leyland cypress trees an impossibility.

Answer choice (D): This is the correct answer choice. Here, there are two alternatives for the necessary condition:

$$\text{path} \longrightarrow \begin{array}{c} \text{concrete} \\ \textit{or} \\ \text{stone} \end{array}$$

It is then stated that the concrete path is an impossibility. Therefore, if there is to be a path, it will have to be stone:

$$\text{path} \longrightarrow \text{stone}$$

Thus, the necessary condition, like that in the stimulus, is left as the lone remaining alternative. The pattern of reasoning in this answer choice perfectly mirrors that found in the stimulus.

Answer choice (E): In this answer choice, there are two viable alternatives:

$$\text{space the size of this meadow} \longrightarrow \begin{array}{c} \text{potentially playground} \\ \textit{or} \\ \text{picnic area} \end{array}$$

The author then points out that the picnic area would create litter and the playground would be noisy, so it is best that the space remain a meadow:

$$\underline{\text{Playground and picnic area}} \longrightarrow \text{remain meadow}$$

Since both necessary variables are ruled out in this case, this pattern of reasoning does not parallel that found in the stimulus.

Question #6: Flaw in the Reasoning. The correct answer choice is (C)

This stimulus provides a statement from Deirdre regarding some philosophers' views of happiness: Many philosophers argue that the goal of every person is to achieve happiness, which is satisfaction derived from living up to one's potential. Furthermore, this happiness is elusive and can be achieved only after years of sustained effort. Deirdre disagrees with these philosophers, since they have "clearly" overstated the difficulty of achieving happiness. She argues that a simple walk on a sunny afternoon causes many to experience feelings of happiness.

The question stem asks us to describe the flaw in Deirdre's argument. Have the philosophers "clearly" overstated the difficulty of achieving happiness? "Clearly" seems to be used in this case more as a statement of persuasion than as a statement of empirical fact. Apparently Deirdre has redefined "happiness" to mean something different from the philosophers' definition of living up to one's full potential. This knowledge should direct us to any answer choice that reflects this shift in the definition of "happiness."

Answer choice (A): This answer choice describes an *ad hominem* attack– an attempt to discredit a position by attacking character. Since Dierdre does not launch a personal attack against the referenced philosophers, this is not the correct answer choice.

Answer choice (B): Although the definition of happiness did shift within the stimulus, this is not the same as *Dierdre's* definition changing over *time*. Since this is not the flaw reflected in Dierdre's argument, this answer choice is incorrect.

Answer choice (C): This is the correct answer choice. As prephrased above, Deirdre's reasoning is flawed because it allows the meaning of "happiness" to shift in the course of the argument. Initially, "happiness" is defined as living up to one's full potential. Yet when Deirdre discusses walks on a sunny afternoon, "happiness" has clearly taken on a different meaning—something more like peace or simple contentment. Since the meaning of this key term has changed, Deidre's reasoning is flawed.

Answer choice (D): It is the philosophers who state that happiness is the goal of life, not Deirdre, so this answer choice is incorrect.

Answer choice (E): Dierdre's claim is only that "many" philosophers have a particular view. Since she makes no broad claims, this does not represent a generalization based on the testimony of an unrepresentative group.

Question #7: Assumption. The correct answer choice is (C)

This stimulus provides a series of statements involving the application of the law of supply and demand to global ecology. Global ecological problems are created when there is an imbalance between demand and sustainable supply, and global supply is inherently limited, but potential global demand is not. Based on these premises, the author concludes that any solution to global ecological problems would require reducing current human demand:

Premise: Global ecological problems are created by an imbalance between demand and sustainable supply.

Premise: Global supply is limited, but *potential* global demand is not.

Conclusion: The only way to solve the natural tendency toward imbalance is to reduce *current* global demand.

Note the leap from a premise about the *potential* global demand to a conclusion about *current* global demand. The author apparently equates these two, with the *assumption* that current global demand causes the same tendency toward imbalance. As we seek an answer choice that addresses this issue, one way to verify the correct assumption is to apply the Assumption Negation Technique. When the negated version of an answer choice weakens (or destroys) the argument in the stimulus, we know that the given answer choice reflects an assumption on which the argument relies.

Answer choice (A): The stimulus discusses the natural tendency toward imbalance between demand and sustainable supply, which is the problem for which the author is suggesting a solution, so this assertion may run counter to the information provided in the stimulus. Even if supply and demand were to balance themselves out in the "long run," it is unclear how long this might take. It is the general tendency toward imbalance that causes the problems the author seeks to solve.

If we apply the assumption negation technique to check our work, this is the negated version of this answer choice:

"Supply and demand don't tend to balance themselves out in the long run."

Since this would not weaken or destroy the argument in the stimulus, this answer choice cannot reflect an assumption on which the author's argument depends.

Answer choice (B): We don't need to be able to determine the precise limitations on the earth's sustainable supply in order for that supply to be outpaced by human demand, so this cannot be an assumption on which this argument relies. To check our work, we can apply the Assumption Negation technique and note whether the negated version of the answer choice would have any effect on the strength of the author's argument:

"It is not possible to determine the limitations of the earth's sustainable supply."

Even if this were impossible, this would not necessarily hamper our ability to deplete the supply completely and this would not affect the conclusion that human demand must be lowered as a part of any solution to the ecological problem, so this cannot be an assumption on which the argument is based.

Answer choice (C): This is the correct answer choice. For the argument's conclusion to be logically drawn, we must assume that there is not only *potential* for demand to outpace supply—actual current demand must exceed the earth's supply for there to be an imbalance which requires a solution. Applying the Assumption Negation technique to the answer choice would yield the following:

> "Human demand does not exceed supply."

If this were the case, then lowering human demand as called for in the conclusion would not necessarily be so vital. Because the negated answer choice weakens the conclusion in the stimulus, this must be an assumption required by the argument.

Answer choice (D): If it were never possible to achieve a balance between environmental supply and human demand, there would be no long term solution to the global ecological problem, presuming that actual current demand were to outpace global supply. Since the stimulus discusses prospects for finding a solution, this answer choice cannot be an assumption on which the author's argument relies. To check our work, we can apply the assumption negation technique by logically negating this answer choice:

> "It is sometimes possible to achieve a balance between the environmental supply and human demand."

Since this would not weaken the argument in the stimulus in any way, this answer choice cannot reflect an assumption on which the conclusion of the stimulus relies.

Answer choice (E): The argument in the stimulus is based in part on the idea that there are no limits on potential human demands. If these demands did not decrease the earth's supply, the problem that the author is looking to solve would not really exist, so this cannot be an assumption on which the argument relies. To check our work, we can again apply the assumption negation technique, to arrive at the following negated version of this answer choice:

> "Human consumption does decrease environmental supply."

As we can see, the negated version of this answer choice has no weakening effect on the argument in the stimulus, so this cannot be an assumption on which the argument relies.

Question #8: Weaken. The correct answer choice is (C)

This stimulus discusses the impact of sugar consumption on hyperactivity in children with ADD (attention deficit disorder). The stimulus begins with the author's conclusion: We can now dismiss the notion that sugar consumption exacerbates hyperactivity in ADD children. This conclusion is based on a "scientific study" (be wary of the vague appeal to authority here) which showed that hyperactivity levels among ADD children who were given three common sugars was not distinguishable from those of ADD children who received a sugar substitute (we should also note the vague description of the sugar substitute—its effects must be distinguishable from those of sugar for it to facilitate an effective control group).

The question stem asks which of the answer choices most weakens the argument.

Answer choice (A): The fact that only one of the sugars used in the study was widely suspected of exacerbating hyperactivity does not change the observed behavior of the study's subjects. This does not weaken the conclusion drawn in the stimulus.

Answer choice (B): Since the stimulus is concerned exclusively with ADD children, information about children in general is not relevant to the argument.

Answer choice (C): This is the correct answer choice. If the sugar substitute used in the study had the same or similar effect as the three sugars, it would not facilitate a good control group for the study, and no conclusions about distinguishing characteristics of the sugars could be logically drawn.

Answer choice (D): As long as all groups participated in these activities, it would not affect the outcome of the study (of course if the control group participated in these activities but the sugar groups did not, the study would be severely flawed).

Answer choice (E): The fact that some children have this belief would not necessarily have an effect on this study, as it is unclear whether any of the subjects would have actually been able to make this distinction, nor whether such knowledge would have had any effects on their behavior.

Question #9: Must Be True—Principle. The correct answer choice is (E)

The philosopher in this stimulus sets out a basic conditional reasoning principle: if an action achieves its intended goal, and it benefits someone else, then it is good:

Achieved intent *and* benefit to others ⟶ morally good

From the conditional statement above, we can also draw the contrapositive:

M̶o̶r̶a̶l̶l̶y̶ good ⟶ a̶c̶h̶i̶e̶v̶e̶d̶ intent *or* benefit t̶o̶ others

The question asks us to find the answer choice that conforms to the above principle.

Answer choice (A): In this answer choice, Colin displayed malicious intent, but his plan backfired and the intent was not achieved. Further, there was only detriment for Colin and his friends, and no benefits derived by others. The **flawed** conditional reasoning applied in this answer choice is as follows:

A̶c̶h̶i̶e̶v̶e̶d̶ intent *and* benefit t̶o̶ others ⟶ morally good

In this choice, the intent was not achieved, and the outcome was detrimental, so this would not meet the philosopher's definition of a morally good action.

Answer choice (B): In this answer choice, although Derek's neighbors were vegetarians, his intentions to be welcoming were achieved. The benefit to others is something of a grey area—even though the neighbors didn't eat, they still arguably derived the benefits of being made to feel welcome. Regardless, the stimulus does not provide enough information to justifiably rule Derek's act "not morally good." That is, we know that achieved intent and benefits to others are sufficient to define an act as "morally good":

Achieved intent *and* benefit to others ⟶ morally good

We are never informed, however, of criteria sufficient to define an act as "not morally good." To draw such a conclusion would require a mistaken negation of the conditional diagram above.

In this choice, the welcoming intentions were achieved, and there may have been benefit to others. But even if there were no benefits, this would not be sufficient to determine that Derek's acts were "not morally good."

Answer choice (C): In this answer choice, Ellen did not achieve her original intent, which was to get a promotion. She was able to put her extra money to good use, but this is not the same as achieving one's intent. There were benefits to others, since her family got to take a vacation, but since this was a different benefit than originally intended, this would not meet the philosopher's criteria to define an act as morally good.

The **flawed** reasoning in this answer choice runs contrary to the stimulus as follows:

Achieved̶ intent   *and*   benefit to others ⟶ morally good

In this example, there was benefit to others, but the initial intent was not achieved, so this would not meet the philosopher's definition of a morally good action.

Answer choice (D): In this scenario, Louisa displayed malicious intent, planning to frame Henry, but her intent was not achieved, and there was no benefit to others. However, according to the conditional reasoning in the stimulus, we cannot assert based on this scenario that Louisa's action was not morally good. This answer choice reflects the following **flawed** reasoning, which is contrary to the information in the stimulus:

Achieved̶ intent   *and*   benefit t̶o others ⟶ morall̶y good

As we can see, this is a mistaken negation of the conditional statement provided in the stimulus (Achieved intent *and* benefit to others ⟶ morally good), so this answer choice is incorrect.

Answer choice (E): This is the correct answer choice. In this scenario, Yolanda's intent was for her children to enjoy a visit to their grandfather. This intent was achieved, bringing the intended benefits to Yolanda's children, reflecting the following conditional reasoning, which is valid based on the stimulus:

Achieved intent   *and*   benefit to others ⟶ morally good

The good intentions are there, as are the benefits for others, so this would be defined as a morally good act, regardless of the fact that Yolanda was also able to derive some benefit as well.

Question #10: Flaw. The correct answer choice is (E)

In this stimulus, a columnist discusses recent research suggesting that *vigorous* exercise can significantly lower one's chances for certain cardio-respiratory diseases. The columnist then concludes that one should ignore older studies that claim the same effect could be achieved by *non-strenuous* walking.

The question stem asks for the vulnerability in columnist's reasoning. The columnist draws a conclusion based on the mistaken notion that because benefits can be derived in one manner, the same benefits can't be achieved by other means:

Premise:	Strenuous walking reduces one changes of getting certain diseases.
Flawed Conclusion:	Non-strenuous walking must not be effective.

Answer choice (A): The fact that other means might be effective in reducing certain illnesses does not weaken the columnist's conclusion, because the columnist is only discussing <u>exercise</u> and whether or not the exercise needs to be vigorous. Whether there are other means of reducing the risks of cardio-respiratory diseases is irrelevant.

Answer choice (B): If the discussion were about overall health, this could be seen as weakening the columnist's conclusion, but this discussion is only about the effect of exercise on cardio-respiratory diseases and whether that exercise must be vigorous. The fact that vigorous exercise may bring some outside risk does not play into an argument about its effects on the certain cardiovascular respiratory illnesses referenced in the stimulus.

Answer choice (C): Overlooking another possible benefit of vigorous exercise is not a flaw in this case. The discussion in the stimulus only concerns the beneficial effects of exercise on cardio-respiratory diseases and whether such exercise must be vigorous.

Answer choice (D): The discussion in the stimulus is not about perceptions of health, and we could only speculate as to the relationship between perception and physical manifestation. In any case, people who perceive themselves as healthy can still acquire cardio-respiratory diseases, and the columnist's conclusion involves the effect of exercise. Since this answer choice does not discuss exercise at all, it does not reflect the flaw in the author's reasoning.

Answer choice (E): This is the correct answer choice. The argument is weak because it fails to show that the conclusion of the recent report is better justified than an opposing conclusion reached in older studies. This mirrors our prephrased answer; no logical justification is offered for ignoring the old studies in favor of the new report.

Question #11: Must be True. The correct answer choice is (B)

This stimulus discusses extreme value theory (EVT), which predicts that the limit on human life spans is more than likely between 113 and 124 years, while under traditional statistical models, some humans would live beyond 130 years. Thus far, no one has lived longer than 124 years, the upper limit indicated by EVT analysis.

Premise: Traditional statistical models estimate human longevity at 130 years.
Premise: EVT predicts human longevity to be between 113 and 124 years.
Premise: No one so far has lived beyond the age predicted by EVT analysis.

This stimulus contains no conclusions, so a Must be True question is likely to follow. We might note that current statistics seem to conform more closely to models that employ EVT analysis.

Answer choice (A): According to the stimulus, it is not clear that EVT offers a more reliable means of predicting future trends. This answer choice reflects a far broader conclusion than is justifiable based on the information provided in the stimulus. While we can infer that EVT might be somewhat accurate, we cannot conclude that this method is more reliable in general.

Answer choice (B): This is the correct answer choice. This is accurate; no human life span has exceeded the upper limits suggested by EVT, while the highest limit suggested by traditional methods is significantly higher. Thus, based on empirical evidence to date, EVT appears to produce a more accurate model of human life's upper limit than more traditional models.

Answer choice (C): EVT is a tool of statistical analysis, and just because no person has exceeded the upper limits of EVT projection does not mean that it is physically impossible to do so.

Answer choice (D): The assertion in this answer choice is not supported at all by the stimulus. The fact that EVT projects the upper limit of human life span does not mean that there is no point in conducting research on increasing this upper limit.

Answer choice (E): While the stimulus offers some limited evidence of EVT's predictive value, the author does not take the rather strong stand represented here, that EVT should eventually replace all traditional forms of statistical analysis, so this answer choice is incorrect.

Question #12: Flaw in the Reasoning. The correct answer choice is (D)

The author begins this stimulus by pointing out that the number of synthetic carcinogenic chemical compounds, used as pesticides, preservatives, or food additives, is small in comparison to the number of non-synthetic carcinogenic compounds found in plants and animals. Based on this premise the author concludes that one cannot point to synthetic carcinogens as the cause of the increased cancer rates of the last few decades.

Since we are searching for a weakness in the argument, we should consider that a numbers comparison like the one offered might not be applicable to this inquiry—that is, even if there are many non-synthetic carcinogens in existence, we cannot draw conclusions about their practical effects on cancer rates without knowing how much cancer they cause. Instead of considering whether there are more natural or synthetic carcinogens, we should consider which type offers the greatest practical threat (which type leads to the greatest *actual* number of cancer cases, for example).

Answer choice (A): Pollutants are not the same as carcinogens. Furthermore, by offering an alternative cause this answer choice would actually strengthen the conclusion that the increased cancer rates are not attributable to synthetic carcinogens.

Answer choice (B): This does not weaken the conclusion regarding non-synthetic carcinogens and would, like answer choice (A), actually strengthen that conclusion.

Answer choice (C): Toxic is not synonymous with carcinogenic, so this answer choice would not weaken the argument in the stimulus in any way.

Answer choice (D): This is the correct answer choice. While there is a large number of non-synthetic carcinogens, exposure to these compounds is limited. On the other hand, there is increased exposure to synthetic carcinogens that is coincident to the increased cancer rate. As stated in the prephrased answer, it is the exposure to the carcinogens, not their numbers, which is responsible for the increased cancer rate.

Answer choice (E): Varied susceptibility is not overlooked; it is simply irrelevant to the argument in the stimulus, which concerns the possible causes of cancer rates that we *know* to have increased in recent decades.

Question #13: Main Point. The correct answer choice is (B)

This stimulus provides that no set of attributes could prepare an organism for every condition, so perfect adaptation is impossible. Thus, natural selection will not result in perfectly adapted organisms.

The question stem asks us to identify the main conclusion of the passage, which is prephrased in the first sentence of the stimulus.

Answer choice (A): It is accurate to assert that, according to the stimulus, perfect adaptation is impossible, but it does not reflect the author's main conclusion, rather, it supports the author's main conclusion, which is that perfect adaptation will not result from natural selection.

Answer choice (B): This is the correct answer choice, as it restates the prephrased answer above: Since there can be no perfect adaptation, it would be a mistake to presume that natural selection will result in perfect adaptation.

Answer choice (C): This is a restatement of one of the premises of the stimulus, offered in support of the main conclusion, that it would be a mistake to presume that natural selection will result in perfectly adapted organisms.

Answer choice (D): This statement is accurate but does not reflect the main conclusion of the argument; rather, it restates one of the premises provided in support of the main conclusion, which is stated in the first sentence.

Answer choice (E): This too is true, but the author of the stimulus asserts that it would be a mistake to hold such beliefs, so this certainly does not represent the main conclusion of the passage.

Question #14: Method of Reasoning—AP. The correct answer choice is (C)

This author of this stimulus discusses the trade route between China and the West, and concludes that it wouldn't be surprising to learn that it was opened centuries or millennia before 200 B.C., the widely-accepted date. The first statement of this stimulus provides the author's conclusion. The rest of the stimulus provides premises for that conclusion: the same things that made the Great Silk Road attractive as a trade route after 200 B.C. were present during the early emigration to China one million years ago. If there was migration, there just as easily could have been trade along the same route:

Premise:	The route that was valuable to China and the West would also have been valuable to those traveling to China from Africa and the Middle East.
Premise:	The immigration from Africa and the Middle East began at least one million years ago.
Conclusion:	It would not be surprising to discover that the trade routes between China and the West were opened well before 200 B.C.

The question stem asks what function the statement about the migration to China from Africa and the Middle East one million years ago serves in the passage. This is a premise that is offered in support of the main conclusion.

Answer choice (A): The conclusion in the stimulus is that it would not be surprising, not that it definitely occurred. This quote is not intended to provide "conclusive" evidence, so this choice is a safe elimination.

Answer choice (B): Intermediate conclusions can serve as premises for the main conclusion, but since this piece of information is provided as a fact, unsupported by other premises, this cannot be properly characterized as a subsidiary conclusion.

Answer choice (C): This is the correct answer choice. With migration from the Middle East and Africa to China, early trade between these two regions would seem a reasonable possibility. This migration occurred one million years ago, far earlier than the trade routes were believed to have been established.

Answer choice (D): The stimulus does not make a distinction between respective routes to Africa and the Middle East, so this answer choice is incorrect.

Answer choice (E): Since the referenced statement does not represent the main conclusion of the stimulus, this answer choice is incorrect.

Question #15: Flaw in the Reasoning. The correct answer choice is (C)

This stimulus presents a discussion of species classification. Under the typological theory, which is not widely used today, species are classified solely on the basis of observable physical characteristics, even though "sibling species" are indistinguishable on the basis of appearance. Because they cannot interbreed, the mainstream theory of species classification distinguishes these sibling species as separate species. The passage concludes that the typological theory of species classification is unacceptable because it does not recognize this distinction:

Premise: The typological theory, which classifies based on physical appearance, does not consider sibling species to be separate species, even though they cannot interbreed.

Premise: The mainstream theory of species classification does distinguish sibling species, based on the fact that they cannot interbreed.

Conclusion: The typological theory must be unacceptable.

The question asks us to identify a weakness in the argument. The author bases the conclusion on the fact that the two theories have different perspectives, apparently presuming the exclusive validity of the mainstream theory.

Answer choice (A): The argument doesn't require that all aspects of the typological theory be discussed. Since this does not weaken the writer's conclusion, this answer choice is incorrect.

Answer choice (B):This answer choice describes a conditional reasoning error that is not reflected in the stimulus.

Answer choice (C): This is the correct answer choice. The author relies on the mainstream theory of classification (and presumes its merit) to discredit the typological theory—the need to recognize sibling species as separate species provides the basis of the argument advanced in the stimulus.

Answer choice (D): This would not necessarily be a flaw if it were accurate; a single fact is in some cases sufficient to determine a theory to be inaccurate. There is no such fact in this stimulus, however, so this answer choice is incorrect.

Answer choice (E): The author does not need to explain why sibling species cannot interbreed. Since this plays no role in the argument, this answer choice is incorrect.

Question #16: Justify the Conclusion. The correct answer choice is (B)

In this stimulus, Chiu asserts that the belief that a person is always morally blameworthy for feeling certain emotions is misguided. Since persons are only responsible for what is under their control, Chiu concludes that a person is not always morally blameworthy for feeling certain emotions.

Premise:　　　People are responsible only for acts under their control:

Individual responsibility ⟶ under individual control

under indi~~vidual~~ control ⟶ Individual ~~re~~sponsibility

Premise:　　　Whether one feels the referenced emotions is sometime not under one's control:

Certain emotions ⟶ under indi~~vidual~~ control

Linking the above two premises:

Certain emotions ⟶ under indi~~vidual~~ control ⟶ Individual ~~re~~sponsibility

Conclusion:　　People are not always morally blameworthy for certain emotions:

Certain emotions ⟶ always moral~~ly~~ blameworthy

We can see that this conclusion represents a leap in logic, and in order to justify Chiu's conclusion, we must identify the answer choice that links moral blameworthiness with individual responsibility or control.

Answer choice (A): The conclusion concerns moral blameworthiness for feeling certain *emotions*, and this choice refers to *actions* beyond one's control that are responses to certain emotions. Further, since there is no reference to moral blameworthiness, this answer choice cannot represent the link needed to justify Chiu's conclusion.

Answer choice (B): This is the correct answer choice. This choice, which discusses the variables required to link the loose ends of Chui's argument, can be diagrammed as follows:

Moral blameworthiness ⟶ Individual responsibility

When we draw the contrapositive, we see that if a person is not responsible for something, he or she is not morally blameworthy:

Individual ~~re~~sponsibility ⟶ Moral blame~~worthiness~~

When we add this to the author's premise that people are responsible only for what is within their control, Chiu's conclusion is logically justified:

Under control ⟶ Individual responsibility ⟶ Moral blameworthiness

From the above conditional statement, we can conclude that, according to Chiu, in cases where emotions are beyond one's control, moral blame should not always be assigned.

Answer choice (C): Chiu's argument involves control of emotions and associated blameworthiness. The relative *appropriateness* of the referenced emotions has nothing to do with Chiu's argument, and this answer choice cannot support or justify Chiu's conclusion in any way, so this choice cannot be correct.

Answer choice (D): This answer choice fails to reference one's own moral blameworthiness for feeling certain emotions, so it cannot provide the link needed to justify Chiu's argument. The reasoning in this choice can be diagrammed as follows:

Under control ⟶ hold *others* responsible

Since this answer choice introduces a new variable, involving the responsibility of *others*, and does not link the elements discussed above, this answer choice does not justify Chui's conclusion.

Answer choice (E): Chiu makes the point that sometimes emotions are not under one's control, and it is these cases to which his argument refers. The proportions of controllable vs. uncontrollable emotions for which people are commonly blamed are irrelevant to the argument. Further, this answer choice fails to tie together the rogue elements of the argument as discussed above, so this answer choice is incorrect.

Question #17: Must Be True—Pr. The correct answer choice is (C)

This stimulus contains two conditional statements provided by an industrial advisor. The first statement is that if two new processes that are being considered have no substantial difference in cost, then the less environmentally damaging alternative should be chosen:

substantial ~~cost~~ difference ⟶ less damaging alternative chosen

There is a different model if a company already uses an environmentally damaging process. If retooling for a less damaging process would involve substantial cost, then that company should retool only if that retooling is legally required *or* would likely bring long-terms savings substantially greater than the cost:

Retooling with substantial cost ⟶ legally required *or* LT savings > cost

The question stem asks which answer choice conforms most closely to the principles as stated by the industrial advisor.

Answer choice (A): The industrial advisor suggests in the stimulus that substantially expensive retooling should be done only if it is legally required or would produce substantial savings. In this answer choice, there is a new law, but this does not suggest a legal *requirement*. The referenced law provides tax credits, a financial incentive, but the savings associated with the more environmentally sound process for manufacturing dye would be *slight*. Since the new process in this answer neither provides substantial savings nor is legally required, the advice that the company should change over to the new process would not accord with the principles provided by the industrial advisor.

Answer choice (B): In this answer choice, the pin cushion company is considering changing its process to one that is more environmentally friendly in order to preserve its image. The first piece of advice from the industrial advisor would not be relevant here, since it is applicable only to a decision between two processes. In the scenario provided by this answer choice, the pin cushion company already has a process in place. According to the advisor, a substantially more expensive new process like the one under consideration by the factory should only be taken on when it is legally required or when it provides substantial savings. This answer choice specifies that both processes are legal, and rather than providing substantial savings, the new process would lead to substantial losses. Since the industrial advisor would advise against change, the advice that the company should change its process would be contrary to that suggested by the author of the stimulus.

Answer choice (C): This is the correct answer choice. In this scenario, the two processes being considered for staple manufacture are not substantially different in cost. Under the advisor's model, the manufacturer should choose the most environmentally friendly process. Process A is slightly more expensive but far more environmentally friendly than Process B. According to the advisor's principles, the manufacturer should choose Process A, which is recommended in this case.

Answer choice (D): In the scenario provided by this answer choice, the company is deciding between two processes of ball bearing manufacture which are not substantially different in cost. The industrial advisor would recommend going with process B, since it would be the more environmentally friendly choice. This answer choice recommends Process A, contrary to the advisor's model, apparently based on the slight savings associated. Since this answer choice does not follow the principles of the industrial advisor, it should be eliminated.

Answer choice (E): In this scenario, the shoelace company already has a process in place, so the first piece of advice offered by the industrial advisor would be inapplicable. The switch to a new, more environmentally friendly process would be costly, and the stimulus provides that an expensive process changeover is only justified by legal requirement or long-term savings that substantially outweigh the associated costs. In this answer choice, the savings apparently do not even equal the cost, so switching processes does not conform to the principles of the industrial advisor.

Question #18: Flaw. The correct answer choice is (E)

This stimulus presents a poll of the residents of a province, in which the provincial capital is the city most often selected as the best place to live. The capital is also the largest city in the province, and the writer's conclusion is that the poll reflects a majority preference among respondents for large cities in general. This flawed reasoning presumes that it was the size of the capital city that was so appealing to respondents, in spite of the fact that other factors might have come into play (access to goods and services would likely be greater in a capital city, for example). Further, looking exclusively at the "winner" of the poll doesn't tell us much about the voting—only that that one capital city got more votes than any other *single* city.

The question asks us to identify a vulnerability of the argument. While there may have been more respondents who chose the capital than any other town, this is not sufficient to conclude that most respondents would prefer large towns to small ones.

Answer choice (A): The stimulus concerns residents of this province. What residents of other provinces believe is irrelevant to the argument.

Answer choice (B): This is not a comparative poll. What occurs in other provinces is totally irrelevant to this poll, this province, and the author's conclusion.

Answer choice (C): This is not a weakness – that is exactly what this poll is seeking to measure: what city residents of a particular province consider the best place to live.

Answer choice (D): The flaw in the stimulus does not involve a misinterpretation of what drove respondents' preferences. Again, the flaw: just because the capital city received more votes than any other single city does not mean that there was a preference for larger cities in general.

Answer choice (E): This is the correct answer choice. This choice reflects the flaw in the interpretation of the survey. While the capital city did receive more votes than any other single city, this does not necessarily mean that large cities received more votes in total than small cities.

Question #19: Justify the Conclusion. The correct answer choice is (B)

In this stimulus, a geneticist states that genes have a strong tendency to self-replicate in a manner similar to that of viruses. Based on this fact, some biologists call genes "selfish." Although the term is not meant to reflect the attitudes or intentions underlying this behavior, the geneticist concludes that the term "selfish" is misapplied to genes, because selfishness only concerns behavior that is best for oneself, and that replicating one's self is not selfish:

Premise:

Selfish ———→ concerns behavior that is best for oneself

From the above statement we can also draw the contrapositive:

concerns behavior ~~that~~ is best for oneself ———→ Sel~~fish~~

Conclusion:

Gene: self-replicating ———→ sel~~fish~~

Since we are asked to find the answer that would justify this conclusion, we should be looking for an answer choice that makes the conclusion of the stimulus undeniable. We should choose the answer choice which would force the conclusion to follow, by tying together the "rogue elements" of the above conditional argument: self-replication and behavior that is not necessarily selfish.

Answer choice (A): The relative importance of selfishness vs. altruism is irrelevant to the geneticist's argument, and the notion of bringing about the best conditions for others is not discussed in the stimulus. Further, it is clear that this answer choice does not provide the link as prephrased above, and does not justify the conclusion that about the applicability of the term "selfish" to replicating genes.

Answer choice (B): This is the correct answer choice. "Creating replicas of oneself (otherwise known as self-replicating) does not help bring about the best conditions for oneself" can be diagrammed as follows:

Self-replicating ———→   concerns behavior that is best for oneself

We can link this with the premise from the stimulus, as follows:

Self-replicating ———→   concerns behavior that is best for oneself ———→ Selfish

As we can see, this extra premise links the elements discussed above, and in so doing justifies the conclusion that self-replication is not selfish, and that such a characterization represents a misnomer.

Answer choice (C): Since the geneticist is concerned with the use of selfish in the behavioral sense, referring to the described use as a misnomer, the geneticist's opinion must be that the same rules should apply, and that there is compatibility between the behavioral and everyday definitions of "selfish." Since this answer choice is contrary to the information provided in the stimulus, it cannot justify the geneticist's conclusion.

Answer choice (D): The geneticist does not ignore the fact that self-replication is a phenomenon that is not limited to genes, and in fact acknowledges that viruses do this as well. The assertion in this answer choice is inapplicable to the geneticist, who does not ignore this fact, so this answer choice is incorrect.

Answer choice (E): According to the stimulus, biologists do have sufficient evidence to determine the applicability of the term selfish. The geneticist just believes that they should not call self-replication selfish, based on current knowledge. Since the geneticist has already rendered an opinion, it cannot be the case that an assumption of the argument is that there is insufficient evidence to do so, and biologists presumably have access to the same evidence as geneticists. This answer choice should therefore be eliminated.

Question #20: Parallel Reasoning – Flaw. The correct answer choice is (C)

The first statement presented in this stimulus is that only experienced salespeople will be able to meet the company's selling quota. In other words, if you are going to meet the company's sales quota, then you must be an experienced salesperson:

> quota ⟶ experienced salesperson

The writer concludes that if one doesn't achieve the quota, one must not be an experienced salesperson:

> q̶u̶o̶t̶a ⟶ experienced s̶alesperson

This is a clear case of Mistaken Negation. We are asked which answer choice reflects the flawed pattern of reasoning in the stimulus, so the correct choice will be the one which reflects an analogous Mistaken Negation.

Answer choice (A): The first conditional statement provided here is that employees are allowed to dress casually only on Fridays. The author of this answer choice concludes, based on Hector's formal dress, that he must not be going to work. The reasoning contained in this answer choice is flawed, because Hector might still go to work on Friday, and opt out of the casual option. This is not a Mistaken Negation, however, so this choice does not parallel the flawed reasoning found in the stimulus.

Answer choice (B): This is the correct answer choice. This answer choice offers a conclusion based on a conditional statement:

Premise:	Only music lovers take this class.
Flawed conclusion:	Since Hillary's not taking the class, she's not a music lover.

Premise:	take class ⟶ music lover
Flawed Conclusion:	tak̶e c̶lass ⟶ musi̶c lover

This flaw is the same as that found in the stimulus: Mistaken Negation.

Answer choice (C): This answer choice provides the following conditional reasoning:

Premise:	Only oceanographers enjoy the Atlantic in midwinter—that is, if you enjoy the Atlantic in the midwinter, you *must* be an oceanographer.
Conclusion:	Since Gerald is not an oceanographer, he can be expected not to enjoy the Atlantic in midwinter. This valid conclusion is the contrapositive of the conditionally stated premise.

The above can be diagrammed as follows:

Premise:	Enjoy Atl MW ⟶ oceanographer
Valid Conclusion:	Oceano̶grapher ⟶ Enjoy A̶tl MW

Since the conclusion above is a valid contrapositive of the original statement, this sound reasoning cannot parallel the flawed reasoning reflected the stimulus.

Answer choice (D): This answer choice presents the following conditional reasoning:

Premise: It is only in the northern latitudes that we would find giant redwoods; that is, if we see a giant redwood, we must be in the northern latitudes.

Conclusion: We are looking at a giant redwood, so we must be in the northern latitudes.

As we can see, the above conclusion represents a restatement of a conditional rule:

Premise: Redwood $\longrightarrow$ Northern latitudes
Conclusion: Redwood $\longrightarrow$ Northern latitudes

Since this choice is based on sound reasoning, it cannot parallel the flaw in the stimulus.

Answer choice (E): This answer choice reflects the following flawed conditional reasoning:

Premise: Only accomplished mountain climbers can scale El Capitan; that is, if one can scale El Capitan, that person is an accomplished climber.

Conclusion: Since Michelle is an accomplished climber, she must be able to scale El Capitan.

The reasoning in this answer choice is flawed, but it is not a mistaken negation, as we can see when we diagram the above conditional statements:

Premise: $EC \longrightarrow AMC$
Conclusion: $AMC_M \longrightarrow EC_M$

This is a Mistaken *Reversal*, rather than a Mistaken *Negation*. Because this answer choice does not employ the same pattern of flawed reasoning as that reflected in the stimulus, this answer choice should be eliminated.

Question #21: Must Be True. The correct answer choice is (D)

In this stimulus, a designer states that any garden and adjoining living room separated by sliding glass doors can become a single space visually. When the doors may be open, as in the summer, the "single space" will be created if it does not already exist. If the visual single space does exist already, this effect will be magnified:

Sliding doors open ⟶ create single space *or* intensify pre-existing single space

Even during the colder months, the effect will remain, *if* the garden is coordinated with the room *and* contributes a strong visual interest on its own:

Garden coordinated *and* contributes strong visuals ⟶ single space effect remains

The question stem asks which answer is most strongly supported by the designer's statements, so we should locate the answer choice in accordance with the above conditional rules.

Answer choice (A): This answer choice provides the following conditional statement regarding a room with the sliding glass doors closed:

Garden coordinated ⟶ contributes strong visual interest

This statement runs contrary to the information provided in the stimulus, referenced above, which states in the winter, when the door is closed, the single space effect will continue if the garden is coordinated with the room <u>and</u> if the garden contributes a strong visual interest of its own:

Garden coordinated *and* contributes strong visuals ⟶ single space effect remains

This answer choice incorrectly characterizes the strong visual interest single space effect as the sole necessary condition for being coordinated with the room, so this answer choice is incorrect.

Answer choice (B): This answer choice provides the following incorrect conditional reasoning:

Single space effect ⟶ garden well coordinated

This answer choice is contrary to the conditional reasoning provided in the stimulus:

Garden coordinated *and* contributes strong visuals ⟶ single space effect remains

Since this answer choice reverses the sufficient and necessary conditions, and leaves out any reference to contribution of a strong visual interest, this choice is incorrect.

Answer choice (C): This answer choice is also contrary to what is said in the stimulus, which tells us that a visual single room effect can be created if the doors are open. The designer also states that the effect can be intensified by opening the doors:

Sliding doors open ⟶ create single space *or* <u>intensify pre-existing single space</u>

Since we are told that the open sliding glass doors have the potential to *intensify* a single space effect, we know that they are not always required to *create* such an effect.

Answer choice (D): This is the correct answer choice. According to the stimulus, the contribution of a strong visual interest doesn't even come into play in the summer, during which the opening of the sliding doors creates a single space effect if it didn't already exist. If this effect was already present, opening the doors intensifies it:

Sliding doors open ⟶ create single space *or* intensify pre-existing single space

Because a garden can visually merge with an adjoining living room and form a single space in the summer, even if it does not contribute a strong visual interest of its own, this answer choice is correct.

Answer choice (E): The designer provides conditional reasoning regarding sliding glass doors. The first rule concerns open sliding doors, and the author points out that this may happen in the summer. This does not imply that the same course of action in the winter would not have the same results, so this answer choice is incorrect.

Question #22: Strengthen. The correct answer choice is (B)

This stimulus discusses a number of people who got sick eating local anchovies. The city of San Martin advised against eating these anchovies, because they were apparently tainted with a harmful neurotoxin called domoic acid. But because of a drop in the local population of a particular type of plankton, the anchovies are apparently safe to eat once again.

We should note that there is a leap from a premise regarding the drop in the plankton population to a conclusion about the safety of the anchovies. Since the question asks us to strengthen the conclusion, we should look for the answer choice that best explains why the decrease in plankton has led to lower levels of domoic acid and more safely edible anchovies.

Answer choice (A): If several types of plankton cause domoic acid in anchovies, this would weaken the conclusion that the noted drop in one particular plankton type would render the anchovies safe to eat.

Answer choice (B): This is the correct answer choice. This answer choice provides sufficient additional information to the stimulus to explain why the anchovies are now safe to eat. When the population of the plankton is extraordinarily large, the anchovies eat so much of it that they become toxic with domoic acid. This answer choice links the rogue elements of the stimulus as prephrased above.

Answer choice (C): While this answer choice does provide a link between the referenced plankton and domoic acid in the lab, it doesn't necessarily explain how a drop in this particular plankton population would affect the presence or absence of domoic acid in nature. Because it does not fully explain why the anchovies are again safe to eat, this answer choice should be eliminated.

Answer choice (D): If a drop in *P. australis* plankton is generally coincident with a drop in anchovies, then fewer plankton might result in fewer anchovies, but not necessarily safer anchovies. Therefore, this choice is incorrect.

Answer choice (E): This answer choice states that there must be significant quantities of domoic acid in the seawater in order to support a large population of *P. australis* (Large population ⟶ significant domoic acid level). But the drop in population does not necessarily mean that the level of domoic acid dropped (large population ⟶ significant domoic acid level). This is a Mistaken Negation, so this answer choice should be eliminated.

Question #23: Point at Issue. The correct answer choice is (A)

In the dialogue presented in this stimulus, Constance states that the traditional definition of full employment is an unemployment rate of 5%, and that a rate lower than 5% will result in a rise in inflation.

Brigita claims that the traditional definition of full employment is no longer applicable because it was developed before the rise of temporary and part-time work and the fall in benefit levels. Because some people have to work several part-time jobs or work in a series of temporary assignments, Brigita argues, one cannot consider 5% unemployment to be full employment.

The question stem asks which of the answer choices reflects an issue on which the two speakers would disagree with one another. In prephrasing an answer, we should note that Constance and Brigita seem to disagree about what constitutes full employment. Constance believes that full employment is achieved when the unemployment rate is 5%; Brigita believes that this definition of full employment is outdated.

Answer choice (A): This is the correct answer choice. This choice reflects the prephrased answer above, stating that Constance and Brigita disagree about what definition of full employment is applicable under present economic conditions.

Answer choice (B): The dialogue surrounds the applicability of the traditional definition of full employment, but Constance and Brigita do not get into a policy based argument about what level of unemployment is a "good idea," so this answer choice is incorrect.

Answer choice (C): Since Constance never even mentions the proper categorization for a part time worker, there is no way to conclude that this would be a point of contention between the two speakers.

Answer choice (D): While this answer choice reflects Brigita's assertion, Constance never weighs in on this issue, and because we cannot presume disagreement based on the information provided in the stimulus, this answer choice must be eliminated.

Answer choice (E): It is known that Constance believes that an unemployment rate below 5% will cause inflation to rise, but no assertion is made by either speaker regarding the effects of a higher unemployment rate on inflation.

Question #24: Strengthen. The correct answer choice is (B)

Current theory regarding supernovas states that when there is a supernova event the size of the one that occurred in 1987, a neutron star should have remained afterward. Yet there is still no evidence of any such neutron star or of the pulse of radiation normally associated with such an event, in spite of searches conducted using some of the most sensitive instruments ever developed. The writer then concludes that current theory is wrong with regard to the assertion that supernovas of a certain size always produce neutron stars.

This stimulus presents the following conditional relationships: If there is a supernova, there is a neutron star, and if there is a neutron star, there is generally a pulse of radiation:

$$\text{Supernova} \longrightarrow \text{neutron star} \longrightarrow \text{pulse of radiation}$$

We are asked which of the answer choices most strengthens the argument, the conclusion of which is that current theory is wrong with regard to supernovas and neutron stars.

Answer choice (A): This answer choice lends support to *current* theory, which would actually weaken the author's conclusion that current theory must be wrong.

Answer choice (B): This is the correct answer choice. If these instruments have detected neutron stars at a greater distance than the 1987 supernova, this would strengthen the case that these instruments would detect a neutron star that resulted from the 1987 supernova, if such a star existed. This lends support to the author's assertion that current theory must be wrong.

Answer choice (C): This statement neither strengthens nor weakens the writer's conclusion that the current theory is wrong.

Answer choice (D): Since this answer choice lends credibility to current theory, this weakens the writer's conclusion that current theory must be wrong.

Answer choice (E): None of this explains the absence of the neutron star in this instance. This information is irrelevant to the writer's argument regarding current theory. Because it certainly does not strengthen the author's conclusion, this answer choice should be eliminated.

Question #25: Weaken. The correct answer choice is (A)

According to this stimulus, corporations that encourage frequent social events in the workplace show higher profits than those businesses that rarely encourage such events. The writer concludes, based upon this, that EZ Corp. could raise its profits by having more staff parties during business hours. This conclusion is apparently based on the author's questionable assumption that there must be a cause and effect relationship: increased socializing in the workplace *causes* higher profits.

The question stem asks which answer choice most weakens the conclusion.
To weaken a causal conclusion, we have several options to consider:

1. Show that an alternative cause exists.
2. Show that the supposed cause exists without the supposed effect.
3. Show that the hypothesized effect exists without the assumed cause.
4. Show that the elements thought to be cause and effect were reversed.
5. Show an effective attack on the data.

Answer choice (A): This is the correct answer choice. If the great majority of corporations that encourage frequent social events in the workplace do so *because* they are already earning higher profits, this appears to be a case of mistaken cause and effect (as prephrased fourth above).

Answer choice (B): The writer's conclusion is that staff parties during business hours will lead to higher profits. The fact that there are some corporations with higher profits who throw parties after hours is not relevant to the value of business hour staff parties, so this choice is incorrect.

Answer choice (C): Some might be tempted to equate the "above average profits" in this answer choice with boosting profits as concluded in the stimulus. These are different effects, and therefore, this answer choice does not weaken the conclusion in the stimulus which deals with *boosting* profits, not profits that happen to be "above average."

Answer choice (D): This answer choice states that frequent social events in a corporate workplace leave employees with less time to perform their assigned duties than they otherwise would have. This does not address why companies with frequent workplace social activities tend to have higher than average profits. Because it does not address this, it cannot be said to weaken the writer's conclusion.

Answer choice (E): This answer choice does not present an alternative cause, but it may show that the cause (workplace parties) has existed in the past. The stimulus states that EZ Corporation has not always been one of the most profitable companies for its size. But how did it compare to other similar companies at that time? Were these parties boosting the corporation's profitability? Since we don't know, this limited information has little effect on the strength of the argument in the stimulus.

Overview: The first passage, which presents a discussion of South African writer Ezekiel Mphahlele, is nicely structured, and those who understand the highlights regarding the writer and his critics shouldn't find the questions too difficult. The second passage focuses on the "late heavy bombardment," a barrage of projectiles in our planetary system that seems to have taken place about four billion years ago. Test-takers found this passage more challenging than the first, likely attributable in part to significant use of scientific terminology. The third passage deals with the cultural ramifications of television programming exports to developing nations. While the passage itself is not difficult to read, understanding the author's reasoning and perspective are vital to a strong performance on the questions. The final passage in this section, which deals with the prospect of computer-based legal reasoning systems, focuses on the challenges associated with application of artificial intelligence to the subtleties of the law. This passage has some sophisticated language, but a very nice structure—the author introduces the broad concept and challenges, discusses the problems with early approaches, and ends the passage with a focus on the latest approach and associated challenges.

Passage 1: Ezekiel Mphahlele

Paragraph 1 Overview

This passage is a literary criticism passage regarding the work of Ezekiel Mphahlele, a South African writer whose works have confused literary critics, "especially those who feel compelled to draw a sharp distinction between autobiography and fiction." From this we know that Mphahlele apparently blurs this line.

Mphahlele's two best-known works are *Down Second Avenue* and *The Wanderers*; the former work has been criticized as "too autobiographical," and the latter as overly fictional. *Down Second Avenue*, published in 1959, is an account which details Mphahlele's life from age five to the beginning of his self-imposed exile at age 38. *The Wanderers* was published in 1971 and is a fictionalized account of his life from the beginning of his exile. The author's perspective on Mphahlele can be found in the last sentence of this first paragraph: "those who focus on traditional labels inevitably miss the fact that Mphahlele manipulates different prose forms purely in the service of the social message he advances."

Paragraph 2 Overview

Continuing with the theme that literary critics do not understand Mphahlele, the author asserts that even favorable critical reviews of Mphahlele often carry a negative subtext. The author cites an example of a review which compliments *The Wanderers*, while at the same time questioning whether the book meets the criteria for great literature. The chief criticism of *The Wanderers* is that it is largely autobiographical and is filled with real-world characters. Mphahlele's defense points to the fictional father-son relationship that opens and closes *The Wanderers*. The author then describes Mphahlele's social activism – the writer is described as a humanist and an integrationist – and points out that his writings are meant to reflect his vision of the future. Reviews are often still critical, however, because Mphahlele provides no plan for bringing this vision to fruition.

Paragraph 3 Overview

In this paragraph, the author of the passage notes that Mphahlele does not seem concerned with drawing a clear distinction between autobiography and fiction. Instead, Mphahlele asserts that no novelist can write pure fiction or absolute fact – details must be drawn from the writer's experiences, dictating that they be somewhat factual, but are conveyed to maximize the effectiveness of the work's social message, and therefore "inevitably fiction." Mphahlele believes that the writing is not about classification, but about the transmission of important ideas. Without some sort of social criticism, Mphahlele asserts, writers are irrelevant.

SUMMARY: This passage introduces the reader to Ezekiel Mphahlele and critics' discomfort with the fact that his two best-known works blur the line between autobiography and fiction. The author's attitude: "Mphahlele manipulates different prose forms purely in the service of the social message he advances." The passage provides criticisms of Mphahlele's works, discusses the writer's social message, and points out Mphahlele's view that social criticism is a vital component of any relevant work.

Passage Structure

Paragraph 1: Introduces Mphahlele, the author's two best known books, and critical response to the works which blur the line between autobiography and fiction in an effort to convey a social message.

Paragraph 2: Cites critiques of Mphahlele's *The Wanderers* based on the work's autobiographical framework. Mphahlele is characterized as a humanist and integrationist looking to provide a vision for the future, but reviewers remain critical because this vision is unaccompanied by plans for its achievement.

Paragraph 3: Points out that Mphahlele is largely unconcerned with literary classification, because the writer believes that every work represents of mix of fact and fiction, and because a more important concern for any relevant writer, according to Mphahlele, is to provide social criticism.

Question #1: Must Be True. The correct answer choice is (B)

The question stem asks for the statement with which Mphahlele would most likely agree, based on the passage. Mphahlele's views are primarily discussed in the third paragraph (lines 41-58).

Answer choice (A): The author of the stimulus never mentions Mphahlele's perspective concerning the necessity of articulating a vision for the future. There is mention of Mphahlele's own vision of the future in the second paragraph, but only in regard to the criticism he received arising from his failure to provide a roadmap to achieve his vision.

Answer choice (B): This is the correct answer choice. Because Mphahlele's works did not fit into predetermined categories, he would likely agree with this statement (lines 41-43). In fact, the passage states that he shows little interest in establishing guidelines to distinguish autobiography from fiction (also lines 41-43). Additionally, in the third paragraph it is stated that Mphahlele asserts that no novelist can write pure fiction or absolute fact, indicating that a blurring of the lines of distinction is inevitable (lines 45-50).

Answer choice (C): Mphahlele did not concern himself with literary categories, even in the case of his own unjustifiably dismissed works, so there is no reason to believe that the South African author would agree with this statement.

Answer choice (D): Because this passage does not get into the definitions of the classifications of work, this answer choice is incorrect. Furthermore, while he did state that no novelist could write complete fiction and that details must be drawn from the writer's personal experiences, Mphahlele never asserted that novels could properly be classified as autobiographies.

Answer choice (E): The passage does not distinguish these classifications at all, so this answer choice is incorrect.

Question #2: Must Be True. The correct answer choice is (B)

The question stem asks for the answer choice that states Mphahlele's beliefs. His beliefs are primarily discussed in the third paragraph, which provides that the writer was less concerned with classification than with social criticism, and that the lines of distinction between fiction and autobiography blur regardless.

Answer choice (A): From paragraph two of the passage we know that one criticism of Mphahlele's vision of the future is that it was presented without providing a roadmap for its achievement. In paragraph three, we are told that Mphahlele believes that all good writing conveys a social message, but even when combined with a vision for the future, this is not the same as a *guide* for social change, so this answer choice is incorrect.

Answer choice (B): This is the correct answer choice. This reflects the assertion found in lines 53-55 ("in all forms writing is the transmission of ideas").

Answer choice (C): Because Mphahlele used real people and events to tell his stories (lines 25-30), he would not be certain to share the perspective that writing is most effective when it minimizes the use of real people and events to embellish a story.

Answer choice (D): Mphahlele asserted that the details must come from the writer's experiences, making them somewhat autobiographical, but must maximize their effectiveness in conveying the social message, which invites a somewhat fictional approach. Mphahlele apparently believed both facets to be important, and never made the assertion reflected in this answer choice.

Answer choice (E): Mphahlele would disagree with this statement since, as noted above, the author believed that all important literary work must have some elements of both fiction and autobiography.

Question #3. Specific reference. The correct answer choice is (E)

In the passage, the author notes that even when Mphahlele received a favorable review, there was often a negative subtext. In other words, even when they were complimentary, the critics often found a way to slip in some negative criticism. In this context, one critic of *The Wanderers* stated that if anger, firsthand experiences, compassion, and topicality were the sole requirements for great literature, *The Wanderers* would be one of the masterpieces of this part of the twentieth century – backhanded praise indeed.

Answer choice (A): It is true that Mphahlele has little interest in establishing such guidelines, but these are not the *critic's* words, nor do they reflect the *critic's* belief. This is a common LSAT ploy – to take an otherwise accurate assertion from the passage and misattribute it, rendering it incorrect.

Answer choice (B): The negative subtext referred to is a negative comment couched in the form of a positive review, which is quite different from a comment that is "one-sided."

Answer choice (C): The critic never states what the requirements for fiction are, nor are there any references to the belief that firsthand experiences are in direct contradiction to those requirements.

Answer choice (D): The critic's comments were presented as hypothetical: "*if* these factors *were* the sole requirements for great literature, this *would* be a masterpiece." Since the critic never makes the claim that these are the *actual*, ill-conceived sole requirements, this answer choice is incorrect.

Answer choice (E): This is the correct answer choice. Since the critic's comment is framed as a hypothetical (in the conditional tense), the critic's implication is that anger, firsthand experiences, compassion and topicality must *not* be the sole requirements for great literature, and Mphahlele's work should not be characterized as such. The critic's assertion is that *if* this were all that was required to be great literature, *The Wanderers* would be great literature.

Question #4: Must Be True. The correct answer choice is (A)

The question stem asks for the reason, according to the passage, that the critics dismissed *The Wanderers*. Relevant discussion is found in paragraph two of the passage, wherein the author states, at lines 27-30, that "there are those who are outright dismissive of *The Wanderers* because it contains an autobiographical framework and is populated with real-world characters." The author goes on to discuss the critics' balking at Mphahlele's vision, because of the South African's failure to provide a specific roadmap for its achievement.

Answer choice (A): This is the correct answer choice. The use of real-world characters was one of the specific criticisms discussed in reference to *The Wanderers*.

Answer choice (B): While the criticism referenced the autobiographical framework, it was the framework itself that was dismissed when questioning the book's literary contribution, not the failure to present the book as an autobiography.

Answer choice (C): The relevant criticism concerning Mphahlele's vision was not that the writer's vision was unclear, but rather that the writer provided no specific instruction for bringing this vision to fruition.

Answer choice (D): While Mphahlele considers social criticism vital to any important work, this was not the basis of the criticisms discussed in the passage, so this answer choice is incorrect.

Answer choice (E): At no point does the passage refer to criticisms regarding Mphahlele's emphasis on relationships.

Question #5: Method—Function. The correct answer choice is (C)

This question stem asks why the author of this passage provided the following Mphahlele quote in lines 55-58: "Whenever you write prose or poetry or drama you are writing a social criticism of one kind or another. If you don't, you are completely irrelevant – you don't count." This quote offers insight into Mphahlele's priorities, and his belief that social criticism is the factor that makes a work important.

Answer choice (A): The referenced portion was a direct quote from the author about his beliefs, not a sample of his writing. The quote at issue would not be evidentiary of Mphahlele's eloquence as a writer, but rather as a reflection of his priorities.

Answer choice (B): The referenced quote reflects Mphahlele's perspective, but is never implied to reflect a common goal of writing among novelists in general.

Answer choice (C): This is the correct answer choice. This is exactly what Mphahlele is stating here, very clearly–social criticism in some form is an absolute requirement for a serious writer; unless a writer is writing social criticism, that writer does not count. Mphahlele values writers who write social commentary—so much so that he disregards writers who do not offer social commentary.

Answer choice (D): Mphahlele's quote is not about his own work, or his three preferred literary forms; it is about all writing. Answer choice (D) is incorrect.

Answer choice (E) This is true with regard to social criticism: Mphahlele believes that all writing must convey social criticism. But Mphahlele does not go so far as to assert that there is *no* distinction between these forms.

Question #6: Author's Attitude. The correct answer choice is (A)

The question stem asks which of the aspects of Mphahlele's work the author seems to value most highly. This is an Author's Attitude question which we can prephrase, by noting the author's appreciation of Mphahlele's emphasis on social criticisms.

Answer choice (A): This is the correct answer choice. This is the choice which is consistent with the prephrased answer above; it was Mphahlele's commitment to social criticism which seems to have made the greatest impression on the author of the passage.

Answer choice (B): While the author does note Mphahlele's blending of these writing categories, it was the social criticism in a work that was important to Mphahlele, and this was what most impressed the author of the passage.

Answer choice (C): This choice, somewhat related to answer choice (B), might reflect a portion of the discussion from the passage, but, again, this was not the aspect of Mphahlele's work that the passage writer values most highly.

Answer choice (D): While the author mentions Mphahlele's use of detail in bringing an autobiographical nature to his writing, this is not the aspect that the passage author values most highly in Mphahlele's work.

Answer choice (E): Mphahlele was specifically criticized for failing to offer a plan to bring about his vision of the future; this plan, which was apparently lacking in Mphahlele's work, cannot therefore be the aspect that the passage writer values most highly.

Question #7: Must Be True. The correct answer choice is (D)

The question stem asks which of the answer choices is most strongly suggested by the information contained in the passage, which most likely means that we should seek an inference supported by the information provided by stimulus.

Answer choice (A): In the first paragraph of that passage, the author provides that Mphahlele's work blurs the line between autobiography and fiction, so this answer choice is incorrect.

Answer choice (B): It may be true that the literary critics referred to in the passage are largely compelled to find distinct literary categories, but it is not necessarily true that Mphahlele's social vision is irrelevant to these critics.

Answer choice (C): While this may be true, it is not discussed or implied in the passage, so this answer choice is incorrect.

Answer choice (D): This is the correct answer choice. Since the author of the passage mentions that many criticize Mphahlele for failing to provide a plan to bring about his vision, it seems logical to infer that more critics could find his vision acceptable if a plan were provided.

Answer choice (E): The author points out that Mphahlele's novel, *The Wanderers*, contains many autobiographical elements, so this answer choice cannot be correct.

Passage 2: The Late Heavy Bombardment

Paragraph 1 Overview

The initial paragraph of this passage introduces the reader to the late heavy bombardment (LHB) theory, which concerns the formation of the major craters of the Moon. According to this theory, this rigorous bombardment occurred about four billion years ago, and it is likely that these projectiles also struck the Earth, and that no life could have survived on Earth until this bombardment ended.

Paragraph 2 Overview

In this paragraph, we are introduced to various theories that were developed with evidence based on Moon rock, and on the size and distribution of the craters on the Moon. Because of the size of the craters, some astronomers believe that the LHB is the result of the disintegration of an asteroid or comet. According to this theory, the large astronomical body broke apart and spread debris throughout the inner solar system.

A second theory discussed is that LHB is a misnomer, and that such a cataclysmic event is not necessary to explain the available evidence. According to the proponents of this second theory, the evidence on the Moon simply reflects the period concluding billions of years of a continuous, but declining, heavy bombardment throughout the inner solar system. Impacts from the latter part of the bombardment, according to this theory, erased evidence of earlier bombardment.

A third theory holds that the Moon's evidence supports a defined cataclysmic cratering period which did not extend to the inner solar system, because of its brief duration. Proponents contend that the disintegration occurred solely within the Earth-Moon system, based on the fact that debris from this event would have been swept up quickly.

Paragraph 3 Overview

The final paragraph provides a new piece of evidence to support the theory that the bombardment extended into the inner solar system, in the form of a rock that was apparently knocked from the surface of Mars and eventually arrived on Earth. With an age estimated at four billion years old, and if this rock is from Mars, it would have been knocked from the planet at about the same time that the Moon went through the LHB. This supports the suggestion that at least two inner solar system planetary systems experienced simultaneous bombardment. The author closes this paragraph by pointing out that to fully determine the scope of the late heavy bombardment, many more such rocks will need to be located, and other surface samples from inner solar system planets may need to be obtained.

SUMMARY: This passage introduces the reader to the concept of late heavy bombardment and the debate that surrounds the explanation of lunar rock samples. Three theories about the LHB are discussed, and recent evidence is introduced, and the author emphasizes the need for more samples and further exploration.

Passage Structure

Paragraph 1:   Provides a definition of the late heavy bombardment (LHB), and a brief explanation of the basic principles, and points out that human life would not have been able to exist before the LHB ended.

Paragraph 2:   Discusses three major theories which deal with differing perspectives on the LHB.

Paragraph 3:   Introduces evidence to support the notion of simultaneous bombardment of systems within the inner solar system, but points out the necessity of further evidence to determine the pervasiveness of the LHB.

Question #8: Main Point. The correct answer choice is (E)

This question stem asks for the Main Point of the passage. If we are to prephrase this answer, the correct choice should likely allude to theories about the LHB and the emphasized need for further exploration.

Answer choice (A): While this answer choice may be consistent with the information in the passage, the main point was not simply to provide a definition of the LHB, so this choice is incorrect.

Answer choice (B): Although the stimulus provides that further evidence is needed to determine the pervasiveness of the LHB, the author never makes the assertion in this choice, so this answer should be eliminated.

Answer choice (C): While it seems that our perspective continues to grow clearer with each new piece of evidence, the author of the passage does not assert that a clear picture will emerge "soon."

Answer choice (D): This answer choice involves the stimulus' third theory, discussed at the end of the second paragraph, but this does not reflect the main point of the passage, so this answer choice is incorrect.

Answer choice (E): This is the correct answer choice. Although there has been new evidence uncovered which enables us to develop our understanding of the LHB, further evidence still needs to be gathered, as prephrased above.

Question 9: Author's Attitude. The correct answer choice is (B)

The question stem asks for the author's attitude toward arguments based on the evidence from the Mars rock (lines 44-46). The passage is largely void of the author's own opinions or attitudes until the last sentence. While the rock from Mars is mentioned in lines 44-46, the real answer to this question lies in the last sentence (lines 54-57), where the author reflects a conservative attitude, cautioning that more evidence is needed before conclusions can be drawn.

Answer choice (A): While the author's tone is cautious, it does not reflect ambivalence, but rather the awareness of the need for further evidence.

Answer choice (B): This is the correct answer choice. The author is not particularly skeptical about the origins of the referenced Mars rock, but is clearly wary of drawing conclusions before more evidence is gathered.

Answer choice (C): The author does not appear to be skeptical regarding the rock's origin; "it seems to be a rare example…" implies belief, so this answer choice is incorrect.

Answer choice (D): This answer choice is more focused on the one particular rock, while the author is more focused on the need to gather more such rocks and samples.

Answer choice (E): While the author does appear to accept the purported origins of the Mars rock, this does not imply outright acceptance of all possible arguments based on the evidence of the rock; in fact, the author specifically asserts that we need to gather more evidence before drawing conclusions about the pervasiveness of the LHB, so this answer choice is incorrect.

Question #10: Method of Reasoning – AP. The correct answer choice is (D)

The question stem asks why the author mentioned that LHB "should have also struck Earth" at lines 8-9. Apparently the author considers this relevant because of the "profound consequences for the history of the Earth since, until the LHB ended, life could not have survived here."

Answer choice (A): The referenced phrase does not address any particular theory regarding the extent of LHB, so this answer choice is incorrect.

Answer choice (B): The author's quote does not question the lack of LHB evidence on earth—the author only discusses the need for more evidence toward the end of the passage.

Answer choice (C): The phrase is not used to advocate any scientific model, but rather to point out the relevance of the timing of the LHB, so this answer choice should be eliminated.

Answer choice (D): This is the correct answer choice. The referenced quote is a part of the author's explanation of the relevance of the LHB, and its profound consequences for the history of the Earth, which is why scientists are interested in studying it.

Answer choice (E): The referenced quote does not provide additional support for the dating of the LHB—the author apparently *relies* on the LHB theory to make this assertion, which is made in the interest of highlighting the relevance of the LHB to the history of life on Earth.

Question #11: Must Be True. The correct answer choice is (C)

This question stem asks for the answer choice that would be supported by all the theoretical approaches to LHB. This is similar to a Resolve the Paradox question from Logical Reasoning. The correct answer choice will provide a premise that is consistent with (that is, does not disagree with) all of the LHB theories, discussed in paragraph two of the passage.

Answer choice (A): Although the third group discussed in the passage apparently perceives the LHB as "brief," this is somewhat vague. Besides, the other two theories don't make any claims regarding how long the LHB lasted, so there is no way to know whether all theories are in agreement regarding its duration.

Answer choice (B): This answer choice is incorrect, because the third theory asserts that the debris came from within the Earth-Moon system, while the other two theories hold that it could have been an asteroid or comet.

Answer choice (C): This is the correct answer choice, since this assertion is consistent with the beliefs of all three groups of theorists discussed in the passage. All three theories hold that the Late Heavy Bombardment included heavy bombardment, and that the barrage decreased after the LHB, allowing life on Earth to flourish.

Answer choice (D): While all of the theories would agree that life could not have survived the LHB, there is nothing in the passage that suggests that any life existed on Earth to be destroyed by the LHB, so this answer choice is incorrect.

Answer choice (E): Since the author doesn't discuss the amount of debris hypothesized by the various theories, there is no way to know, based on the passage, whether all three theories would agree on this issue, so this answer choice is incorrect.

Question #12: Specific reference—MBT. The correct answer choice is (B)

The question stem asks for the beliefs of the third group of scientists regarding the LHB—this is discussed at the end of the second paragraph. From the passage, it is known that these scientists believe that the LHB was a sharply defined relatively brief cataclysmic event, and the debris was swept up quickly.

Answer choice (A): This assertion is false according to the information found in the passage. The event affected the Moon, the Earth and the object that was within the Earth-Moon system that produced the debris.

Answer choice (B): This is the correct answer choice. The scientists subscribing to this theory of LHB believe that it was confined to the Earth-Moon system and was of relatively short duration.

Answer choice (C): The scientists subscribing to the second theory of LHB do not believe its effects extended beyond the Earth-Moon system, so therefore there was nothing to be absorbed by the other planets of the inner solar system.

Answer choice (D): In the initial paragraph, the author states that the LHB occurred approximately four billion years ago. There is nothing in the subsequent discussion of the third theory that would indicate disagreement with this dating of the LHB.

Answer choice (E): Since proponents of the third theory assert that the LHB was relatively brief, they would be unlikely to agree that it "may have lasted a long time," so this answer choice is incorrect.

Question #13: Strengthen. The correct answer choice is (A)

The question stem asks which answer choice gives the most strength to the view that the LHB was limited to the Earth and Moon, consistent with the third theory of LHB, so it would include a relatively brief event that was confined to the Earth-Moon system. The problem with this theory is the Mars rock. How would a scientist explain the rock from Mars if LHB was confined to the Earth-Moon system? Any other evidence of LHB outside the Earth-Moon system would tend to weaken the third theory. Conversely, lack (or disproof) of such evidence would strengthen the theory of confinement to the Earth-Moon system.

Answer choice (A): This is the correct answer choice. If further testing shows that it is unlikely that Mars experienced any increase in projectile intensity of during the LHB (about 4 billion years ago), this would tend to weaken the assertion that Mars was involved, which makes it more likely that the effects of the LHB were not felt beyond the Earth and Moon.

Answer choice (B): Since there doesn't appear to be much issue with the notion that there was such a bombardment that included both Earth and the Moon, such a discovery would probably do little to alter current hypotheses, and certainly wouldn't help to disprove any possibility of other planetary bodies being affected by the LHB, so this answer choice is incorrect.

Answer choice (C): As with answer choice (B), this might strengthen the conclusions about the involvement of the Earth and the Moon, but wouldn't help to disprove the inclusion of other planetary bodies in the phenomenon.

Answer choice (D): Although the Mars rock provides evidence for the assertion that Mars was involved with the LHB, the author cautions that further evidence needs to be gathered before conclusions can be drawn. The discovery of an alternate explanation for the origin of the Mars rock might tend to strengthen a theory that states that LHB is exclusive to the Earth-Moon system, but it would not serve to disprove other theories that are not restricted to the Earth-Moon system, so this answer choice is incorrect.

Answer choice (E): While this evidence would help to explain what was really represented by the LHB (the conclusion of billions of years of heavy bombardment), it would not support the view that the LHB was confined to the Earth and the Moon, so this answer choice is incorrect.

Passage 3: Cultural Effects of Television Exports

Paragraph 1 Overview
The author begins the first paragraph of this passage with the presentation of a consensus view to be later refuted. In this case, the "almost unanimous" assertion among communication specialists is that with television programming exports, industrialized countries tend to overwhelm developing nations' cultures. The author is quick to point out that this belief has no real empirical foundation. In fact, developing nations' television industries are rarely threatened by such imports, and most viewers tend to show a preference for domestic programming.

Paragraph 2 Overview
The second paragraph begins with a restatement of the assertion that the "specialists" are off base. The author discusses an anthropological study which notes the popularity of domestic serial dramas, comparing them to oral poetry used at gatherings to publicly discuss events of interest.

Paragraph 3 Overview
The third paragraph opens with the assertion that communications specialists should use an *empirical* approach to this topic, much like that of anthropologists. The first inquiry, according to the author, must concern the proper model to represent the relationship between imported cultural productions and domestic ones: Perhaps cultures are enriched by absorbing imported productions, or perhaps imports only connect with local culture where mutually relevant themes, situations, or characters provide some cultural overlap.

Paragraph 4 Overview
In this paragraph the author continues the discussion of relevant considerations for communications specialists, underscoring the importance of assessing the particular experiences of diverse individual viewers, and in particular the experiential contexts and the manner in which such productions' meanings are ascribed.

SUMMARY: The main point of this passage is to present and dispute a consensus view regarding the phenomenon of television productions' export from industrialized to developed nations, providing a different model from which to understand the phenomenon. The author's attitude is that the cultural imperialism perspective adopted by most experts, the belief that the referenced export results in the detrimental overwhelm of the developing culture, lacks empirical basis, and appears to run contrary to available evidence. The author believes that communication specialists should develop their understanding of the complex relationship between imported and domestic productions, and that a new perspective should be based on empirical evidence, as would be the case with an anthropologist-like approach. The proper model is vital, as are considerations of diverse individual preferences and ascriptions of meaning.

Paragraph 1:   Introduces consensus opinion among specialists regarding the imperialistic view of the effects of industrialized programming's overwhelm of domestic culture. Refutes this view based on lacking empirical evidence, pointing out that the viability of domestic programming is generally not threatened by imports, and that there is usually a preference for domestic programming.

Paragraph 2:   Reasserts that specialists' assertions are off base and points to anthropological study regarding the popularity of serial dramas, comparing them to oral poetry.

Paragraph 3:   Argues that communication specialists should use an empirical approach like that of the anthropologists, first seeking the proper model to develop an understanding of the relationship between domestic and imported cultural productions. Presents two possible perspectives on this relationship: absorption/enrichment, and domestic selection based on mutual relevance.

Paragraph 4:   Offers a second important consideration of the assessment of individuals, their diverse experiences, the contexts in which they experience the imported productions, and how they ascribe meanings to them.

Question #14. Primary Purpose. The correct answer choice is (C)

The question stem asks for the primary purpose of the passage. The main point is prephrased above, in the summary of the passage.

Answer choice (A): Although it is clear that the author believes the prevailing perspective to be unfounded, the intent of the passage is not to determine the correct hypothesis, but rather to suggest a framework from which to study the phenomenon.

Answer choice (B): The author's purpose is not so much to discredit the evidence offered, but to point out that the prevailing view seems to be based on ungrounded assumptions rather than empirical evidence, and to suggest a different perspective.

Answer choice (C): This is the correct answer choice. Part of the author's purpose, as prephrased above, is to argue that the prevailing specialists would be well served to take on a different perspective with regard to the ramifications of importing programming to developing nations, a perspective which takes empirical evidence into consideration.

Answer choice (D): Since this passage only involves the methodological weaknesses of one discipline, this answer choice is incorrect.

Answer choice (E): Like answer choice (D), this choice cannot be correct, because the author of the stimulus discusses only one discipline.

Question #15: Structure. The correct answer choice is (A)

This question asks for an overview of the structure of the passage. As prephrased in the discussion of the structure above, this passage introduces a prevailing view, and then refutes it with empirical evidence and suggests developing a different perspective.

Answer choice (A): Although the author does indeed take issue with an assertion, the author does not speculate as to why the proponents are supportive, so this answer choice is incorrect.

Answer choice (B): This is the correct answer choice, as it restates the prephrased answer discussed above. The author takes issue with a common assertion among communication specialists, offers examples which show that the assertion in some cases runs counter to empirical fact, and suggests a more anthropologist-like approach, with two specific issues to consider.

Answer choice (C): This answer choice correctly asserts that the author takes issue with an assertion. The author, however, then introduces *examples* that prove that the referenced assertion sometimes run counter to factual evidence, rather than presenting a new view and supporting *it* with examples. The author then offers two considerations relevant to the *development* of a new view.

Answer choice (D): This answer choice is correct inasmuch as the author takes issue with an assertion, presents counter examples, and suggests a change to the conventional approach. However, the author then discusses two considerations relevant to the new approach, rather than two benefits to the proponents, so this answer choice is incorrect.

Answer choice (E): The author does take issue with an assertion, and present examples that run counter to that assertion. And although the author does suggest considerations for the *development* of a new view, the author never suggests a compromise between the old assertion and the new view, so this answer choice is incorrect.

Question #16: Must Be True. The correct answer choice is (C)

The question stem asks which of the answer choices would be the best continuation of the last paragraph. These questions can be among the most confusing in the Reading Comprehension sections of the LSAT, but if one understands the paragraph and the overall flow of the passage, the right answer might be more obvious.

The last paragraph discusses the role of the individual viewer in the model of cultural relationships. The correct answer choice will likely continue along this theme.

Answer choice (A): The degree to which cultural relationships can be described by an abstract model is not a focus in the passage, and this would not be a likely continuation to the final paragraph.

Answer choice (B): The author suggests considerations relevant to developing a new perspective, but the focus, especially toward the end of the passage, is not on ensuring the overturn of the dominant view.

Answer choice (C): This is the correct answer choice. The inclusion of this aspect in the study is essential for the study to be accurate—this is a logical continuation of the ideas from the last paragraph.

Answer choice (D): This is not the focus toward the end of the passage, and there is no reference to communications specialists' cravings for scientific credibility. It is the author who believes that the consensus perspective lacks empirical foundation.

Answer choice (E): Because neither the last paragraph nor the passage as a whole focuses on the economic relationship between cultures, this answer choice is incorrect.

Question #17: Method of Reasoning—AP. The correct answer choice is (D)

The question stem asks for the most likely reason the author discusses the anthropological study in the second paragraph. The reason is given in the first sentence of that paragraph, immediately before the introduction of the anthropological study: "The role of television in developing nations is far removed from what the specialists assert." In other words, the anthropological study is used as evidence to show that the assertion made by the international communications specialists is wrong.

Answer choice (A): The study is not discussed to provide specialists with a model, but rather to refute their perspective, so this answer choice is incorrect.

Answer choice (B): The reference to the anthropological study is not meant to describe new ways of conducting research, but rather to refute the beliefs of the specialists, so this answer choice is incorrect.

Answer choice (C): The anthropological study was not meant to highlight flaws in a similar study, but rather to highlight flaws in the specialists' perspective.

Answer choice (D): This is the correct answer choice. The study is meant to provide empirical evidence which contradicts the consensus perspective of communications specialists.

Answer choice (E): The study is meant to underscore the popularity of domestic dramas, rather the diversity of individual viewing habits, which is discussed in the last paragraph of the passage.

Question #18: Specific Reference. The correct answer choice is (E)

This question stem asks what can be concluded about the subjects of the study cited in the second paragraph. This anthropological study was used to contradict the conclusions of the specialists. Because residents enjoyed following domestic drama story lines day to day, television in the referenced community served a function analogous to that of oral poetry.

Answer choice (A): There is no information provided to support the idea that the referenced viewers will for some reason gradually change their preferences, so this answer choice is incorrect.

Answer choice (B): The tradition of oral poetry to keep up with the day's events explains the popularity of domestically produced dramas, but the passage contains nothing to suggest that these dramas will eventually phase out oral poetry completely.

Answer choice (C): It is the popularity of oral poetry that helps to explain the popularity of the domestically produced drama, but it is a logical fallacy to conclude that people would watch more television if they did not have more oral poetry.

Answer choice (D): Since the author notes that imported programs were available, so this answer choice cannot be correct.

Answer choice (E): This is the correct answer choice, as noted in lines 32-36: "because viewers enjoy following the dramas from day to day, television in the community can serve an analogous function to that of oral poetry, which the residents often use at public gatherings as a daily journal of events of interest."

Question #19: Specific Reference. The correct answer choice is (B)

This question stem asks how, according to the author, an empirical study of the effect of external cultural influences on the lives of people in a society must begin. This is discussed in the third paragraph of the passage, specifically in lines 41-45: "what model best represents the true relationship" between imported programs and domestic ones.

Answer choice (A): This answer choice is incorrect, because the author identifies a different first consideration.

Answer choice (B): This is the correct answer choice, as prephrased above.

Answer choice (C): This is drawn from the first sentence of the third paragraph (lines 37-40), but it is the general goal of the empirical study, as opposed to the first task of the study.

Answer choice (D): This is one of two possibilities mentioned in paragraph three of the passage and is an example of the model of how imported productions influence domestic ones. It is not identified as a first question to ask in developing an empirical study.

Answer choice (E): Social factors are discussed in the fourth paragraph at the end of the passage in lines 60-61: *After* the model has already been formed, the study must examine the complex manner in which individuals ascribe meanings to those productions.

Question #20: Must Be True. The correct answer choice is (A)

This question stem asks whether an imported programming airtime allotment study would be relevant to various possible questions provided as answer choices.

Answer choice (A): This is the correct answer choice. The referenced study would allow one to determine various nations' access to imported cultural productions.

Answer choice (B): The study would not provide such information because it would only examine the airtime schedule of the broadcasts in developing nations, not the specific viewing habits of the residents therein.

Answer choice (C): A study of the airtime devoted to domestic versus imported programming would not necessarily be conducive to an understanding of degree of influence.

Answer choice (D): A study of airtime devoted to imported programs would not offer insight into relative audience sizes, so this answer choice is incorrect.

Answer choice (E): Answering this question is the first task of the proposed study in the author's passage, but the study discussed in the question stem would not assist with this inquiry at all, so this answer choice should be eliminated.

Passage 4: Legal Reasoning Systems

Paragraph 1 Overview
The author begins this passage by pointing out that computers have been commonly used for basic functions in law, with interesting prospects in the area of "legal reasoning systems," utilizing artificial intelligence to apply the law and resolve disputes. Early efforts, however, have been unable to provide expert advice, which is to be expected, considering the complexity of any system of legal rules.

Paragraph 2 Overview
In this paragraph the author discusses early attempts at legal reasoning systems, which began with programs based on sets of rules. These were found ineffective because of the interpretations required at every level. Because of this, and since many laws are written vaguely to require some degree of interpretation, the comprehensive information that would be required to enable such interpretation is beyond computer capability at present or in the foreseeable future.

Paragraph 3 Overview
The final paragraph begins with the suggestion by systems proponents that basing decisions on past cases may improve prospects for a successful system. Such a system would base its decisions on precedents set by previous similar cases. The problem is that the criteria for similarity would have to be fixed within the program, and eventually, a complete reasoning system would require the ability to determine relevant points of similarity on its own.

SUMMARY: The main point of this passage is to discuss the prospects for the development of "legal reasoning systems"—programs which use artificial intelligence to produce sound legal judgment— and the associated challenges. The author introduces the problems with previous attempts at a doctrinal approach, and then discusses the next effort, programming which bases its judgments on precedent. This new approach, the author points out, is sure to have serious challenges as well, because at some point it will be necessary to enable the program to determine relevant precedent.

Passage Structure

Paragraph 1:   Defines concept of computer-based legal reasoning systems and points to challenges associated with such programs.

Paragraph 2:   Discusses early attempts to base legal reasoning systems on sets of legal rules; this doctrinal approach required interpretations at each level, necessitating a knowledge of the law more comprehensive can be achieved at present or in the near future.

Paragraph 3:   Introduces another approach suggested by legal reasoning systems proponents—basing decisions on relevant precedent to arrive at sound legal judgments. This approach will bring significant challenge, necessitating that a program determine which precedents are relevant to a given case or judgment.

Question #21: Main Point. The correct Answer choice is (A)

The question stem asks for the main point of the passage, which is prephrased above, in the summary of the passage—to introduce the concept and challenges associated with the development of artificial intelligence-based legal reasoning systems.

Answer choice (A): This is the correct answer choice, discussing the same points emphasized in the prephrased answer above.

Answer choice (B): This answer choice is incorrect, because computer programs are presently used in law, as discussed in the first sentence of the passage, and because there is likely great potential value in developing such programs—the author's point is that there are sure to be challenges in the development.

Answer choice (C): While earlier, doctrinal approaches apparently were not successful, and case-based programs represent the latest effort to develop legal reasoning systems, it is still unclear whether they will prove any more effective, so this answer choice is incorrect.

Answer choice (D): While there is promise, the author highlights the challenges involved going forward, and never makes the assertion that revolutionary results will be achieved in the near future.

Answer choice (E): While this may be true, the main point of the passage involves the challenges associated with developing legal reasoning systems, so this answer choice is incorrect.

Question #22: Specific Reference. The correct answer choice is (A)

The question stem asks the logical relationship between the portion of the passage at lines 8-13 and the portion at lines 23-25 and lines 49-53 of the passage. At lines 8-13, the author is summarizing his main point: the benefits of legal reasoning systems have fallen short of predictions. At lines 23-25, the discussion focuses on how rule-based systems have proven inadequate because of the problems of interpretation. At lines 49-53, the discussion surrounds how case-based systems are limited. The first statement is a general statement: the benefits of legal reasoning systems have fallen short of expectations. The second statement is one example of how the first portion of the passage is true. The third statement is another example to support the first referenced assertion.

Answer choice (A): This is the correct answer choice, restating the prephrased answer above.

Answer choice (B): Since both later points support the first, this answer choice is incorrect.

Answer choice (C): The first reference is a general assertion, but the later two referenced excerpts are facts, not assertions.

Answer choice (D): Since the two observations support the first assertion, this answer choice should be eliminated.

Answer choice (E): This answer choice is incorrect because the first referenced quote is a general assertion, rather than a specific observation.

Question #23: Author's Attitude. The correct answer choice is (B)

The question stems asks for the author's primary concern. Again, the author is primarily interested in discussing the concept of legal reasoning systems and the associated challenges.

Answer choice (A): Although the author does allude to the potential benefits of legal reasoning systems, this is not the primary concern.

Answer choice (B): This is the correct answer choice, as the author is interested in discussing the challenges of such systems—the subtleties of law that make interpretation and determination of relevance difficult.

Answer choice (C): There is no such demonstration—the author focuses on the challenges that are sure to come with systems based on precedent, so this answer choice should be eliminated.

Answer choice (D): The passage provides no such suggestion, and while this may be true, it is not supported by the passage and certainly not the primary focus.

Answer choice (E): While the author could be a proponent of the use of computers in the law office, the primary concern is to note that legal reasoning systems are sure to bring challenges during development.

Question #24: Author's Attitude. The correct answer choice is (E)

The question stem asks with which answer choice the author would most likely agree concerning computerized automated legal reasoning systems.

Answer choice (A): The passage specifically states at line 10 that these systems have fallen short of original predictions, so this choice is incorrect.

Answer choice (B): The hindrance to progress has come from difficulties in subtle interpretations, not lack of accessibility to legal documents, so this answer choice should be eliminated.

Answer choice (C): The author highlights the challenges that will go along with developing a system for legal analysis, but is not so skeptical as to presume that such efforts will be futile, so this answer choice is incorrect.

Answer choice (D): Rule systems represented the early attempts at legal reasoning systems, while case-based systems are the latest approach.

Answer choice (E): This is the correct answer choice. In rule systems, at line 34-37, the author notes that systems would have to be equipped with knowledge "that is far beyond their capabilities at present or in the foreseeable future." For case-based systems, lines 50-57 state that the criteria for these systems are system dependent and fixed by their designers, and that there is a problem of developing a system that can flexibly determine the factors that make cases relevant precedents.

Question #25: Author's Attitude. The correct answer choice is (D)

The question stem asks for the answer choice with which the author would most reasonably agree concerning the requirements for developing effective automated legal reasoning systems.

Answer choice (A): With regard to the doctrinal model, the author discusses the challenges associated but does not suggest that the choice of this focus was a fundamental error. Rather, the challenges go along with the task itself, for which a solution has not yet been found.

Answer choice (B): The chief problem with legal reasoning systems is not memory but the limitations of the programming, so this answer choice is incorrect.

Answer choice (C): In the examples provided in the second paragraph of the passage, it is not rules programming that is the problem; it is inability to equip the systems with the comprehensive knowledge required for expert interpretation.

Answer choice (D): This is the correct answer choice. The author notes the "intractable problem of developing a system that can discover for itself the factors that make cases similar in relevant ways."

Answer choice (E): The incompetence of the legal practitioners is not the source of the problems with legal reasoning systems; the challenge lies in the creation of the programming.

Question #26: Must Be True. The correct answer choice is (C)

The question stem asks what can be inferred concerning case-based reasoning systems, which were discussed in the last paragraph of the passage.

Answer choice (A): At lines 49-57, the author notes that the major problem is the human limitations created by the programmers, not the lack of storage capacity. In fact, inadequate storage is not mentioned at all.

Answer choice (B): The author will likely agree that case-based systems currently appear to have more potential than rule-based systems, but this is not because they are based on a simpler view of legal reasoning.

Answer choice (C): This is the correct answer choice, rephrasing the author's assertion at the end of the passage that there remains the "intractable problem of developing a system that can discover for itself the factors that make cases similar in relevant ways."

Answer choice (D): The author is focused on the challenges associated with developing a program that can independently provide such advice, but such programs have not yet been successfully developed, so this answer choice should be eliminated.

Answer choice (E): There is nothing in the passage to suggest that there is a more ambitious goal for case systems versus rules systems. Rather, the two models simply represent two different approaches to the same problem.

Question #27: Specific Reference. The correct answer choice is (C)

This question stem asks which of the answer choices is mentioned in the passage as an important characteristic of many statutes that frustrates the application of computerized legal reasoning systems: This is the vagueness that is written into many statutes to allow for flexible interpretation.

Answer choice (A): Since the complexity of the syntax is never mentioned, this answer choice is incorrect.

Answer choice (B): It is not the *unavailability* of relevant precedents that is the problem, it is the flexible determination of relevance of various precedents, so this answer choice should be eliminated.

Answer choice (C): This is the correct answer choice, reflecting our prephrased answer above. This is noted at lines 31-33: "a statute may be deliberately left undefined so as to allow the law to be adapted to unforeseen circumstances."

Answer choice (D): The problem is not an overly narrow intent. It is the opposite—the built-in flexibility—that is mentioned as a challenging attribute.

Answer choice (E): There is no reference to statutes' incompatibility, so this answer choice cannot be correct.

Question #28: Method of Reasoning—AP. The correct answer choice is (B)

This question stem asks what function is served by the examples of situations that are open to differing interpretations (lines 25-30). These are offered to show that rule-based systems underestimated the complexity of interpretation that can arise at each stage of a legal argument.

Answer choice (A): Given the fact that the author focuses on the inability thus far to create legal reasoning systems, this answer choice is incorrect.

Answer choice (B): This is the correct answer choice, consistent with our prephrased answer above.

Answer choice (C): Since the issues exemplify the challenges of rule based systems, this answer choice is incorrect.

Answer choice (D): The referenced examples show the *difficulties* of adapting to novel situations, so this answer choice should be eliminated.

Answer choice (E): The discussion of precedents is pertinent to case-based systems rather than rule-based systems, which is the context for the referenced examples, so this answer choice is incorrect.

Overview: Between the two logical reasoning sections, this was the more difficult for most students. As with Section 1, Flaw in the Reasoning questions were well represented here, with four Flaw questions and one Parallel—Flaw question. The questions were generally more challenging toward the latter half of this section, which included the more difficult of the five Must Be True questions of the section, along with two challenging Assumption questions (#15 and #18, a tricky Supporter Assumption), two difficult Justify the Conclusion questions, and two Method—Argument Part questions which require a solid understanding of logical argumentation.

Question #1: Weaken. The correct answer choice is (A)

In this stimulus we are told that with regard to the treatment of certain illnesses, studies have shown treatment X provides the same benefits as treatment Y. The author concludes that because treatment X is less expensive and faster acting than treatment Y, but still provides the same patient benefits as treatment Y, treatment X should be preferred to treatment Y for such illnesses.

The question stem asks which of the answer choices most weakens the argument contained in the stimulus. It seems that treatment X is the better alternative. But what would weaken the conclusion that treatment X should be preferred? The correct answer choice will convey some sort of inequality that favors treatment Y; this will come in the form of either an added benefit associated with treatment Y or a previously unstated detriment associated with treatment X.

Answer choice (A): This is the correct answer choice. This is an example of an inequality between treatments X and Y that favors treatment Y, by pointing to a new detriment associated with treatment X, thereby weakening the conclusion that treatment X should be the preferred treatment.

Answer choice (B): The conclusion in the stimulus specifically refers to "these illnesses," not other illnesses. Because this answer choice does not deal with the referenced illnesses, it is incorrect and should be eliminated.

Answer choice (C): The conclusion in the stimulus is concerned with the present, not the past. Once upon a time, treatment Y may have been preferred on the basis of cost, but now it is more expensive than treatment X. Since this is not a present inequality that favors treatment Y, this answer choice is incorrect.

Answer choice (D): Just because a treatment is more popular does not mean that it should be the preferred treatment, and this is merely a simple comparison of total prescriptions, inapplicable to our limited discussion about particular illnesses. Because this answer choice does not present an inequality that favors treatment Y, it does not weaken the argument in the stimulus.

Answer choice (E): If the stimulus stated that treatment X should be preferred to *all* other treatments, this answer choice would weaken the conclusion. But because the conclusion in the stimulus only concerns treatments X and Y, new information about treatment Z is irrelevant to the argument.

Question #2: Assumption. The correct answer choice is (D)

The initial statement of this stimulus introduces an assertion to be refuted: "Some political thinkers hope to devise a form of government in which every citizen's rights are respected." In typical LSAT fashion, in the next statement the author concludes that such a form of government is impossible to achieve. The author then provides bases for this conclusion.

The first premise is that any government is defined by and controlled by laws that determine its powers and limits. The second premise is that some will interpret these laws to afford themselves a greater share of political power than others possess. In other words, there will be laws, and some people will interpret those laws to gain a power advantage, and therefore, the author concludes, it is impossible to achieve a form of government wherein all citizens' rights are respected:

Premise:	Any government is defined and controlled by its laws and powers.
Premise:	Some will interpret such laws to maximize their own political power.
Conclusion:	It is impossible to create a form of government in which every citizen's rights are respected.

We are asked to identify an assumption required by the conclusion. Since there is a leap from the idea that there will be inevitable power inequity to the conclusion that there cannot be a society where all citizens' rights are respected, the Supporter Assumption required by the argument will link the referenced power advantage with the inability to form a government which respects the rights of all. To prephrase this supporter assumption, we must look for an answer choice that reflects the idea that inequitable distribution of political power invariably leads to the failure to respect some citizens' rights.

Answer choice (A): If any form of government that leads to unequal power distribution will surely violate the rights of the majority of citizens, this answer choice would certainly *justify* the conclusion in the stimulus, but it is not an assumption that is *required* in order to properly draw the conclusion. That is, we don't need to assume that the *majority* of citizens' rights will be violated as a result of the referenced power inequity—only that the rights of *some* will be disrespected—in order for the author's conclusion to be properly drawn. To confirm, we can always apply the assumption negation technique, to determine whether the negated answer choice will weaken the stimulus:

> "In any form of government with unequal power distribution, the rights of the majority of citizens will not be violated."

If the rights of the majority will *not* be violated, this doesn't weaken the conclusion in the stimulus, so we know that this is not an assumption on which that argument depends.

Answer choice (B): Keeping citizens ignorant of the laws may prevent the citizens from *knowing* when their rights are not being respected, but that is entirely different from not *having* their rights respected at all. This answer choice does not link the rogue elements of the argument by expressing a connection between unequal distribution of political power and failure to respect the rights of all citizens. As such, this choice is irrelevant to the justification of the conclusion in the stimulus, so this cannot be the correct answer choice. To check our work, we can apply the Assumption Negation Technique to determine whether the negated form of this answer choice has any weakening effect on the conclusion in the stimulus:

> "A government cannot ensure that every citizen's rights are respected by keeping the citizens ignorant of the laws."

Since the above assertion would not weaken the conclusion in the stimulus, it is confirmed that this answer choice does not provide an assumption on which the author's conclusion relies.

Answer choice (C): This answer choice basically says that there are some laws that cannot be misinterpreted. This is not really relevant to the argument in the stimulus. One of the author's premises is that a nation's laws will invariably be interpreted to afford some with more power than others, but the author doesn't assert that this requires *mis*interpretation, so this answer choice doesn't come into play and should be eliminated. To check our work, we can always apply the Assumption Negation Technique to determine the effects of the negated version of the answer choice:

> "All the laws that define a government's power can be misinterpreted."

This assertion would not weaken the argument in the stimulus at all, so we can confirm that this answer choice does not provide an assumption on which the argument relies.

Answer choice (D): This is the correct answer choice, as it links the rogue elements referenced above:

Premise:	A government is defined by its laws.
Premise:	These laws will be interpreted to give some greater power.
Assumption:	*This uneven power distribution will violate some citizens' rights.*
Conclusion:	Therefore, it is impossible to create a form of government in which everyone's rights are respected.

With the assumption that there is always a violation of rights that comes with uneven distribution of power, the author's conclusion is properly drawn, reflecting the concepts prephrased in the discussion above.

Answer choice (E): This answer choice deals with the continuing effects of the power inequity referenced in the stimulus. While this assumption would make the power disparity greater, this answer choice does not assert that the acquired political power has anything to do with the failure to respect the rights of all citizens. Because there is no such connection between power inequities and respecting other's rights, this cannot be the supporter assumption we seek.

Question #3: Strengthen. The correct answer choice is (C)

This stimulus begins with its conclusion: Nuclear power plants are not economically feasible. Although the fuel costs associated with nuclear plants are lower, favoring nuclear power, nuclear power plants are far more expensive to build than conventional power plants. These additional expenses outweigh the fuel savings associated with nuclear plants as compared with conventional plants.

The question stem asks which of the answer choices, if true, most strengthens the argument. The correct answer choice will be one that further demonstrates that nuclear plants are not economically feasible, either by introducing other detriments associated with nuclear plants, or more information on further benefits provided by conventional plants.

Answer choice (A): Because this answer discusses increased safety costs which can apply to *both* types of power plants, it cannot strengthen the argument that nuclear power plants are not economically feasible. While this statement would strengthen an argument that *both* types of power plants are too costly, the correct answer choice must offer evidence which distinguishes the two types of plants, in favor of conventional power.

Answer choice (B): If conventional plants spend more time out of service than nuclear plants, this weakens the argument. Since this statement would strengthen an argument in favor of nuclear plants, based on their apparently greater reliability, this answer choice is incorrect.

Answer choice (C): This is the correct answer choice. If the average life expectancy of a nuclear plant is shorter than that of a conventional one, this would strengthen an argument against nuclear plants—this choice provides, as prephrased, a further demonstration of the greater costs associated with nuclear plants, supporting the conclusion that they are not economically feasible.

Answer choice (D): If nuclear power plants cost less to build today than when the technology was first developed, thus increasing their cost effectiveness, this would weaken the author's conclusion that nuclear power plants are not economically feasible.

Answer choice (E): If the cost of running a conventional power plant will increase, this would lend support to the notion of building nuclear power plants for economic reasons. Since this weakens the author's conclusion, it is incorrect.

Question #4: Flaw in the Reasoning. The correct answer choice is (B)

The pundit in this stimulus states that because the average salary for teachers is lower than the average salary for athletes, it must be the case that our society values sports more than it values education.

The question stem asks for the reason that the pundit's argument is questionable: Is the average salary the best means to determine how much a society values education? Perhaps there are indicators other than this one simple comparison that would more accurately reflect our societal priorities.

Answer choice (A): While sports may have some sort of educational value, the pundit doesn't make any such presumption in the stimulus. Regardless, such a presumption would not play into the author's conclusion that society values sports more than education.

Answer choice (B): This is the correct answer choice. If the total spent on education is much greater than the total spent on sports, this would provide evidence against the pundit's assertion that our society values sports more than education. The failure to consider this fact renders the pundit's conclusion questionable, since information on total money spent might provide a better means to judge the value that our society places on education.

Answer choice (C): The argument in the stimulus provides a simple comparison of salary—how much each profession makes, on average, in a year. Information about the vacation time afforded to the respective professions would not be relevant to the comparison offered by the pundit, so the failure to consider such would not be a vulnerability in the argument, and this answer choice is incorrect.

Answer choice (D): Comparing teachers' salaries only to those of professional athletes is not a flaw in the pundit's reasoning; when the relevant comparison is between the society's valuation of sports and education, further comparisons between teachers' salaries and the salaries of other professionals would be irrelevant, so this answer choice should be eliminated.

Answer choice (E): The pundit's argument deals exclusively with *our* society's valuation of sports vs. education, so further comparisons to the salaries of other teachers from other nations would be irrelevant to the argument. The pundit is making a judgment about his or her society alone. What other societies do in terms of teachers' salaries or athletes' salaries does not play into the author's conclusion regarding *this* society.

Question #5: Must Be True. The correct answer choice is (A)

This stimulus involves a discussion of mathematical theories and their applications. The "gauge field theory" was investigated in the nineteenth century, but the theory wasn't applied to quantum mechanics until fairly recently. Another area of mathematics, differential geometry, was also investigated by Gauss, well ahead of Einstein's application of related, "offspring" concepts to his theory of general relativity.

The question stem asks which one of the answer choices is best illustrated by the examples presented. In an effort to prephrase this answer choice, we should note that the main link between the two examples presented in the stimulus is that they both reflect mathematical discoveries which were applied to concepts a long time after they were initially conceived.

Answer choice (A): This is the correct answer choice. New theories are often applied long after their initial discovery—this reflects the concept prephrased above, and the example of Gauss' investigation of differential geometry, the offspring of which was later applied by Einstein to the exploration of general relativity.

Answer choice (B): The author of the stimulus alludes to the point that there are sometimes wide spans of time between the conception of a mathematical idea and its application, but there is no reference made to any such specific anticipation on the part of the mathematicians.

Answer choice (C): It is not clear that modern discoveries in physics would have been *impossible* without 19th century mathematical advances—even though they may have facilitated the later discoveries, this does not necessarily mean that the modern discoveries would have been impossible without earlier advances. Rather, the examples in the stimulus are offered to reflect the lapse that sometimes occurs before an idea is applied.

Answer choice (D): While it *may* be true that the nineteenth century stands out as a period of great mathematical progress, there is no way to know based on the information provided; since the stimulus contains no reference whatsoever to the degree of progress during any other time periods, there is no basis for such comparison. Since we cannot conclude that the nineteenth century held any such distinction based on the stimulus, this cannot be the correct answer choice.

Answer choice (E): While mathematics might advance more quickly than other sciences, this is not illustrated by the information contained in the stimulus. If anything, the stimulus points out the time lapse between conception and application, indicating that mathematics in some cases advances rather slowly, but there is no basis for comparison to other fields.

Question #6: Flaw in the Reasoning. The correct answer choice is (A)

This stimulus deals with recently discovered bird fossils that are 20 million years older than the fossils of some birdlike dinosaurs. Most paleontologists claim that birds descended from these birdlike dinosaurs. But the author of this stimulus concludes that no birds could have descended from any dinosaur.

The question stem asks how the reasoning is flawed. What is wrong with the conclusion above? The author concludes that birds did not descend from any dinosaur because some bird fossils are older than the fossils of some dinosaurs from which the birds are believed to have descended. The argument breaks down as follows:

> Premise: There are *some* bird fossils older than *some* dinosaur fossils.
>
> Conclusion: Therefore, *no* bird could have descended from *any* dinosaur.

This conclusion is overly broad, and is not justified based on the information provided in the stimulus (for example, hypothetically, birds could have descended from dinosaurs with the two species coexisting for 50 million years. If this were the case, we could conceivably find *some* of the older bird fossils to be 20 million years older than *some* recent dinosaur fossils, even though the birds in this hypothetical scenario descended from the dinosaurs).

Answer choice (A): This is the correct answer choice. The author draws a generalization that is broader than warranted by the findings cited. In other words, the premise that there are *some* bird fossils that are older than *some* dinosaur fossils is not sufficient to draw such a broad conclusion about birds and dinosaurs in general, as discussed above.

Answer choice (B): While the author of this stimulus does indeed reject a consensus view, there is not necessarily a requirement to provide a counterexample when doing so. Since this is not a flaw, this answer choice should be rejected.

Answer choice (C): This answer choice describes the classic source argument, or *ad hominem* attack. The author of the stimulus does not personally attack the paleontologists who hold the majority opinion, so this answer choice is incorrect.

Answer choice (D): Since the argument in the stimulus concerns whether or not any bird descended from any dinosaur, the possibility referenced in this answer choice is irrelevant. Since this possibility need not be considered, this answer choice cannot be correct.

Answer choice (E): The argument does not explicitly discuss the possibility that the two species discussed share a common ancestor, but this is irrelevant to the author's conclusion that no bird descended from any dinosaur, and that the prevailing paleontologist view is wrong.

Question #7: Must Be True—Principle. The correct answer choice is (B)

The stimulus is comprised of two pieces of advice regarding fashion:

Premise:	A classic suit may be in style for as long as five years, so one should pay more to be sure it is well constructed.
Premise:	A trendy hat that will go out of style in a year or two should be purchased as cheaply as possible.

The question stem asks which of the answer choices most accurately expresses the principle underlying the reasoning above. In prephrasing an answer, one should look for an answer choice that indicates that it is acceptable to spend more for clothes that will last, but not much should be spent on clothes that will be likely to fall out of fashion in the short term.

Answer choice (A): The author of the stimulus asserts that better quality should be paid for when the item is likely to stay fashionable. The author does not make the assertion that formal attire generally lasts longer or is better constructed. In fact, no comparison of design and construction between formal and casual wear is ever made in the stimulus, so this answer choice should be eliminated.

Answer choice (B): This is the correct answer choice, as it articulates the principle prephrased above: The amount of money one spends on clothing should be proportional to the length of time one expects to be wearing the article of clothing.

Answer choice (C): This answer choice provides a universal rule that ignores the second conditional statement in the stimulus, which advises that one spend as little as possible on an item like a trendy hat. One should only opt for the available well-constructed garment, according to the author of the stimulus, when that garment is likely to be in style for five years or longer.

Answer choice (D): This answer choice is a "could be true," but the stimulus contains no information at all distinguishing men's clothes versus women's, so there is no way to know whether or not this would be the advice suggested by the author, so this choice should be eliminated.

Answer choice (E): This incorrect answer choice might look appealing, because some test takers may have the opinion that the purchase of office attire might provide a more appropriate use of funds. Because the author of the stimulus does not distinguish between office attire and casual attire, however, there is no way to draw this conclusion based on the information provided in the stimulus.

Question #8: Resolve the Paradox. The correct answer choice is (D)

This stimulus contains information regarding two commissioned erosion reports which concern the suitability of a new bridge site at Wantastiquet Pass, with a focus on the prospect that erosion might weaken the new bridge's foundation. Both of the reports are accurate, but they come to different conclusions about the degree of erosion at the site. One report holds that the area suffers relatively little erosion, while the other report states that regional erosion is heavy enough to cause concern.

We are asked how to resolve this apparent paradox, so we should find the answer that explains what might distinguish these two reports from one another (while still allowing for the fact that both reports are accurate), and offers some explanation as to why the different conclusions were drawn.

Answer choice (A): Even if neither report presents an extensive chemical analysis, this does not distinguish the two reports in any way, and thus provides no resolution to the discrepancy in the findings regarding the impact of erosion, so this answer choice should be eliminated.

Answer choice (B): If *both* reports include enhanced satellite photos, then we would still expect that the findings would be similar. This answer choice provides no distinction between the two reports, and no insight into a resolution of the reports' disparate findings.

Answer choice (C): If one report came from a university and the other came from a private consulting firm, this would provide one distinguishing characteristic between the two sets of findings. However, the author of the stimulus asserts that the findings of both reports are accurate, so we would still expect similar conclusions, and information regarding their respective sources doesn't help to resolve the discrepancy in the respective findings.

Answer choice (D): This is the correct answer choice. If the results of one report were based on general findings concerning regional topsoil erosion, and the other focuses instead on flood-caused riverbank erosion, then we wouldn't necessarily have the expectation that the reports would arrive at similar conclusions. It makes sense that both could be accurate, since one type of erosion can be light while the other can be significant. This resolves the paradox and allows for the given fact that both reports are accurate.

Answer choice (E): While this answer choice provides a point of distinction between the two reports, the relative costs of the reports should not differentiate the results, especially considering that we already know that both reports are confirmed accurate according to the stimulus.

Question #9: Flaw in the Reasoning. The correct answer choice is (D)

This stimulus introduces a letter to the editor complaining of the reasoning in a recent article on speed limits. In that article, it was noted that areas with lower speed limits had lower vehicle fatality rates. But the letter writer concludes that it will not be that way for long, based on the fact that vehicle-related fatalities are increasing in areas with lower speed limits.

The question stem asks why the reasoning in the letter writer's argument is flawed. Whenever we see simple numbers comparisons, we should be wary of the author's tendency to draw unwarranted conclusions. The problem here is that a simple increase in the number of vehicle related fatalities does not provide sufficient evidence to logically draw any conclusions about whether these fatalities are attributable to the lower speed limits. If we are seeking to determine whether or not safety is increased by lower speed limits, a more relevant comparison would be between the respective fatalities of high vs. low speed limit areas.

Answer choice (A): Reliance upon empirical evidence cited in the original article is not a flaw in the letter writer's argument—it is quite common on the LSAT to see two different viewpoints or interpretations based on the exact same evidence. The author of the letter is not refuting the evidence provided by the original report, but rather the interpretation of that evidence, so this answer choice is incorrect.

Answer choice (B): The term "often" is extremely vague, and provides no insight into the relative likelihood of fatalities at high speeds vs. low speeds. The reason the conclusion in the stimulus is flawed is that it rests on a shaky premise, not that it fails to consider all outside evidence. This answer choice does not provide an effective attack on the stimulus' reasoning.

Answer choice (C): The fact that some drivers don't want to drive any faster plays no role in the editorialist's argument, since an increased speed limit would not *require* anyone to drive faster. The fact that some don't wish to drive faster is irrelevant, and certainly does not represent a flaw in the author's reasoning, so this answer choice should be eliminated.

Answer choice (D): This is the correct answer choice. If vehicle fatality rates are increasing everywhere, not just in the low speed limit areas, then we cannot logically draw any justifiable conclusions about the increase in fatality rates that has taken place in the low speed limit areas, and raising the speed limit based on these figures would not necessarily be advisable.

Answer choice (E): The letter writer does provide some evidence (though questionable) against the opposing viewpoint—the evidence that the vehicle fatality rate is increasing in the low speed limit areas. This evidence may be weak, but the claim is presented, so this answer choice is inaccurate and incorrect.

Question #10: Resolve the Paradox. The correct answer choice is (E)

In this stimulus, the writer discusses the fact that while human settlement of previously vacant lands tends to endanger wildlife, the Mississippi kite has nevertheless flourished in areas where people have settled—starting in 1985, the Mississippi kite population increased more during the following five-year period in towns than in rural areas, contrary to what we would generally expect of wildlife.

The question stem asks us to resolve this apparent discrepancy, or explain why the Mississippi kite population has not followed the typical pattern of diminishing in settled areas. In Resolve the Paradox questions we look for the answer choice which provides a premise that is consistent with both of the seemingly contrary premises in the stimulus. In this case, we should seek an answer choice that reflects some benefit that this species derives from human-populated lands.

Answer choice (A): Loud firecrackers near roosting spots would clearly be intended to hinder these birds, which is what we would expect. Since the kites have flourished regardless, this answer choice only serves to widen the apparent discrepancy, so this answer choice should be eliminated.

Answer choice (B): While this answer choice provides that towns might be more nature-friendly than big cities, it does not help explain the ability of the kites to thrive *more* in towns than in rural areas, contrary to the normal reaction of bird populations to settlements, so this answer choice fails to provide resolution to the paradox presented in the stimulus.

Answer choice (C): While such a treaty and its enforcements explain some degree of legal protection for the birds when they do come into contact with humans, it still does not explain why these birds have been doing better in prairie towns than in areas with *no* human population at all.

Answer choice (D): While the experiences of the pigeons and raccoons might show that it is possible to *adapt* successfully to towns, this would imply that they have learned to co-exist successfully where humans live. This doesn't explain why the Mississippi kite has not only adapted, but flourished *more rapidly* in towns than in rural areas, so this answer choice is incorrect.

Answer choice (E): This is the correct answer choice. This answer choice gives a reason why the kites have flourished in towns along the North American prairie. If these towns' trees tend to grow more densely and thus offer more protection for the birds' nests and eggs, this would explain why the Mississippi kite's population has increased more rapidly in towns.

Question #11: Method of Reasoning – AP. The correct answer choice is (E)

When a record label signs a band, it takes a financial risk, which includes the costs for videos, album art, management and promotions. All of these costs would have to be covered by the band if it were to take the independent route rather than signing with a label. The writer concludes that it is fair for the record company to take a large portion of profits from record sales of a band signed to its label.

The question stem asks for the role played in the argument by the claim that a band signed with a major label does not assume nearly as much risk as it would if it produced its own records independently. Evidence is provided to support this assertion, so it must be some sort of conclusion. But this claim about risk is also a premise in support of the main conclusion, so this must be a secondary, or subsidiary, conclusion, which supports the main conclusion found at the end of the stimulus:

Label covers costs ————→ *thus, not as much band risk* ————→ thus, fair for label to take profits

Answer choice (A): The assertion regarding the reduced risk for a label-signed band is a conclusion, but it is not the main conclusion of the argument in the stimulus, so this answer choice is incorrect.

Answer choice (B): The two conclusions *are* related to each other—the subsidiary conclusion supports the main conclusion:

Subsidiary Conclusion:	Thus, not as much band risk for label-signed bands
Conclusion:	Thus, fair for record labels to take large portion of profit

Since these are not two unrelated conclusions, this answer choice is incorrect.

Answer choice (C): The claim that a label assumes much of a band's risk is not a general principle—it is an assertion which provides support for the main conclusion, that a large part of a band's profits should justifiably go to the label.

Answer choice (D): The referenced claim is not a phenomenon to be explained, but rather a supported assertion that provides support for the main conclusion, so this answer choice should be eliminated.

Answer choice (E): This is the correct answer choice, as this choice provides a perfect description of this subsidiary conclusion:

Premise:	The label takes on significant risk
Subsidiary Conclusion:	*Thus, not as much band risk for label-signed bands*
Conclusion:	Thus, fair for record labels to take large portion of profit.

Here the referenced subsidiary, or secondary, conclusion is supported by a premise, while lending support to the main conclusion that record labels are justified in taking large portions of the profits.

Question #12: Must Be True. The correct answer choice is (A)

The commentator in this stimulus notes that articles criticizing the environmental movement have been appearing regularly in newspapers. The commentator introduces Winslow's belief that this is not the result of an anti-environmental bias among the media, but is due instead to editors' preference for "daring" articles that challenge prevailing political viewpoints.

The commentator agrees with Winslow regarding what drives newspapers to run articles that challenge prevailing political orthodoxy. There is also disagreement with Winslow, however: The commentator asserts that environmentalism is not politically orthodox, so anti-environmentalists are not the rebels that they may portray themselves to be.

The question stem asks which answer choice is most strongly supported by the commentator's remarks. The correct answer choice will likely be a conclusion or an inference that can be logically drawn from the stimulus.

Answer choice (A): This is the correct answer choice. The commentator does agree with Winslow about newspaper editors' preferences for controversial articles, apparently chosen in an effort to appear daring.

Answer choice (B): In the last sentence of the stimulus, the commentator notes that the anti-environmentalists have succeeded somewhat in selling themselves as renegades, so it would be inaccurate, according to the information in the stimulus, to claim that the author doesn't believe there has been such successful self-promotion. This answer choice should therefore be eliminated.

Answer choice (C): Winslow's explanation *does* provide reasons why such critiques are published regularly, so this assertion is inaccurate, and this answer choice is incorrect.

Answer choice (D): The commentator would not agree with the assertion that the refuted position is the prevailing political position, having stated that the refuted position is serious environmentalism, which is not politically orthodox according to the commentator, so this answer choice should be eliminated.

Answer choice (E): The commentator says that serious environmentalism is by no means politically orthodox, but does not make the claim, or the implication, that it will eventually become a prevailing political position. While the assertion in this answer choice could in time prove to be accurate, it is not supported by the information in the stimulus, and this choice should be eliminated.

Question #13: Strengthen. The correct answer choice is (B)

The philosopher in this stimulus notes that some of the most ardent philosophical opponents to democracy have correctly noted that both the inherently best and inherently worst forms of government are those which concentrate power in the hands of few. Based on this premise, the philosopher concludes that democracy is a better form of government than rule by few, even though democracy is consistently mediocre—that is, according to the philosopher, reliable mediocrity is preferable to the prospect of a worse form of government.

The question stem asks which of the answer choices *most* helps to justify the philosopher's argument—that is, which answer choice lends the greatest strength to the argument that, as a mediocre but consistent form of government, democracy is preferable to both the best and worse forms of government.

Answer choice (A): The philosopher's conclusion is that democracy is the better form of government, regardless of the preference of the majority.

Answer choice (B): This is the correct answer choice. This choice asserts that it is better to eliminate the worst form of government, even if the cost is not being able to attain the best form of government.

Answer choice (C): This answer choice is incorrect, because the philosopher's conclusion excludes both the best and worst forms of government, in favor of the consistently mediocre form of government which is democracy.

Answer choice (D): The philosopher's conclusion is not about which forms of government are the most equitable, just which ones are "better" than others. Since this answer choice is irrelevant to the argument in the stimulus, it is incorrect.

Answer choice (E): While the philosopher might agree with the notion that sound philosophical reasoning provides a better basis than popular preference for decisions about government, this assertion does not lend any strength to the stimulus' argument. The philosopher's theory is that it is better when choosing a form of government to avoid the worst in favor of safe mediocrity.

Question #14: Must Be True. The correct answer choice is (C)

The expert in this stimulus discusses addictive versus non-addictive substances. Some suggest that any substance that habitual users can stop using is non-addictive. The author believes that this definition of non-addictive is overly broad, as it would deem some expert-classified addictive substances erroneously, as non-addictive.

The expert states that any definition should define a substance as addictive only if withdrawal from its habitual use causes most users extreme psychological and physiological difficulty. This conclusion provides a conditional statement: A substance is deemed to be addictive *only* if withdrawal must cause most users extreme psychological *and* physiological difficulty. So in this case, the sufficient variable is "addictive," and the necessary variables are extreme psychological and physiological addiction:

$$\text{Addictive} \longrightarrow \begin{array}{c} \text{extreme psychological difficulty for most} \\ \textit{and} \\ \text{extreme physiological difficulty for most} \end{array}$$

The question stem asks which of the answer choices can be inferred from the expert's statements. When a Must Be True question follows a conditional statement, it is worthwhile to consider the contrapositive as well: In this case, if withdrawal from a substance lacks extreme psychological difficulty for most, *or* if such withdrawal lacks physiological difficulty for most, then it is non-addictive:

$$\begin{array}{c} \text{extreme psychological \cancel{difficulty} for most} \\ \textit{or} \\ \text{extreme physiological \cancel{difficulty} for most} \end{array} \longrightarrow \cancel{\text{addictive}}$$

Answer choice (A): This answer choice reverses the sufficient and necessary variables provided by the stimulus, providing the following conditional reasoning:

$$\begin{array}{c} \text{extreme psychological difficulty for most} \\ \textit{and} \\ \text{extreme physiological difficulty for most} \end{array} \longrightarrow \text{addictive}$$

Since this statement reflects a Mistaken Reversal of the conditional statement in the stimulus, this answer choice is incorrect.

Answer choice (B): According to the stimulus, the view in question defines non-addictive substances too *broadly*. This means that the author believes that non-addictive substance should be defined more narrowly, which would define fewer substances as non-addictive, and characterize more substances as addictive. Thus, it is not likely that in the author's view, an adequate definition would *reduce* the number of substances that are deemed addictive.

Answer choice (C): This is the correct answer choice. This answer choice provides the exception to the conditional statement found in the stimulus, which applies to most users. Even if some users can cease use of a habitual substance, then that substance can still be deemed addictive, *only* if most users have stronger ties to the substance. This aligns with the conditional rule provided by the stimulus:

extreme psychological difficulty for *most*

Addictive ——————→ *and*

extreme physiological difficulty for *most*

A substance is properly characterized as addictive *only* if most users will have extreme psychological and physiological difficulty in ceasing the use of this substance. This conditional rule focuses on the majority of users, regardless of the fact that *some* users might be able to quit with little difficulty.

Answer choice (D): This answer choice presents the following conditional reasoning:

Significant psycho~~lo~~gical difficulty

and ——————→ addi~~c~~tive

Significant physi~~o~~logical difficulty

This looks attractive, because of its similarity to the contrapositive version of the conditional reasoning presented in the stimulus. There are important distinctions, however: The author of the stimulus made this conditional statement with reference to the experiences of *most*, while this answer choice focuses on *one* individual's experience. Additionally, the stimulus deals with the experiences associated with the *cessation* of use of a substance, while this answer choice focuses on the habitual *use* of a substance. Because of these two vital differences, this answer choice cannot be properly inferred from the information in the stimulus.

Answer choice (E): The stimulus presents two attributes which, according to the expert, must be present in every case in order for a substance to be addictive (the necessary variables: psychological difficulty and physiological difficulty associated with cessation of use). This is not presented as an exhaustive definition—this could represent only a small part of what it takes for a substance to be addictive. Thus we cannot draw any conclusions regarding even the precise definition of an addictive substance, let alone such a definition of addiction. Since the expert does not specifically discuss the definition of the term "addiction," or the precision with which one could define the term, this answer choice is incorrect.

Question #15: Assumption. The correct answer choice is (A)

This stimulus starts as many LSAT questions do—with a prevailing view to be disputed. In this case, the prevailing view is that the difference in wages between highest and lowest will eventually become a source of social conflict. The sociologist disputes this claim, concluding that the difference will have an opposite effect, because companies will be able to hire freely. He claims that social friction does not arise from high wage differences, but rather from static or slowly changing wages.

> Premise: Social friction arises from static or slow changing wages.
>
> Conclusion: The ability to hire freely will reduce social friction.

In order for this conclusion to be properly drawn, the author must believe that the ability to hire freely must somehow make static or slow changing wages less likely.

The question stem asks for the assumption required by the sociologist's argument; this is a Supporter Assumption question, and the correct answer choice should provide some link between the ability to hire freely and the absence of static or slow changing wages—for the author's conclusion to hold, it must be the case that the ability to hire freely must allow companies to avoid static or slow changing wages.

Answer choice (A): This is the correct answer choice, as it provides the link between the rogue elements referenced above: When companies can hire freely, wage levels tend not to be static or slow changing:

> Premise: Social friction arises from static or slow changing wages.
>
> *Assumption: There tend not to be slow or static changes to wages when companies are able to hire freely.*
>
> Conclusion: The ability to hire freely will reduce social friction.

Once we make this Supporter Assumption explicit, we can see that the argument flows logically.

Answer choice (B): The conclusion in the stimulus does not concern *reactions* to wage change expectations, but rather the relationship between static or slowly changing wages, social friction, and companies' ability to hire freely. Since the sociologist's conclusion makes no distinction regarding how people react to disparities in income, and this choice makes no reference to the unlinked elements of the author's argument, this answer choice is incorrect.

Answer choice (C): Expansion of business operations is completely irrelevant to the sociologist's conclusion, and this answer does not tie together the prephrased elements listed above, so this answer choice is incorrect.

Answer choice (D): It may be the case that a company's ability to respond swiftly to change always benefits workers, but since this choice does not provide the necessary link between the rogue elements referenced above, this is not the Supporter Assumption we are seeking.

Answer choice (E): If well-paid workers become dissatisfied if their wages never change, this may help to support or explain the author's assertion that static wages lead to social friction, but this answer choice does not link the premise about static wages causing social friction with the conclusion that when companies can hire freely, social friction is reduced.

Question #16: Main Point. The correct answer choice is (D)

In this stimulus, a book publisher discusses the need to do "whatever it takes" to ship exercise and fitness books in time to meet the seasonal demand that accompanies the new year. The publisher's competitors have shown a high level of organization and the publisher "cannot afford to be outsold":

Premise: The competition has shown a high level of organization.

Premise: This publisher cannot afford to be outsold.

Conclusion: This publisher must therefore do whatever it takes to ship out its books and meet increased seasonal demand.

The question stem asks for the main conclusion of the publisher's argument. The correct answer choice will convey the urgent need to ship these books in a timely manner.

Answer choice (A): While shipping books in a timely manner should apparently be a priority ("do whatever it takes"), the publisher does not specify that it should be the *highest* priority. Since there could be other, higher priorities, this answer choice does not accurately reflect the conclusion of the publisher's argument.

Answer choice (B) The publisher does not mention maintaining the company's competitive edge by increasing its efficiency—only that it is urgent that the books ship on time. In fact, it is not clear that this publisher even has a competitive edge to maintain, so this answer choice is incorrect.

Answer choice (C): Although the stimulus makes it clear that shipping is a high priority, the author offers no information about the potential repercussions of failing to keep up with the high level of organization maintained by the competition.

Answer choice (D): This is the correct answer choice. This is the main point of the publisher's statement: The publisher must do whatever it takes to ship out its fitness and exercise books on time to meet the increased seasonal demand, and avoid being outsold by the competition.

Answer choice (E): The publisher mentions that the competitors have a high level of organization, and that this publisher cannot afford to be outsold, but does not discuss a need to copy the competitors' shipping practices.

Question #17: Flaw in the Reasoning. The correct answer choice is (D)

The advertiser in this stimulus asserts that because the advertiser's product, the VersaTool, performs more functions than any other tool, a VersaTool user will need other tools less often than when using alternative multi-function tools.

The question stems asks how the advertiser's reasoning is most vulnerable to criticism. In prephrasing an answer, one should look skeptically at the advertiser's claims. The claim here is that using a VersaTool will require one to use fewer tools and use them less often than if he or she were to use another multi-purpose tool.

The legitimacy of this claim rests entirely on how commonly or often the functions on the VersaTool are used, so the vulnerability in the argument lies in the fact that if the VersaTool's functions are not commonly used or needed, the claim in the ad is invalid regardless of how many functions it has.

Answer choice (A): This answer choice might be attractive because it notes the inclusion of useless tools on the VersaTool. But it is not the tools that are *not* used that are important; it is how often the VersaTool's tools *are* used that will determine the credibility of the claims in the ad.

Answer choice (B): If anything, the fact that the VersaTool would perform such difficult functions would strengthen the advertiser's claims, because one would be still be using the VersaTool to perform functions that would normally require other tools. This would serve to bolster the claim that the VersaTool might make other multi-tools less useful by comparison.

Answer choice (C): If the claims in the ad concerned relative cost effectiveness, this assertion might come into play. Since the comparison deals with functionality, however, the fact that the VersaTool is more expensive is irrelevant to the advertiser's actual claims, so this answer choice is incorrect.

Answer choice (D): This is the correct answer choice. If the VersaTool might be able to perform fewer often-needed functions than some other multi-function tool, this is another way of saying that another tool might perform a greater number of the often-needed functions, rendering the advertiser's claims invalid.

Answer choice (E): The ad's claims compare the number of functions, rather than how well the VersaTool performs each of those functions; this statement is irrelevant to the advertiser's claim that a user of the VersaTool would need additional tools less often than with other multi-function tools.

Question #18: Assumption. The correct answer choice is (B)

This stimulus discusses the flagellum, which is used by bacteria to swim and requires many parts before it can propel the bacteria at all. Based on this premise, the writer concludes that an evolutionary ancestor of bacteria that had only a few flagellum parts gained *no* survival advantage from those parts:

> Premise: The flagellum requires many parts in order to propel a bacterium.
>
> Conclusion: A bacterial ancestor that was missing some flagellum parts would gain *no* survival advantage from the flagellum.

We should note that there is a significant logical leap represented here, from the premise, which concerns an inability to aid in swimming, to a conclusion about an inability to provide *any* survival advantage.

The question stem asks us to identify the assumption on which the stimulus' conclusion depends. This is a Supporter Assumption question, and the correct answer choice should link together the two elements discussed above to allow the author to properly draw the conclusion that an incomplete flagellum would offer no advantages if it were unable to propel a bacterium.

Answer choice (A): If an incomplete flagellum actually served as a disadvantage, this would justify the conclusion in the stimulus, but it is not an assumption *required* by the argument. That is, the assertion in this answer choice goes beyond what is necessary for the argument to stand—we don't need to know that such ancestors would be at a *disadvantage*—only that there would be no survival *advantage* associated with limited parts of the flagellum. Since the assumption provided by this answer choice is not *required* by the argument, this answer choice is incorrect.

Answer choice (B): This is the correct answer choice. This answer choice provides the required link between the survival advantage, the parts of the flagellum and the ability to swim:

> Premise: The flagellum requires many parts in order to propel a bacterium.
>
> *Assumption:* *For the flagellum to offer any survival advantage, it would have to aid in the ability to swim (that is, it would have to be able to propel the bacterium).*
>
> Conclusion: Therefore, a bacterial ancestor that was missing some flagellum parts would gain no survival advantage from the flagellum.

The above assumption is required to allow the author's conclusion to be logically drawn from the premise provided in the stimulus.

Answer choice (C): While this assertion might lend support to the conclusion in the stimulus, it is not *required* by the argument, so this answer choice cannot be correct.

To check our work, we can apply the Assumption Negation Technique to determine whether the negated assumption would weaken the conclusion:

"Not all parts of the flagellum are vital to each of its functions."

Even if *some* of the flagellum's parts don't play a role in every flagellum function, this doesn't weaken the argument asserting the need for a full flagellum to derive any survival benefits.

Answer choice (D): The fact that no evolutionary ancestor of bacteria had been limited to a few parts of the flagellum—if this were the case—would not play into the argument, which is phrased in the conditional tense, asserting that if there *were* such an ancestor, no survival advantage would be gained. The assertion in this answer choice is not an assumption required by the argument in the stimulus.

Again, we can apply the assumption negation technique by determining the effects of the negated version of the answer choice:

"Some evolutionary ancestors of bacteria had only a few of the parts of the flagellum."

Since this assertion would not weaken the argument in the stimulus, it is confirmed that this answer choice does not supply an assumption on which the conclusion relies.

Answer choice (E): This answer choice reinforces a point already covered by the stimulus—that bacteria use their flagella to swim. This is not, however, an assumption required by the argument, and since there is no mention of survival advantage, this cannot be the supporter assumption that ties together the author's argument.

To check our work, we can apply the assumption negation technique and determine whether the argument in the stimulus is weakened by the negated version of the answer choice:

"Not all of the bacteria's flagellum-lacking evolutionary ancestors also lacked the capacity to swim."

Again, this assertion has no effect on the argument that an incomplete flagellum provides no survival advantage, so this answer choice is incorrect.

Question #19: Must Be True. The correct answer choice is (D)

This stimulus provides instruction regarding the correction of archaic spelling and punctuations in direct quotations from older works. The general rule is that they are to be preserved if they occur infrequently <u>and</u> they do not interfere with a reader's comprehension of the quotation:

frequent
   and ⟶ preserve
interfere

On the other hand, if they occur frequently, the editor may modernize them, inserting a note in the text, or if a similar modernizing procedure has been done before, inserting a general statement in the preface:

Frequent occurrence ⟶ modernize w/note or general statement

Finally, if the quotations are from modern works, they are to be corrected without explanation:

Obvious typos ⟶ correct w/o explanation

The question stem asks which answer choice flows from the statements in the stimulus or which of the answer choices must be true.

Answer choice (A): The stimulus states that if an error is infrequent and interferes with the reader's comprehension, the error should be corrected. The stimulus does not state how this correction should be noted, if at all. Furthermore, if the error in question does not interfere with the reader's comprehension of the text, correcting this error may be contrary to the style manual's instructions.

Answer choice (B): The rule about modern works contained in the stimulus only refers to obvious typographical errors, which may be corrected without explanation. Because the stimulus does not discuss archaic spellings found in modern works, this answer choice is incorrect.

Answer choice (C): The stimulus states that such errors are to be preserved if they occur infrequently <u>and</u> they do not interfere with a reader's comprehension of the quotation. Because this answer choice omits one of these two criteria for modernizing an archaic spelling that is quoted from an older work, it is not necessarily true.

Answer choice (D): This is the correct answer choice. The style manual holds that if examples of archaic punctuation occur frequently, the editor may modernize, with an explanation in the text or preface, so this answer choice is accurate according to the information in the stimulus.

Answer choice (E): The stimulus states that if the modernizing has been done in more than one place, a note should be placed in the preface. This answer choice states that if modernizing occurs *once* out of several instances, then a note should be placed in the preface. Since this action would be contrary to directives of the stimulus, it is incorrect.

Question #20: Justify the Conclusion. The correct answer choice is (C)

This stimulus provides something of a murder mystery. Jansen's murderer was in the victim's office on the day of the crime, and Samantha and Herbert were both in Jansen's office on that day. Had Herbert committed the crime, the police would have found his fingerprints or footprints at the scene. Had Samantha committed the crime, she would have avoided leaving behind any fingerprints or footprints. Fingerprints were found at the scene, but there were no footprints. The fingerprints did not belong to Herbert, so it makes sense to conclude that he is not the murderer. Once Herbert has been ruled out as a suspect, however, the writer jumps to the conclusion that Samantha must have been the culprit. This argument has many premises, breaking down as follows:

Premise:	Jansen's murderer was in Jansen's office the day of the crime.
Premise:	Samantha and Herbert were both in Jansen's office that day.
Premise:	If Herbert were the culprit, he would have left prints.
Premise:	If Samantha were the culprit, she'd have avoided leaving prints.
Premise:	The police found fingerprints, but no footprints.
Premise:	The fingerprints were not Herbert's.
Subsidiary Conclusion:	Therefore, Herbert is not the murderer.
Conclusion:	Therefore, Samantha must be the killer.

This conclusion is not fully justified based on the information provided. It is *possible* that Samantha is the killer, because we only know that she would have *avoided* leaving prints, so the prints found at the scene could have belonged to her. However, this argument is not air-tight, because only two possible suspects have been identified. Could there have been another culprit entirely? There simply is not enough information to justifiably conclude that Samantha was the only conceivable murderer.

The question stem asks which of the answer choices allows the conclusion in the stimulus to be properly drawn. The correct answer choice will allow the reader to justifiably rule out *all* other possible suspects.

Answer choice (A): Since Herbert has already been ruled out, this answer choice merely lends support to the assertion that Herbert could not have been the culprit.

Answer choice (B): We were told in the stimulus that the murderer was in Jansen's office on the day the crime took place, so this answer choice provides no additional relevant information to help justify the conclusion that it must have been Samantha.

Answer choice (C): This is the correct answer choice. If all other possible culprits have been eliminated (since the murderer was in the office that day, and Herbert and Samantha were the only ones in the office on the day of the crime), then we can justifiably conclude that the only remaining possible offender would have been Samantha.

Answer choice (D): The stimulus describes the death as a murder, so we already know that the culprit must have been someone other than Jansen. This answer choice, therefore, offers no relevant information to justify the conclusion about Samantha.

Answer choice (E): If the fingerprints found at the scene did not belong to Samantha, this obviously weakens the conclusion that she was the culprit, so this answer choice does not provide an assumption on which the argument depends.

Question #21: Must Be True. The correct answer choice is (E)

In this stimulus, it is stated that most opera singers who add demanding roles to their repertoires early in life later lose their voices prematurely. This phenomenon has been attributed to their immature voices and insufficient vocal power. In typical LSAT fashion, the writer dismisses this attribution, asserting that the real reason is that most young singers have insufficient technical training to avoid straining their vocal chords, especially when singing at full strength.

The question stem asks which answer choice the stimulus most strongly supports.

Answer choice (A): The author of the stimulus primarily discusses young opera singers *with* great vocal power, so we have no basis for drawing any conclusion about young opera singers *without* great vocal power.

Answer choice (B): The assertion that some young opera singers with immature vocal chords ruin their voices singing demanding roles is specifically dismissed by the author of the stimulus, so this answer choice is incorrect.

Answer choice (C): While the author hypothesizes that the problem with many of these singers is a lack of training, the time required for such training is never specified, so we cannot draw the conclusion that many years of training are required before singing demanding roles.

Answer choice (D): It is not maturity that allows one to safely take on demanding roles, according to the author, but proper training. A young opera singer with proper training could tackle a demanding role, the author would likely assert, and still manage to avoid strained vocal chords, so this answer choice is incorrect.

Answer choice (E): This is the correct answer choice. From the first sentence of the stimulus we know that most young opera singers who take on demanding roles at young ages lose their voices early, and we are later told that *the real problem* is that most young singers lack the technical training to avoid straining their vocal chords, so it is a logical inference that the referenced loss of voice would be attributable to vocal strain.

Question #22: Parallel Reasoning—Flaw. The correct answer choice is (B)

This stimulus provides that food that is high in fat tends to be unhealthy. The writer then concludes that a particular type of fat-free brownies is healthier than a particular type of cookies with a high fat percentage.

The question stem asks for the answer choice that exhibits flawed reasoning similar to the flawed reasoning in the stimulus. In the case of the stimulus, the author draws an overly broad conclusion based on a single criterion: Fat content. All other things being equal, low fat or no fat foods might be healthier than high fat foods, but generally there are other factors to consider in making a complete determination.

Answer choice (A): If canned foods *always* contain more salt than frozen foods do, then it must be the case that the referenced canned peas contain more salt than the frozen peas do. This reasoning is not flawed, so this answer choice cannot possibly parallel the flawed reasoning reflected in the stimulus.

Answer choice (B): This is the correct answer choice. Here, the conclusion about overcooked carrots appears to be based on a single factor: Overcooking. If we don't have any information on the vitamin content of carrots relative to peas in their respective uncooked states, then it is impossible to draw any logical conclusions about the vitamin content of overcooked carrots relative to that of uncooked peas. This conclusion, overly broad and based on a single factor, perfectly parallels that of the stimulus.

Answer choice (C): This conclusion provides the following flawed logic:

Human Body:	Remain Healthy $\longrightarrow$ minerals
Distilled water:	M~~inerals~~ $\longrightarrow$ healthy t~~o~~ drink

This reasoning is flawed, although the second statement above looks almost like a contrapositive of the first statement. It is not the contrapositive, however, because the two statements deal with different variables. The first statement discusses needs of the human body, which requires minerals to *remain in a state of good health*. The second statement discusses ingredients in water, which may or may not require minerals to be *healthy to consume*. This reasoning, although flawed, does not parallel the argumentation found in the stimulus, so this answer choice is incorrect.

Answer choice (D): This answer choice reflects flawed logical reasoning, because without specific information about which nuts make Roy's throat itch, we can draw no conclusions about how relatively likely the referenced pie and cookies are to make his throat itch. Although the argumentation in this answer choice is flawed, this is mistaken logic of a different sort, and thus does not reflect that found in the stimulus.

Answer choice (E): If eating food at a restaurant *always* costs more than eating the same food at home, this home cooked meal must be less expensive than the same meal in a restaurant would be. Because the dishes are the same, all other things remain equal and the reasoning used here is valid. This logically sound answer choice cannot parallel the flawed logic found in the stimulus.

Question #23: Method of Reasoning – AP. The correct answer choice is (B)

The ethicist in this stimulus states that a person deserves praise for doing what is right, even if that person is not inclined to do wrong. The ethicist asserts that while people are considered virtuous for resisting a wrongful desire, they are no less virtuous if they have successfully extinguished such desires completely.

The question stem asks what role in the argument is played by the assertion that people are considered especially virtuous if they successfully resist a desire to do wrong. The referenced phrase provides some conventional wisdom: Those who can suppress wrongful desires are often *considered* especially virtuous. The author references this belief in order to then refute its overly broad application, with the assertion that those who have successfully extinguished wrongful desires actually deserve the same consideration.

Answer choice (A): The author does not attempt to justify the referenced claim; on the contrary, the ethicist goes on to refute the belief that it is more virtuous to resist desires than to extinguish them.

Answer choice (B): This is the correct answer choice. The author references this point in order to later refute its overly exclusive application: Although those who can suppress wrongful desires are considered by some to be especially virtuous, the ethicist asserts that we cannot conclude that those who have extinguished such desires are any less virtuous.

Answer choice (C): While a refutation of the referenced claim is offered, the author does not specify that this claim is a *primary* obstacle to an adequate conception of virtue, so this answer choice is incorrect.

Answer choice (D): The language in this answer choice is stronger than intended by the assertions in the stimulus. The author does not assert that it is *false* to consider those who can suppress wrongful desires as virtuous, but rather that those who are able to extinguish such desires deserve the same consideration.

Answer choice (E): The phrase in question serves as a premise to be refuted, not as evidence of the ethicist's conclusion, so this answer choice is incorrect.

Question #24: Parallel Reasoning. The correct answer choice is (C)

Ecologists predict that malaria will increase if global warming continues or if the use of pesticides is not expanded. The use of pesticides contributes to global warming, so the author of this stimulus concludes that an increase in malaria in the coming years will be inevitable. The initial conditional statement can be diagrammed as follows:

global warming increases
        or   ⟶   increase in malaria
use of pestic~~id~~es expanded

use of pesticides expanded ⟶ global warming increases ⟶ increase in malaria

Valid conclusion: There will be an increase in malaria.

Since increasing the use of pesticides causes global warming to increase, either use of pesticides will be expanded, causing global warming, which would lead to an increase in malaria, or use of pesticides won't be expanded, which would lead to an increase in malaria. Either way, one of the sufficient variables will surely come to pass, which dictates an inevitable increase in malaria.

The question stem asks for the answer choice which uses the same pattern of reasoning used in the stimulus. In the stimulus, there are two options that causally contribute to the effect that is contained in the conclusion. But if one of the causes doesn't come to fruition, the other surely will, thus creating an inevitability, since at least one of the causes will always be present. The correct answer choice will be one in which there are two possible causes of a given phenomenon. Additionally, one of those causes will be causally linked to the other, creating an inevitability analogous to that found in the stimulus.

Answer choice (A): The reasoning provided in this answer choice is as follows:

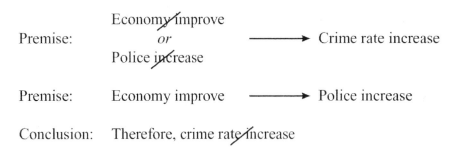

Premise: Economy ~~improve~~
                    or   ⟶   Crime rate increase
                 Police i~~n~~crease

Premise: Economy improve ⟶ Police increase

Conclusion: Therefore, crime rat~~e~~increase

This conditional reasoning is flawed, because there it no reason to presume that the economy *will* improve—and if it doesn't, the crime rate will increase. Unlike the conditional reasoning reflected in the stimulus, where the increase in malaria would surely come to pass, this answer choice concludes that the crime rate will surely *not* increase, and bases this conclusion on flawed reasoning, so this choice fails to parallel the author's reasoning.

Answer choice (B): This answer choice reflects the following conditional reasoning:

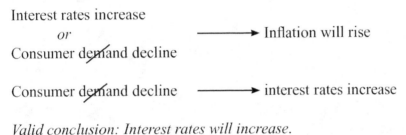

Educational funds current level
or
Recruit qualified teachers ⟶ Student performance worsen

Valid conclusion: Recruit qualified teachers ⟶ Student performance worsen

This reflects valid reasoning, since one of the causes will certainly be present, and this is enough to ensure that the necessary variable (worsening student performance) will come to pass. Unlike the reasoning presented in the stimulus, however, the two alternative causes are not themselves causally linked in this case. Since the conditional reasoning presented in this choice does not parallel the reasoning found in the stimulus, this answer choice is incorrect.

Answer choice (C): This is the correct answer choice. This answer choice presents the following conditional reasoning:

Interest rates increase
or
Consumer demand decline ⟶ Inflation will rise

Consumer demand decline ⟶ interest rates increase

Valid conclusion: Interest rates will increase.

Since a non-declining consumer demand will cause inflation to rise, and a decline in consumer demand would cause interest rates to increase, which in turn would cause inflation to rise, it is logical to conclude that inflation will increase regardless.

This answer choice presents two potential causes for the given effect. Additionally, if one of those causes (non-declining consumer demand) fails to come to fruition, this will bring about the other cause (rising interest rates). Since these two possible causes are themselves causally linked, increased inflation is the inevitable outcome and the reasoning in this answer choice provides a parallel to the conditional reasoning found in the stimulus.

Answer choice (D): The conditional reasoning provided by this answer choice is as follows:

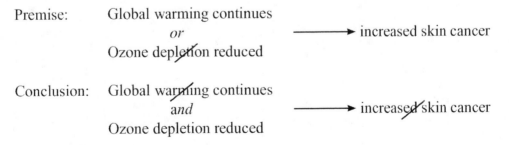

Premise: Global warming continues
or
Ozone depletion reduced ⟶ increased skin cancer

Conclusion: Global warming continues
and
Ozone depletion reduced ⟶ increased skin cancer

This reasoning clearly reflects a mistaken negation, a flaw not found in the reasoning of the stimulus. Further, this answer choice contains two sufficient variables which are then both *ruled out*, so this choice does not parallel the author's argumentation and should be eliminated.

Answer choice (E): The conditional reasoning found in this answer choice can be diagrammed as follows:

Deforestation maintains current rate
            and   ⟶ wildlife extinction will continue
Use of che~~m~~icals curtailed

Deforestation will maintain rate
            and   ⟶ thus, extinction will continue
Use of chem~~i~~cals curtailed

The reasoning in this answer choice is valid, but the cause and effect relationship in this case does not present two alternative causes for the given effect. Instead, there are two causes, *both* of which are required, in order to achieve the given effect. A third piece of evidence (increase in population worldwide) ensures that both of the needed causes will indeed be present, allowing for the conclusion to be logically drawn.

The reasoning in this answer choice is different from that found in the stimulus, in which there is no further evidence needed to draw the conclusion, because one of the two sufficient variables mentioned will surely come to pass. Because this answer choice does not present two alternative causes that are *themselves* causally linked, this choice fails to parallel the reasoning in the stimulus.

Question #25: Strengthen. The correct answer choice is (C)

In ancient Greece, this stimulus tells us, there was no cross-examination of witnesses, and juries were given no legal guidance, so it was imperative for litigants to make a good impression on the jury. Based on this, the author concludes that courtroom records of litigants' testimony provide good sources of data on the Greek culture's common perceptions of morality during that era.

The question stem asks for the answer choice that would most strengthen the argument contained in the stimulus. The correct answer choice will bolster the claim that the referenced courtroom oratory would provide an accurate reflection of cultural perceptions of morality at the time.

Answer choice (A): This answer choice links personality with jurors' preferences. If jurors were impressed by those whose personalities they preferred, this would provide incentive for litigants to be personable, but not necessarily to reflect common cultural perceptions of morality, so this answer choice should be eliminated.

Answer choice (B): It would seem likely that jurors would apply closer scrutiny to the morals of litigants than others might. Such a belief on the part of a litigant (that his or her moral codes would be under closer scrutiny by juries) might provide incentive for that litigant to try to reflect strong moral values, but would not necessarily lead that litigant to profess moral beliefs which reflect *those of the society*—the societal morals may not have been the same as those appreciated by juries or aspired to by litigants of the time.

Answer choice (C): This is the correct answer choice. If the belief was that jurors were likely to be more impressed by morals similar to their own, this would provide incentive for those litigants to reflect the personal moral code of *the jurors*, and, more generally, of that *society*. This strengthens the conclusion that litigants' courtroom testimony serves as a good source of data for perceptions of morality in that culture.

Answer choice (D): If the belief was that jurors would be more impressed by litigants of an economic class similar to their own, courtroom oratory might be a good source of data on the economic classes of ancient Greek society, but that society's common conceptions of *morality* would not necessarily be reflected.

Answer choice (E): If the belief was that jurors made decisions based on strong legal principles, litigants would have incentive to base their testimony on the laws of the time, but this would not necessarily render the courtroom oratory an accurate reflection of that society's common conceptions of *morality*.

DECEMBER 2006 SECTION 4: LOGIC GAMES

Overview: Although this section features a fairly broad range of game types (Grouping, Basic Linear, Advanced Linear, Sequencing) and approaches (Numerical Distributions and Identify the Templates), the section as a whole is fairly easy. Specifically, none of the games in this section is especially difficult *if* the correct setup is used, and the game that is probably the hardest to diagram appears last. Thus, if a student takes an extra minute or two to make sure the rules are clear and the diagram is complete, the questions can be completed very quickly with a high degree of accuracy. The one negative is that the section only contains 22 questions, and thus the impact of this section on your overall score is somewhat diminished.

Game #1: This Grouping game features two powerful fixed numerical distributions that lead to three templates. In total, there are only six solutions to the game, and the three templates capture these solutions very easily. Students who spend an extra minute or two on the setup will find the questions extremely easy. Thus, this game, which can appear a bit intimidating at first glance, is actually a great starting point for a successful attack on this Games section.

Game #2: This balanced Linear game features two very interesting conditional sequencing rules that, when used in conjunction with the last rule, create two mutually exclusive super-sequence templates that control the game. Students who identify the two templates will find the game relatively easy (but still somewhat challenging to diagram). Students who fail to construct the two templates typically find the game somewhat difficult and time-consuming.

Game #3: The third game is an Advanced Linear game featuring three variable sets. There are six disparate rules, but they work together nicely to form a fairly complete diagram. Although the setup may take an extra minute to create, the questions are relatively easy once the correct setup is constructed.

Game #4: The final game is a Pure Sequencing game that features a challenging setup. On recent tests, the makers of the exam have sought to make sequential relationships more complex, and the rules in this game create a diagram that takes some expertise to construct. While Pure Sequencing is not generally considered a difficult game type, if the relationships are hard to represent then the game itself becomes difficult. However, with good diagramming technique games of this type can be handled without excessive difficulty. The test makers raise the difficulty level by adding some complex conditions into the questions, but overall this game would only be considered of medium difficulty.

This is a Grouping game, with colors assigned to two distinct groups, the jacket and the overalls. One of the initial steps in any grouping game is to attempt to establish, if possible, the number of elements in each group. In this instance, it takes a combination of the game scenario and rules to determine how many elements are in each group.

The second sentence of the game scenario establishes that one of the two items will always be entirely one color, and then the first two rules establish the number of colors in each costume piece if the piece is plaid. Each rule creates a separate fixed numerical distribution:

Distribution #1

> This distribution comes from the first rule, which states that "If the jacket is plaid, then there must be exactly three colors in it."
>
> The rules states that if the jacket is plaid, then it must have exactly three colors. From the second sentence in the game scenario, then, the overalls must be exactly one color. This creates a 3-1 fixed distribution:

<table>
<tr><td>____</td><td></td></tr>
<tr><td>____</td><td></td></tr>
<tr><td>____</td><td>____</td></tr>
<tr><td>Jacket</td><td>Overalls</td></tr>
</table>

Distribution #2

> This distribution comes from the second rule, which states that "If the overalls are plaid, then there must be exactly two colors in them."
>
> The rules states that if the overalls are plaid, then they must have exactly two colors. From the second sentence in the game scenario, then, the jacket must be exactly one color. This creates a 1-2 fixed distribution:

<table>
<tr><td></td><td>____</td></tr>
<tr><td>____</td><td>____</td></tr>
<tr><td>Jacket</td><td>Overalls</td></tr>
</table>

Because all the possibilities are established when each costume piece is plaid (or, alternately, when each costume piece is entirely one color), these are the only two possible distributions in the game.

With all the numerical possibilities established, you must now focus on the contents of each grouping. In this case, the contents are the colors, and the last three rules of the game address the colors of each piece of the costume. Accordingly, we will examine each of the last three rules against the two numerical possibilities.

Rule #3

This rule states that "The jacket and overalls must have exactly one color in common." From a representational standpoint, an easy way to diagram this rule would be:

However, this diagram, while useful, is not the best possible representation. A better approach would be to use internal diagramming and represent this rule directly on the diagram of each numerical possibility:

The 3-1 distribution: The 1-2 distribution:

In examining rules #4 and #5, we will keep in mind the operating effects of this rule.

Rule #4

This rule specifies that the colors of the jacket can only be green, red, and violet. In the 1-2 distribution, there is not an immediate impact from this rule (there will be an impact when this rule is combined with the rules #3 and #5). In the 3-1 distribution, however, since the jacket is a total of three colors, all three slots are filled:

The 3-1 distribution: The 1-2 distribution:

```
   G
   R
   V  <------->  ____              ____  <------->  ____
 Jacket      Overalls           Jacket      Overalls
```

Note that at this point we have not yet considered the effects of the last rule, but even so we are not going to fill in the remaining slots with options that will ultimately be impossible. For example, in the 3-1, from rule #3 and rule #4, one could assume that the overalls must be either green, red, or violet. While this is true from those two rules, rule #5 will alter those possibilities to only red or violet, and so we will refrain from diagramming further at this time in order avoid confusion.

<u>Rule #5</u>

This rule specifies that the colors of the overalls can only be red, violet, and yellow. A comparison of the color sets of the jacket and overalls shows that they share only two colors: red and violet. Thus, in the 3-1 distribution, because the jacket has already been determined to be green, red, and violet, the effect of rule #3 is that the overalls can only be red or violet:

The 3-1 distribution:

$$\frac{\quad G \quad}{\displaystyle \frac{R}{\displaystyle \frac{V}{\text{Jacket}}}} \qquad \frac{R/V}{\text{Overalls}}$$

In the 1-2 distribution, the jacket must be red or violet (it cannot be green because it would not have a color in common with the overalls). Thus, one color selection for the overalls must be red or violet. The color selection for the overalls can be any color (other than the color the jacket and overalls have in common, of course):

The 1-2 distribution:

$$\frac{R/V}{\text{Jacket}} \longleftrightarrow \frac{R/V/Y}{\displaystyle \frac{R/V}{\text{Overalls}}}$$

This representation, while helpful, is not entirely satisfactory because it creates the possibility that an interpretation mistake could be made (for example, accidentally selecting the same color for both color selections for the overalls while visually scanning the arrangement). Since the jacket can only be two colors, a better approach is to create a template for each color option:

The 1-2 distribution, jacket is red:

$$\frac{R}{\text{Jacket}} \longleftrightarrow \frac{V/Y}{\displaystyle \frac{R}{\text{Overalls}}}$$

The 1-2 distribution, jacket is violet:

$$\frac{V}{\text{Jacket}} \longleftrightarrow \frac{R/Y}{\displaystyle \frac{V}{\text{Overalls}}}$$

Overall, there are three templates containing six solutions: two solutions in the 3-1 scenario, and four solutions in the 1-2 scenario (two solutions when red is the common color, two solutions when violet is the common color).

In reviewing the color contents of six templates, the controlling effect of the color sets and rule #3 becomes apparent: red and violet are featured prominently, whereas green and yellow do not appear as much. In fact, green and yellow cannot appear in the same costume together, an inference that is tested in question #4.

Combining all of the information above leads to the following optimal setup for the game:

Jacket: G, R, V
Overalls: R, V, Y

$Jacket_{Plaid}$ ⟶ 3 colors

$Overalls_{Plaid}$ ⟶ 2 colors

J ⟷₁ O

G ⟷|⟷ Y

Template #1	Template #2	Template #3
The 3-1 distribution:	The 1-2 distribution: jacket is red:	The 1-2 distribution: jacket is violet:

Template #1

The 3-1 distribution:

```
  G
 ___
  R
 ___
  V          R/V
_____     _____
Jacket     Overalls
```

Template #2

The 1-2 distribution: jacket is red:

```
                V/Y
               ____
   R    ⟷       R
 _____       _____
 Jacket       Overalls
```

Template #3

The 1-2 distribution: jacket is violet:

```
                R/Y
               ____
   V    ⟷       V
 _____       _____
 Jacket       Overalls
```

At this point we are ready to attack the game with confidence since the setup elegantly captures all six solutions to the game.

Question #1: Global, List. The correct answer choice is (D)

As with any List question, simply apply the rules to the answer choices. In this game, the easiest approach is to apply the rules in the order given. Note that rule #1 does not eliminate any answer choices because none of the answers feature a plaid jacket.

Answer choice (A): This answer choice is eliminated by the rule in the game scenario that indicates that one of the pieces will be plaid (and thus contain multiple colors). Always remember that in a List question the game scenario might contain conditions that can eliminate answer choices.

Answer choice (B): This answer choice is eliminated by rule #3 because the pieces do not have a color in common.

Answer choice (C): This answer violates rule #5 because the overalls cannot be green.

Answer choice (D): This is the correct answer choice.

Answer choice (E): This answer violates rule #2 because when the overalls are plaid they only contain two colors.

Question #2: Local, False to True, Cannot Be True. The correct answer choice is (A)

The first item to attend to is converting the "false" statement in the question stem into terms of "true." "Must be false" is functionally equivalent to "cannot be true," and thus this is really a Cannot Be True question.

Proceeding, the condition in the question stem indicates there are only two colors in the costume. Thus, the only applicable scenarios feature the 1-2 fixed distribution (because the 3-1 distribution features three colors in the jacket). Before attacking the answers, quickly scan templates #2 and #3, which feature the 1-2 distribution, and then use those templates to attack the answer choices.

Answer choice (A): This is the correct answer choice. None of the solutions in templates #2 and #3 contain green as a color, and thus it cannot be true that green is a part of the jacket.

Answer choice (B): This answer choice is incorrect. Template #2 has a red jacket.

Answer choice (C): This answer choice is incorrect. Both templates #2 and #3 allow for red and violet overalls.

Answer choice (D): This answer choice is incorrect. Template #2 allows for red and yellow overalls.

Answer choice (E): This answer choice is incorrect. Template #3 allows for violet and yellow overalls.

Question #3: Local, Could Be True. The correct answer choice is (E)

The condition in the question stem establishes that part of the jacket is green, and that can only occur in the 3-1 fixed distribution. Accordingly, refer to template #1 to answer this question.

Answer choice (A): This answer choice is incorrect. In template #1, the jacket is plaid, not the overalls.

Answer choice (B): This answer choice is incorrect. In template #1, part of the jacket is red.

Answer choice (C): This answer choice is incorrect. In template #1, part of the jacket is violet.

Answer choice (D): This answer choice is incorrect. In template #1, the overalls must be red or violet.

Answer choice (E): This is the correct answer choice. In template #1, the overalls must be red or violet, and therefore it could be true that the overalls are violet.

Question #4: Global, False to True, Cannot Be True. The correct answer choice is (C)

This is the most difficult question of the game, and one that is not easy to answer from a quick glance at the rules.

First, convert the "False" statement into terms of "true." "Must be false" is functionally equivalent to "cannot be true," and thus this is really a Cannot Be True question.

Second, because this is a Global question, refer to your inferences for any negative deductions. In this case, when discussing the effects of rule #3, rule #4, and rule #5, we arrived at the inference that green and yellow cannot appear in the same costume together:

$$G \longleftrightarrow\mkern-18mu| \longrightarrow Y$$

This inference is directly tested in the correct answer, answer choice (C).

However, consider for a moment the approach to take if you did not see that inference while creating the setup. In this game, that would involve two separate steps:

1. Refer to the templates and eliminate incorrect answer choices. Template #1 (the 3-1) quickly eliminates answer choices (A) and (B), template #2 eliminates answer choice (D), and template #3 eliminates answer choice (E). Thus, answer choice (C) is the only remaining answer choice and must be correct.

2. Refer to the hypotheticals created in other questions. This approach is often helpful in Global questions with no obvious answer, and the hypothetical in question #1 eliminates answer choice (D). This approach could be used if step 1 failed to eliminate all incorrect answer choices.

Answer choice (A): This answer choice is incorrect. Template #1 proves that both green and red can be used in the costume together.

Answer choice (B): This answer choice is incorrect. Template #1 proves that both green and violet can be used in the costume together.

Answer choice (C): This is the correct answer choice. As discussed in the game setup, green and yellow can never appear in the costume together.

Answer choice (D): This answer choice is incorrect. Template #2 proves that both red and violet can be used in the costume together.

Answer choice (E): This answer choice is incorrect. Template #3 proves that both violet and yellow can be used in the costume together.

Question #5: Local, Must Be True. The correct answer choice is (E)

The question stem states that there must be exactly three colors in the costume. Templates #2 and #3 feature exactly two colors, and therefore template #1 is the template that applies to this question. The question stem also references the overalls, and since in template #1 the overalls are either red or violet, the correct answer must indicate that the overalls are red or violet, or indicate that the overalls are *not* yellow.

Answer choice (A): This answer choice is incorrect. In template #1, the overalls cannot be plaid.

Answer choice (B): This answer choice is incorrect. In template #1, the overalls cannot be plaid (or yellow, for that matter).

Answer choice (C): This answer choice is incorrect. In template #1, the overalls cannot be plaid.

Answer choice (D): This answer choice is incorrect. In template #1, the overalls cannot be yellow.

Answer choice (E): This is the correct answer choice.

Overall, this game is relatively easy as long as you use the numerical distribution to produce templates, which should enable you to complete the game very quickly with perfect accuracy.

This is a Linear game controlled by sequencing rules. The key to this game is to use the last rule to create the two mutually exclusive sequences that control this game.

From the game scenario, we know the following:

F G H J K L [6]

$$\underline{\quad} \quad \underline{\quad} \quad \underline{\quad} \quad \underline{\quad} \quad \underline{\quad} \quad \underline{\quad}$$
$$\ \ 1 \qquad 2 \qquad 3 \qquad 4 \qquad 5 \qquad 6$$

Because there are no ties, this is a balanced game, wherein each of the six hotel suites is assigned to a different space.

Ultimately, the final rule controls the game , and students who begin diagramming before reading all of the rules often find themselves scrambling to re-diagram. Remember, always read the entire scenario and accompanying rules prior to starting your diagram.

For the purposes of clarity, let's review each rule individually. At the conclusion of showing the diagram for each rule, we will combine the diagrams into two super-sequences.

Rule #1. This is a basic sequential rule:

$$H > L$$

Rule #2. This is a conditional rule, and the sufficient condition is that G is more expensive than H. When that occurs, then J is more expensive than both K and L:

$$G > H \longrightarrow J > \begin{matrix} K \\ \text{------} \\ L \end{matrix}$$

Rule #3. This is another conditional rule, and the sufficient condition is that H is more expensive than G. When that occurs, then K is more expensive than both J and L:

$$H > G \longrightarrow K > \begin{matrix} J \\ \text{------} \\ L \end{matrix}$$

Rule #4. Initially this rule seems like a simple either/or rule, where F is either more expensive than G (diagrammed as F > G) or F is more expensive than H (diagrammed as F > H). However, the "but not both" portion of the rule means that F is more expensive than *only one* of G or H at a time, and since there are no ties, that means that the other variable must be more expensive than F. So, when F is more expensive than G, then H must be more expensive than F, producing the following sequence:

$$H > F > G$$

And, when F is more expensive than H, then G must be more expensive than F, producing the following sequence:

$$G > F > H$$

Every game solution must conform to one of the two sequences produced by rule #4, and thus you should take those two base sequences and create two templates for the game.

<u>Sequence Template #1</u>

This template is produced by the part of rule #4 that produces the H > F > G sequence. To build a super-sequence that captures the relationship between all six hotel suites, first add rule #1 to the sequence:

```
               L
H > - - - - - - - - -
             F > G
```

The next step is to add rule #3 to the sequence (rule #2 does not apply to this sequence, and can be ignored). This step is more difficult than the first step above because adding the third rule creates an unwieldy diagram:

```
               J
  K > - - - - - - - - -
  - - - - - - - L
H > - - - - - - - - -
             F > G
```

The relationship between K, J, and L is clear when isolated in rule #3, but when added to a sequence where L is already less expensive than another hotel suite, H, the relationship is more difficult to diagram. In the above diagram, K and H have no relationship other than both being more expensive than L, and thus they are separated by a dotted line.

The tricky part comes in analyzing the relationship between H and J, and between K and F > G. In both instances, there is no relationship. That is, J can be more or less expensive than H, and K can be more or less expensive than both F or G. Of course, this difficulty in representation and analysis is exactly what the test makers intended.

To better understand the possibilities inherent in this sequence, consider the following hypotheticals, all of which are valid:

Hypothetical 1: K - H - F - G - J - L
Hypothetical 2: K - J - H - L - F - G
Hypothetical 3: H - F - G - K - L - J
Hypothetical 4: H - F - K - J - G - L
Hypothetical 5: H - K - L - F - G - J

Also, remember to use the Sequencing Diagramming Guidelines from the *PowerScore LSAT Logic Games Bible* and consider which variables can be first and which can be last. In the sequence above, only K or H can be first, and only G, J, or L can be last.

For those of you having difficulty with the diagram of the sequence above, there is an alternate representation of the above relationships that uses arrows:

$$
\begin{array}{c}
\quad\quad\;\; \rightarrow \text{J} \\
\text{K} \leftarrow \\
\quad\quad\;\; \text{L} \\
\text{H} > \text{- - - - - - - - -} \\
\quad\quad\;\; \text{F} > \text{G}
\end{array}
$$

This diagram has the same meaning as the first diagram, but may be easier for some students to use.

Sequence Template #2

This template is produced by the part of rule #4 that produces the G > F > H sequence. To build a super-sequence that captures the relationship between all six hotel suites, first add rule #1 to the sequence:

$$G > F > H > L$$

The next step is to add rule #2 to the sequence (rule #3 does not apply to this sequence, and can be ignored). This step is more difficult than the first step above because adding the second rule creates an unwieldy diagram:

$$
\begin{array}{c}
\text{G} > \text{F} > \text{H} > \text{L} \\
\quad\quad\; \text{J} > \text{- - -} \\
\quad\quad\quad\quad \text{K}
\end{array}
$$

The relationship between K, J, and L is clear when isolated in rule #2, but when added to a sequence where L is already less expensive than three other hotel suites, the relationship is more difficult to diagram (although not as troubling as the first sequence template). The tricky part comes in analyzing the relationship between J and K and the other variables. J must be more expensive than K and L, but J has no relationship with G, F, and H. Similarly, K must be less expensive than H but otherwise K has no relationship to any other variable in the chain. Analyzing which variables can be first and which can be last, in the sequence above, only G or J can be first, and only K or L can be last.

To better understand the possibilities inherent in this sequence, consider the following hypotheticals, all of which are valid:

    Hypothetical 1: G - F - H - J - L - K
    Hypothetical 2: J - K - G - F - H - L
    Hypothetical 3: J - G - F - H - L - K

Hypothetical 4: G - J - F - K - H - L
Hypothetical 5: G - F - J - H - K - L

For those of you having difficulty with the diagram of the sequence above, there is an alternate representation of the above relationships that uses arrows:

G > F > H > L

J ↵

↳ K

This diagram has the same meaning as the previous diagram, but may be easier for some students to use.

Combining all of the information above leads to the following optimal setup for the game:

F G H J K L [6]

```
  ___ ___ ___ ___ ___ ___
   1   2   3   4   5   6
```

H > L

                                                    Sequence Template #1

                    K
G > H ⟶ J > - - - - - -   J
                    L   K > - - - - - - - - - -
                                                    - - - - - - - L
                                                    H > - - - - - - - - - -
                    J   F > G
H > G ⟶ K > - - - - - -
                    L
                                                    Sequence Template #2
      H > F > G
         or   G > F > H > L
      G > F > H   J > - - -
                                                            K

Use the two sequence templates to answer the questions.

Question #6: Global, List. The correct answer choice is (B)

As with any List question, simply apply the rules to the answer choices.

Answer choice (A): This answer choice is incorrect because it violates rule #2. Specifically, when G is more expensive than H, then L cannot be more expensive than J.

Answer choice (B): This is the correct answer choice.

Answer choice (C): This answer choice is incorrect because it violates rule #3. Specifically, when H is more expensive than G, then J cannot be more expensive than K.

Answer choice (D): This answer choice is incorrect because it violates rule #4 because F less expensive than both G and H.

Answer choice (E): This answer choice is incorrect because it violates rule #1.

Question #7: Local, Could Be True. The correct answer choice is (C)

The condition in the question stem specifies that G is the second most expensive suite. Reviewing the two sequence templates, template #1 does not allow for this possibility (at best, G can be the third most expensive suite), and thus template #2 is the only template that applies to this question. In template #2, when G is the second most expensive suite, then J must be the most expensive suite:

$$\frac{\text{J}}{1} \quad \frac{\text{G}}{2} \quad \frac{}{3} \quad \frac{}{4} \quad \frac{}{5} \quad \frac{}{6}$$

The remainder of the spaces are controlled by the following relationship:

$$F > H > L$$
- - - - - - -
$$K$$

Answer choice (A): This answer choice is incorrect because H cannot be more expensive than F in template #2.

Answer choice (B): This answer choice is incorrect because H cannot be more expensive than G in template #2.

Answer choice (C): This is the correct answer choice. Under template #2, K could be more expensive than F. The following hypothetical shows one possible way: J - G - K - F - H - L.

Answer choice (D): This answer choice is incorrect because K cannot be more expensive than J in template #2.

Answer choice (E): This answer choice is incorrect because L cannot be more expensive than F in template #2.

Question #8: Global, Cannot Be True. The correct answer choice is (A)

From our analysis of the two sequence templates, we know that in template #1 only H and K can be the most expensive. This information eliminates answer choices (C) and (E). In template #2 only G and J can be the most expensive, and that eliminates answer choice (B) and (D). Thus, answer choice (A) is proven correct by process of elimination.

Alternatively, answer choice (A) can be proven correct because in template #1, F must be less expensive than H, and in template #2, F must be less expensive than G.

Answer choice (A): This is the correct answer choice.

Answer choices (B) and (D): These two answer choices are incorrect because sequence template #2 allows for G or J to be the most expensive suite.

Answer choices (C) and (E): These two answer choices are incorrect because sequence template #1 allows for H or K to be the most expensive suite.

Question #9: Local, Could Be True. The correct answer choice is (D)

If L is more expensive than F (L > F), then only Template #1 can apply to this question. Let's revisit template #1 with the addition of L > F:

In the above diagram, both K and H are more expensive than the L > F > G chain, and J is simply less expensive than K.

Answer choice (A): This answer choice is incorrect because F cannot be more expensive than H according to the diagram above.

Answer choice (B): This answer choice is incorrect because F cannot be more expensive than K according to the diagram above.

Answer choice (C): This answer choice is incorrect because G cannot be more expensive than H according to the diagram above.

Answer choice (D): This is the correct answer choice. J can be more expensive than L.

Answer choice (E): This answer choice is incorrect because G cannot be more expensive than L according to the diagram above.

Question #10: Local, Could Be True. The correct answer choice is (D)

The question stem adds the following condition:

$$K > H > J$$

Because template #2 specifies that J > K, template #2 cannot apply, and only template #1 is applicable. Adding the question stem condition to template #1 produces the following diagram:

```
                    J
               - - - - - - - -
    K > H >          L
               - - - - - - - -
                  F > G
```

Consequently, K is the most expensive suite and H is the second most expensive suite.

Answer choice (A): This answer choice is incorrect because F cannot be more expensive than H according to the diagram above.

Answer choice (B): This answer choice is incorrect because G cannot be more expensive than F according to the diagram above.

Answer choice (C): This answer choice is incorrect because G cannot be more expensive than H according to the diagram above.

Answer choice (D): This is the correct answer choice. J can be more expensive than L.

Answer choice (E): This answer choice is incorrect because L cannot be more expensive than K according to the diagram above.

Overall, this game is relatively easy *if* you use the last rule to create two super-sequence templates. If you do not see how the game is controlled by the templates, this game can be fairly tricky and time-consuming.

Unlike the previous two games, this Advanced Linear game does not require an Identify the Templates approach. However, the diagram to this game is quite powerful since most of the spaces can be filled in.

From the game scenario, we know that there are three variable sets: the seven tracks, the seven songs, and the two types (new or rock classic). Because the seven tracks have a numerical order, they are the better choice for the base. This choice creates a linear setup with two stacks, one for the songs and one for the types (remember to leave ample vertical space between the two stacks since each row will likely have its own Not Laws):

Types: N R ^{2}
Songs: S T V W X Y Z ^{7}

Type: _____ _____ _____ _____ _____ _____ _____

Song: _____ _____ _____ _____ _____ _____ _____
        1   2   3   4   5   6   7

Because the rules have so many consequences, let's examine each rule:

Rule #1. This rule is the most straightforward rule of the game, and it can be represented by placing an "S" in fourth space of the Song row:

Type: _____ _____ _____ _____ _____ _____ _____

Song: _____ _____ _____ __S__ _____ _____ _____
        1   2   3   4   5   6   7

Rule #2. This rule states that both W and Y precede S on the CD, and this rule can be diagrammed as:

$$\begin{matrix} W \\ \\ Y \end{matrix} \text{---->} S$$

By itself, this rule means that W and Y cannot be tracks 5, 6, or 7 on the CD (because the first rule establishes that S is 4th)

<u>Rule #3</u>. This rule can be diagrammed as:

$$T > W$$

When combined with rule #2, we can create the following sequence:

$$
\begin{array}{c}
T > W \\
\text{-------} > S \\
Y
\end{array}
$$

This sequence indicates that T, W, and Y must all precede S on the CD. Of course, if T, W, and Y precede S, they occupy the first three spaces, and that leaves only spaces 5, 6, and 7 for V, X, and Z:

Type: ____ ____ ____ ____ ____ ____ ____

Song:
$$
\underset{\substack{1 \\ \cancel{W}}}{(\; T > W,} \quad \underset{2}{Y \;)} \quad \underset{\substack{3 \\ \cancel{T}}}{} \quad \underset{4}{S} \quad \underset{5}{(\; V,} \quad \underset{6}{X,} \quad \underset{7}{Z \;)}
$$

Thus, although all songs have not been specifically placed, we do how they are divided on either side of S. Also, because T must precede W, we can ascertain that W cannot be first and T cannot be third.

<u>Rule #4</u>. This rule specifies that the sixth track is a rock classic. This information can be added directly to the diagram:

Type: ____ ____ ____ ____ ____ _R_ ____

Song:
$$
\underset{\substack{1 \\ \cancel{W}}}{(\; T > W,} \quad \underset{2}{Y \;)} \quad \underset{\substack{3 \\ \cancel{T}}}{} \quad \underset{4}{S} \quad \underset{5}{(\; V,} \quad \underset{6}{X,} \quad \underset{7}{Z \;)}
$$

<u>Rule #5</u>. This rule can be diagrammed as:

$$R \longrightarrow \boxed{N\,R}$$

Note that this rule only applies to rock classics. A new song does not have to be followed by a rock classic.

The appearance of this rule creates several inferences. First, because a rock classic must be preceded by a new song, the first song on the CD must be a new song (a rock classic cannot be first because then it would not be preceded by a new song). Second, because the sixth song is a rock classic, we can automatically determine that the fifth song must be a new song. Third, because the sixth song is a rock classic, the seventh song must be a new song (if it were a rock classic then the sixth song would have to be a new song). Adding this information creates the following setup:

Type: N ___ ___ ___ N R N

Song: (T > W, Y) S (V, X, Z)
       1   2   3   4   5   6   7
       W̸   X̸

Rule #6. This rule states that Z is a rock classic. When considered with the fifth rule, this rule can be diagrammed as follows:

```
┌──────────┐
│  N   R   │
│ ___  Z   │
└──────────┘
```

However, we already know from the analysis in rule #3 that Z must be the fifth, sixth, or seventh song on the CD. And, since the analysis in rule #5 indicated that, of those three tracks, only the sixth could be a rock track, we can determine that Z must be the sixth track on the CD. Accordingly, V and X must occupy the fifth and seventh tracks, not necessarily in that order:

Type: N ___ ___ ___ N R N

Song: (T > W, Y) S V/X Z X/V
       1   2   3   4   5   6   7
       W̸   X̸

Compiling all of the information above, we arrive at the final setup for this game:

Types: N R ^{2}
Songs: S T V W X Y Z ^{7}

```
T > W
------- > S
    Y
```

Type: N ___ ___ ___ N R N

R ──────▶ ┌──────┐
          │ N R │
          └──────┘

Song: (T > W, Y) S V/X Z X/V
       1   2   3   4   5   6   7
       W̸   X̸

```
┌──────────┐
│  N   R   │
│ ___  Z   │
└──────────┘
```

Question #11: Global, List. The correct answer choice is (D)

To attack this List question in a foolproof manner, simply apply the first three rules. For an even faster approach, apply the rules and inferences together (for example, first apply the rule that states that S is fourth, then apply the inference that indicates that Z is sixth, etc).

Answer choice (A): This answer choice is incorrect because Y does not precede S, and Z is not sixth.

Answer choice (B): This answer choice can be eliminated because W does not precede S.

Answer choice (C): This answer choice is incorrect because V does not appear (and therefore S appears twice), and T does not precede W.

Answer choice (D): This is the correct answer choice.

Answer choice (E): This answer choice can be eliminated because S is not fourth and Z is not sixth.

Question #12: Global, Must Be True. The correct answer choice is (E)

Use the final diagram to quickly and easily solve this question. Examine each answer choice and determine whether the two songs must be consecutive, or whether they can be separated in a valid hypothetical.

Answer choice (A): This answer choice is incorrect because S and V can be the fourth and seventh tracks, respectively.

Answer choice (B): This answer choice can be eliminated because W and S can be the second and fourth tracks, respectively.

Answer choice (C): This answer choice is incorrect because T is always first or second, and Z is always sixth.

Answer choice (D): This answer choice can be eliminated because T and Y can be the first and third tracks, respectively.

Answer choice (E): This is the correct answer choice. V must be fifth or seventh, and Z must be sixth, so V and Z are always consecutive whether it is VZ or ZV.

Question #13: Global, Must Be True. The correct answer choice is (D)

With Global questions in this game, simply refer to the main diagram. In this case, we know that the first, fifth and seventh songs must be new songs. With the first song, either T or Y must be first, but there is no way to determine which must be first. With the fifth and seventh songs, those two tracks are occupied by V and X, so both V and X must be new songs. A quick scan of the answer choices reveals that X is present, and thus answer choice (D) is correct.

Answer choices (A), (B), (C), and (E): These answer choices are incorrect because each of the listed songs could be rock classics.

Answer choice (D): This is the correct answer choice. X must be fifth or seventh, and both the fifth and seventh songs are new songs.

Question #14: Local, Must Be True. The correct answer choice is (D)

The question stem indicates that W precedes Y on the CD. That sets up the following chain relationship:

$$T > W > Y > S$$

Since S must be the fourth track on the CD, the diagram appears as follows:

Type:	N				N	R	N
Song:	T	W	Y	S	V/X	Z	X/V
	1	2	3	4	5	6	7

Answer choice (A): This answer is incorrect because S could be a new song or a rock classic.

Answer choice (B): This answer choice is incorrect because V is a new song.

Answer choice (C): This answer is incorrect because Y could be a new song or a rock classic.

Answer choice (D): This is the correct answer choice. T must be first, and the first track is a new song as discussed in the setup to the game.

Answer choice (E): This answer choice is incorrect because W could be a new song or a rock classic.

Question #15: Local, Could Be True. The correct answer choice is (E)

The condition in the question stem is worded in a clumsy fashion. Let's examine the statement piece by piece to derive what the test makers meant to say.

The question stem states that "there are exactly two songs on the CD that both precede V and are preceded by Y." The portion that states that "there are exactly two songs on the CD that both precede V," means that there are exactly two tracks in front of V, which would be diagrammed as follows:

The portion that states that "there are exactly two songs on the CD that...are preceded by Y," means that there are exactly two tracks behind Y, which would be diagrammed as follows:

| Y | ___ | ___ |

Combing those two statements (they are combined by the "and" in the question stem) yields the following diagram:

| Y | ___ | ___ | V |

The challenge is now to place that split-block on the main diagram. Because V is restricted to fifth or seventh, V is a logical starting point. If V is seventh, then Y would have to be fourth, which is impossible since S must be fourth. Thus, V must be fifth, and therefore Y must be second under the conditions in this question:

| Type: | N | ___ | ___ | ___ | N | R | N |

Song:	T	Y	W	S	V	Z	X
	1	2	3	4	5	6	7

Of course, when Y is second, then T must be first and W must be third (because T > W). Also, when V is fifth, then Z must be seventh, and thus the entire song order is established.

Answer choice (A): This answer choice is incorrect because V must be fifth.

Answer choice (B): This answer choice is incorrect because X must be seventh.

Answer choice (C): This answer choice is incorrect because Y must be second.

Answer choice (D): This answer choice is incorrect because T must be a new song.

Answer choice (E): This is the correct answer choice. W could be either a new song or a rock classic.

This may be the most difficult game of the section even though it is a Pure Sequencing game. Although sequencing games have traditionally been relatively easy, the rules in this game form an ungainly diagram that requires some skill to create and interpret.

The game scenario establishes that a courier delivers eight packages—G, H, J, K, L, M, N, and O—and no two packages are delivered simultaneously:

G H J K L M N O ^{8}

Packages: ____ ____ ____ ____ ____ ____ ____ ____
            1   2   3   4   5   6   7   8

The rules then establish a pure sequence that controls the placement of every variable. Let's first examine each rule separately, and then link them together afterward:

Rule #1. This rule can be diagrammed as:

   H > L

Rule #2. This rule can be diagrammed as:

   K > O

Rule #3. This rule can be diagrammed as:

   H > M

Rule #4. This rule can be diagrammed as:

   G > O

Rule #5. This rule can be diagrammed as:

   M > G

Rule #6. This rule can be diagrammed as:

       N
    - - - - - > M
       J

Individually, none of the rules is daunting. Linking them together into a workable diagram, however, is not easy.

To create a super-sequence, first start with the last three rules, which connect together easily:

```
    N
    - - - - - > M > G > O
    J
```

Next, add in the second and third rules, using arrows:

```
        H ←          K ←
    N      ┐            ┐
    - - - - - >  M  >  G  >  O
    J
```

Finally, add in the first rule:

```
            ┌→ L
            │
        H ←─┘        K ←
    N      ┐            ┐
    - - - - >  M  >  G  >  O
    J
```

Note that the method of constructing this diagram worked backwards through the rules, which is another reminder that you must read all of the rules before beginning your diagram. (Note that this is not the only possible way to construct this diagram, and at the conclusion of question #22 we present two alternative diagrams that capture the same relationship in different ways).

Now that the main diagram is complete, take a moment to analyze the relationships.

Which packages can be delivered first? Only H, J, K, and N. Note how easy it is to miss K.

Which packages can be delivered last? Only L and O.

What is the earliest L can be delivered? Second, right after H.

What is the latest H can be delivered? Fourth—H can be delivered after J, K, and N.

What is the latest N can be delivered? Fifth—N can be delivered after H, J, L, and K. The same holds true for J, which can also be delivered fifth, after H, L, N, and K.

What is the earliest M can be delivered? Fourth, after H, J, and N have been delivered.

What is the latest M can be delivered? Sixth, just before G and O are delivered.

Whenever you create a complex diagram (sequencing or otherwise), always take a moment to evaluate the relationships contained within because the test makers will surely question you on any confusing relationship.

Using the setup above and keeping the relationships firmly in mind, move ahead and attack the questions.

Question #16: Global, List. The correct answer choice is (D)

To attack this List question, simply apply the rules in the given order. Although the first two rules do not eliminate any answers, there is no way to know this when you begin attacking this question.

Answer choice (A): This answer choice violates the last rule because J is not delivered earlier than M.

Answer choice (B): This answer choice violates the fifth rule because M is not delivered earlier than G.

Answer choice (C): This answer choice violates the fourth rule because O is not delivered later than G.

Answer choice (D): This is the correct answer choice.

Answer choice (E): This answer choice violates the third rule because H is not delivered earlier than M.

The presentation of answer choices by the test makers is interesting because applying the rules in the given order—which is the accepted protocol in a game where the rules are all basically similar—consumes the maximum amount of time possible. This occurs because the first two rules do not eliminate any answers, then the third rule eliminates answer choice (E), the fourth rule eliminates answer choice (C), the fifth rule eliminates answer choice (B), and the last rule eliminates answer choice (A). This presentation forces you to comb through the answers multiple times in order to eliminate all four incorrect answers. Alas, while this presentation is interesting, there is no way to reliably combat this trick—it is simply a weapon the test makers have at their disposal.

Question #17: Global, Must Be True. The correct answer choice is (C)

The only way to attack a Global question in a Pure Sequencing game is to refer to the super-sequence that controls the game.

Answer choice (A): This answer choice is incorrect because K can be delivered first, and thus it is not true that at least one parcel is delivered before K.

Answer choice (B): This answer choice is incorrect because G can be delivered seventh, and thus it is not true that at least two parcels are delivered later than G.

Answer choice (C): This is the correct answer choice. G, L, M, and O must all be delivered later than H.

Answer choice (D): This answer choice is incorrect because only three parcels must be delivered later than J (those parcels are G, M, and O).

Answer choice (E): This answer choice is incorrect because only three parcels must be delivered earlier than M (those parcels are H, J, and N).

Question #18: Local, Must Be True. The correct answer choice is (D)

The condition in the question stem indicates that M is delivered fourth. For M to be delivered fourth, *only* H, J, and N can be delivered before M (all three must be delivered before M regardless, but to allow M to be delivered fourth those can be the only three parcels delivered before M). A diagram including the new condition would appear as:

```
        H
      - - - - -              L
        N  >  M  >  - - - - - - - -
      - - - - -           G  >  O
        J       |_____
                |         |
                |___ K ___|
```

The arrows "bracketing" K indicate that K is delivered after M but before O. K has no relationship with G or L. Other than the placement of K, the diagram is relatively standard.

From a linear standpoint, this creates the following scenario:

Packages: (H,   J,   N)   M   ___   ___   ___   L/O
            1   2   3   4   5   6   7   8

Use the above information to attack the answer choices.

Answer choice (A): This answer choice is incorrect because G could be delivered fifth, sixth or seventh.

Answer choice (B): This answer choice is incorrect because O could be the eighth parcel delivered.

Answer choice (C): This answer choice is incorrect because the relationship between J and H is unfixed, and thus H could be delivered later than J.

Answer choice (D): This is the correct answer choice. N must always be one of the first three parcels delivered and K must be delivered fifth, sixth, or seventh.

Answer choice (E): This answer choice is incorrect because G and L do not have a fixed relationship, and therefore L could be delivered later than G.

Question #19: Local, Could Be True, Except. The correct answer choice is (A)

This question is similar to question #18, except that H is specified as the fourth parcel. Because J and N are already delivered before H, in order to deliver H fourth, K must be among the first three parcels delivered (leaving K, J, and N as the first three parcels, not necessarily in that order). The remaining parcels (L, M, G, O) then align behind H. A diagram including the new condition would appear as:

```
     K
   - - - - -                    L
      N  >  H  >   - - - - - - - - - - - -
   - - - - -              M  >  G  >  O
     J
```

The remainder of the question stem is a Could Be True Except question, which means that the four incorrect answers Could Be True, and the one correct answer Cannot Be True.

Answer choice (A): This is the correct answer choice. Because K must be one of the first three parcels delivered, K cannot be delivered fifth. Note how the test makers immediately examine the most difficult variable to place in this question. In this sense, the question becomes a "gut check" on whether you understand the range of possibilities inherent in K's positioning in the game itself.

Answer choice (B): This answer choice could be true, and is therefore incorrect. L could be delivered fifth, sixth, seventh, or eighth.

Answer choice (C): This answer choice could be true, and is therefore incorrect. M could be delivered fifth or sixth.

Answer choice (D): This answer choice could be true, and is therefore incorrect. G could be delivered sixth or seventh.

Answer choice (E): This answer choice could be true, and is therefore incorrect. O could be delivered seventh or eighth.

Question #20: Global, Could Be True, Except. The correct answer choice is (B)

In this Global question, simply use the main diagram to confirm or eliminate answer choices. If an answer choice Could Be True, then it is incorrect. The correct answer choice Cannot Be True.

Answer choice (A): This answer choice is incorrect because H could be delivered later than K. Remember, K could be delivered first, so even though it appears that K is at the "end" of the diagram, K can "move" forward greatly.

Answer choice (B): This is the correct answer choice. J must be delivered earlier than M, and M must be delivered earlier than G, so J can never be delivered later than G.

Answer choice (C): This answer choice is incorrect because L can be delivered last, so L can be delivered later than O.

Answer choice (D): This answer choice is incorrect. The only relationship that L and M have is that they must both be delivered later than H. However, the rules do not specify if L or M is delivered later, so M could be delivered later than L.

Answer choice (E): This answer choice is incorrect because H can be delivered first, so N can be delivered later than H.

Note that the nature of the answer choices in this question makes this a simple diagram interpretation question. If you can create a main diagram that incorporates all of the rules and also understand the relationships inherent in that diagram, then this question is easy.

Question #21: Local, Could Be True, Except. The correct answer choice is (C)

If K is the seventh parcel delivered, then O must be the eighth parcel delivered (because the second rule specifies that K > O). That leaves the remaining variables to be delivered in the first six spaces:

Answer choice (A): This answer choice is incorrect because G could be the fifth parcel delivered. The following hypothetical shows how: N-J-H-M-G-L-K-O.

Answer choice (B): This answer choice is incorrect because M could be the fifth parcel delivered. The following hypothetical shows how: N-J-H-L-M-G-K-O.

Answer choice (C): This is the correct answer choice. Because L, M, and G must all be delivered later than H, the latest that H can be delivered is third (after J and N).

Answer choice (D): This answer choice is incorrect because L could be the fourth parcel delivered. The following hypothetical shows how: N-J-H-L-M-G-K-O.

Answer choice (E): This answer choice is incorrect because J could be the third parcel delivered. The following hypothetical shows how: N-H-J-M-G-L-K-O.

Question #22: Local, False to True, Cannot Be True. The correct answer choice is (C)

When addressing this question stem, first convert the Must Be False statement into its true equivalent, Cannot Be True. Thus, the one correct answer Cannot Be True, and the four incorrect answers Could Be True.

The local condition in the question stem, L > K, is not easy to handle. The rule adds another layer of complexity to an already complex diagram. The difficulty in the L > K relationship comes from the fact that L and K are already "floating" because of their relationships with H and O, respectively. To show that the two floating variables have a relationship, and most importantly, to understand the implications of that relationship, is challenging. The diagram would appear as:

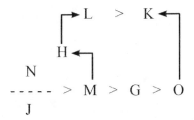

This diagram is deceptive because it makes it appear as though L must be delivered relatively early, and that K must be delivered relatively late. This is not true: L can be delivered as late as sixth (followed by K and O), and K can be delivered as early as third (preceded by H and L). When answering this question—which may be the toughest of the section—be very careful and deliberate.

Answer choice (A): This answer choice is incorrect because N could be the second parcel delivered. The following hypothetical shows how: J-N-H-L-K-M-G-O.

Answer choice (B): This answer choice is incorrect because L could be the third parcel delivered. The following hypothetical shows how: H-N-L-J-M-G-K-O.

Answer choice (C): This is the correct answer choice. Because H must all be delivered earlier than M, G, K, L, and K, the latest that H can be delivered is third (after J and N).

Answer choice (D): This answer choice is incorrect because K could be the fifth parcel delivered. The following hypothetical shows how: N-J-H-L-K-M-G-O.

Answer choice (E): This answer choice is incorrect because M could be the sixth parcel delivered. The following hypothetical shows how: J-N-H-L-K-M-G-O.

Alternate Diagrams for the Main Diagram

In sequencing games, there is sometimes more than one accepted diagram. Basing the diagram on a different starting point (emphasizing a different rule, for example) can lead to a diagram that has a different appearance, although, of course, the inherent relationships will remain identical. The following two diagrams have the same functionality as the main diagram used in attacking this game, but they look different. Some students may find a different look more beneficial, and, in any case, understanding the diagramming options is a useful learning tool.

Diagram #1: This diagram emphasizes the first and third rules as the "start" of the diagram (as a comparison, the main diagram emphasized the last rule as the starting point). Once those two rules are chosen, the other rules are then diagrammed those two:

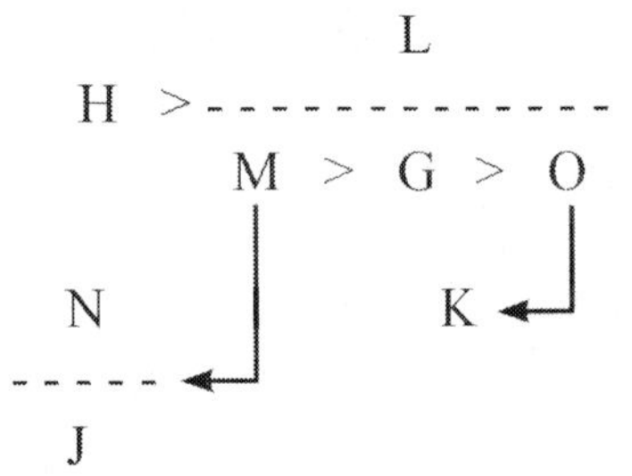

```
                   L
     H  > - - - - - - - - - -
                 M  >  G  >  O
                 |
     N           |        K  ←⌐
                 ↓           |
     - - - - - ← ⌐
     J
```

The challenging element of this diagram is to realize that K can "move" all the way to the front of the diagram, and that N and J have no connection with L.

Diagram #2. This diagram uses the second and fourth rules as the starting point:

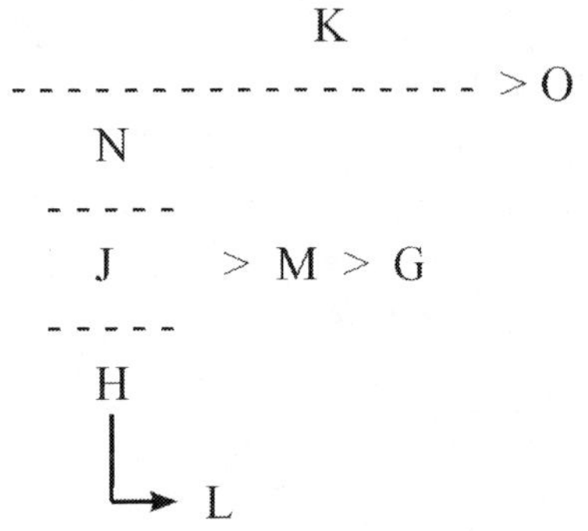

```
                  K
     - - - - - - - - - - - - - - - > O
        N
     - - - - -
        J      > M > G
     - - - - -
        H
         └─→ L
```

This may be the best diagram, but this is the most difficult diagram to construct because you have to work backwards from O. Under the time constraint of the LSAT, most students simply do not have enough time to construct a diagram such as this one. The second challenge is to realize that L is delivered later than H, but not necessarily later than N or J. Creating a diagram with this type of uncertainty is only recommended for students who are comfortable with games, and this is one reason we chose not to use this presentation as our main diagram.

CHAPTER FOUR: GLOSSARY

Introduction

This section contains a brief definition of the terms used in this book. The terms are given in alphabetical order. For more comprehensive explanations of each term or concept, refer to either the *Logic Games Bible* or the *Logical Reasoning Bible*.

Alphabetical Glossary

#%:   See Numbers and Percentages.

Additional Premise: Additional premises are premises that may be central to the argument or they may be secondary. To determine the importance of the premise, examine the remainder of the argument.

Agree/Disagree Test™: This test is used to solve Point at Issue questions. The correct answer must produce responses where one speaker would say, "I agree, the statement is correct" and the other speaker would say, "I disagree, the statement is incorrect." If those two responses are not produced, then the answer is incorrect. The Agree/Disagree Test crystallizes the essence of Point at Issue questions by forcing you to concretely identify the elements that determine the correct answer.

AP: See Author's Perspective and Tone.

Appeal Fallacies: A common error of reasoning that attempts to "appeal" to various insubstantial viewpoints of the reader (emotion, popular opinion, tradition, authority, etc.). However the appeal is not valid, and concrete evidence is needed to support the argument.

Argument: A set of statements wherein one statement is claimed to follow from or be derived from the others. An argument requires a conclusion.

Argument Part Question: A subset of Method of Reasoning questions. In Argument Part questions, the question stem cites a specific portion of the stimulus and then asks you to identify the role the cited portion plays in the structure of the argument.

Assumption: An assumption is an unstated premise of the argument. Assumptions are an integral component of the argument that the author takes for granted and leaves unsaid.

Assumption Question: These questions ask you to identify an assumption of the author's argument. Question stem example:
> "Which one of the following is an assumption required by the argument above?"

Assumption Negation Technique™: This technique requires you to logically negate the answer choice under consideration, which results in a negated answer choice that attacks the argument. If the negated answer does not attack the argument, then it is incorrect. The purpose of this technique is to take an Assumption question, which is generally difficult for most students, and turn it into a Weaken question, which is easier for most students. This technique can only be used on Assumption questions.

Author's Perspective and Tone (AP): These Reading Comprehension questions ask you to select the answer choice that best reflects the author's views, such as, "The author of the passage would most likely agree with which one of the following statements?" Tone questions ask you to identify the author's attitude toward the subject.

Balanced (see also Grouping, Linearity, Unbalanced, Defined, Undefined, etc.): In a Defined game, when the number of variables to be selected is equal to the overall number of available spaces.

Block (See also Linearity): In Linear games, blocks reflect the idea of a fixed spatial relationship between variables. Blocks represent variables that are next to one another, not next to one another, or separated by a fixed number of spaces. Basic blocks indicate adjacency.

C: In diagramming Logical Reasoning questions, "C" indicates Cause. Also see Cause.

Cannot Be True Questions: Ask you to identify the answer choice that cannot be true or is most weakened based on the information in the stimulus.
Question stem example:
"If the statements above are true, which one of the following CANNOT be true?"

Causal Reasoning: Asserts or denies that one thing causes another, or that one thing is caused by another. On the LSAT, cause and effect reasoning appears in many Logical Reasoning problems, often in the conclusion where the author mistakenly claims that one event causes another.

Cause (C): The event that makes another occur.

Cause and Effect (CE): When one event is said to make another occur. The cause is the event that makes the other occur; the effect is the event that follows from the cause. By definition, the cause must occur before the effect, and the cause is the "activator" or "ignitor" in the relationship. The effect always happens at some point in time after the cause.

CE: See Cause and Effect.

Circular Reasoning: A flaw where the author assumes as true what is supposed to be proved. The premise supports the conclusion, but the conclusion equally supports the premise, creating a "circular" situation where you can move from premise to conclusion, and then back again to the premise, and so on.

Circular Sequencing: Games that consist of a fixed number of variables assigned to spaces distributed around a circle (usually a table). Essentially these games are Linear games wrapped around a circular diagram.

Complex Argument: Arguments that contain more than one conclusion. In these instances, one of the conclusions is the main conclusion, and the other conclusions are subsidiary conclusions (also known as sub-conclusions). In basic terms, a complex argument makes an initial conclusion based on a premise. The author then uses that conclusion as the foundation (or premise) for another conclusion, thus building a chain with several levels.

Conclusion: A statement or judgment that follows from one or more reasons. Conclusions, as summary statements, are supposed to be drawn from and rest on the premises.

Conclusion/Premise Indicator Form: The test makers will sometimes arrange premise and conclusion indicators in a way that is designed to be confusing. One of their favorite forms places a conclusion indicator and premise indicator back-to-back, separated by a comma, as in the following examples:

"Therefore, since..."
"Thus, because..."
"Hence, due to..."

Conditional Reasoning: The broad name given to logical relationships composed of sufficient and necessary conditions. Any conditional statement consists of at least one sufficient condition and at least one necessary condition. In everyday use, conditional statements are often brought up using the "if...then" construction. Conditional reasoning can occur in any question type.

Contender: An answer choice that appears somewhat attractive, interesting, or even confusing. Basically, any answer choice that you cannot immediately identify as incorrect.

Contrapositive: Denies the necessary condition, thereby making it impossible for the sufficient condition to occur. Contrapositives can often yield important insights in Logic Games.

Counter-premise: A premise that actually contains an idea that is counter to the argument. Counter-premises, also called adversatives, bring up points of opposition or comparison.

Defender: In the Supporter/Defender Assumption Model™, the Defender assumptions contain statements that eliminate ideas or assertions that would undermine the conclusion. In this sense, they "defend" the argument by showing that a possible source of attack has been eliminated.

Defined: In these Logic Games, the exact number of variables to be selected is fixed in the rules.

Double Arrow: Indicates that the two terms must always occur together. The double arrow is typically introduced in any of the following three ways:

      1. Use of the phrase "if and only if"

      2. Use of the phrase "vice versa" (as in "If A attends then B attends, and vice versa")

      3. By repeating and reversing the terms (as in "If A attends then B attends, and if B attends then A attends")

Double-not Arrow: Indicates that two terms cannot occur together. The double not-arrow only prohibits one scenario—one where the two terms occur together.

Dual Option: When only one of two variables can occupy a single slot. Represented with a slash, as in "A/B."

E: In diagramming, indicates Effect. See also Effect.

Effect: The event that follows from the cause.

Either/Or: For the purposes of the LSAT, the definition of "either/or" is "at least one of the two." Note that this definition implicitly allows for the possibility that both elements occur, and the existence of this possibility makes diagramming sentences containing the "either/or" term confusing. A careful examination of the definition of "either/or" reveals that a conditional relationship is at the heart of the construction: since at least one of the terms must occur, if one fails to occur then the other must occur.

Elemental Attack™: When attacking Parallel Reasoning questions, compare the big-picture elements of the argument: intent of the conclusion, force and use of the premises, the relationship of the premises and the conclusion, and the soundness of the argument. The four tests you can use to evaluate answers are Match the Method of Reasoning, Match the Conclusion, Match the Premises, and Match the Validity of the Argument.

Errors in the Use of Evidence: A common error of reasoning that involves the misuse of evidence in one of these ways:

      1. Lack of evidence for a position is taken to prove that position is false.

      2. Lack of evidence against a position is taken to prove that position is true.

      3. Some evidence against a position is taken to prove that position is false.

      4. Some evidence for a position is taken to prove that position is true.

Errors of Composition and Division: A common error of reasoning that involves judgments made about groups and parts of a group. An error of composition occurs when the author attributes a characteristic of part of the group to the group as a whole or to each member of the group. An error of division occurs when the author attributes a characteristic of the whole (or each member of the whole) to a part of the group.

Errors of Conditional Reasoning: A common error of reasoning that involves confusing the sufficient condition with the necessary condition. Note that the authors can either mistake a necessary condition for a sufficient condition, or mistake a sufficient condition for a necessary condition.

Evaluate the Argument Questions: With Evaluate the Argument questions you must decide which answer choice will allow you to determine the logical validity of the argument. Use the Variance Test™ to prove or disprove answers as needed.
Question stem example:
> "The answer to which one of the following questions would contribute most to an evaluation of the argument?"

Except: When "except" is placed in a question it negates the logical quality of the answer choice you seek. Literally, it turns the intent of the question stem upside down.

Exceptional Case/Overgeneralization: A common error of reasoning that involves taking a small number of instances and treating those instances as if they support a broad, sweeping conclusion.

F: See also Function.

Fact Set: A collection of statements without a conclusion. Fact sets make a series of assertions without making a judgment.

Fact Test™: The correct answer to a Must Be True question (and other First Family questions) can always be proven by referring to the facts stated in the stimulus. An answer choice that cannot be substantiated by proof in the stimulus is incorrect.

False Analogy: A common error of reasoning that involves an author using an analogy that is too dissimilar to the original situation to be applicable.

False Dilemma: A common error of reasoning that involves assuming that only two courses of action are available when there may be others (for example, "You are either rich or impoverished"). Do not confuse a False Dilemma with a situation where the author legitimately establishes that only two possibilities exist. Phrases such as "either A or B will occur, but not both" can establish a limited set of possibilities, and certain real-world situations yield only two possibilities, such as "you are either dead or alive."

First Family: Consists of question types that use the stimulus to prove that one of the answer choices must be true. No information outside the sphere of the stimulus is allowed in the correct answer choice. Includes the following question types: Must Be True, Main Point, Point at Issue, Method of Reasoning, Flaw in the Reasoning, and Parallel Reasoning.

FL: See Formal Logic.

Flaw in the Reasoning Questions: Flaw in the Reasoning questions ask you to describe, in abstract terms, the error of reasoning committed by the author.
Question stem example:
> "The reasoning in the argument is flawed because this argument"

Formal Logic (FL): A standard system of translating relationships into symbols and then making inferences from those symbolized relationships.

Fourth Family: Consists of question types that use the stimulus to prove that one of the answer choices cannot occur. No information outside the sphere of the stimulus is allowed in the answer choices. Includes the following question type: Cannot Be True.

Function (F): These Reading Comprehension questions ask why the author referred to a particular word, phrase, or idea. This is essentially an extended Method of Reasoning question, requiring you to go beyond simply identifying the argument structure, and asking you the reasons behind the author's use of words or ideas.

Game Scenario: In Logic Games, introduces sets of variables, people, places, things, or events involved in an easy to understand activity such as sitting in seats or singing songs.

General Lack of Relevant Evidence for the Conclusion: A common error of reasoning that involves authors misusing information to such a degree that they fail to provide any information to support their conclusion or they provide information that is irrelevant to their conclusion.

Global: These Logic Games questions ask about information derived only from the initial rules, such as "Who can finish first?" or "Which one of the following must be true?"

Grouping: These Logic Games require you to analyze the variables in terms of which ones can and cannot be together.

Horizontality: When a game is diagrammed in a horizontal line (or setup), the relationship between variables arranged horizontally indicates adjacency, while the relationship of variables arranged vertically indicates similarity. This is also true of horizontality in blocks.

Hurdle the Uncertainity™: In Logic Games, during the placement of variables, situations occur where even though you cannot determine the exact variables being selected, you can "leap" that uncertainty to determine that other variables that must be selected. This powerful technique can be used in many different games, and it attacks a concept frequently used by the test makers an appears in virtually every Grouping game.

Hypothetical: A possible solution to a question that you quickly create to gain insight into Logic Game answers. Hypotheticals can be the fastest way to solve a question, and sometimes they give you information that can be used to solve other problems.

Inference: In logic, an inference can be defined as something that must be true. If you are asked to identify an inference of the argument, you must find an item that must be true based on the information presented in the argument.

Internal Contradiction: A common error of reasoning (also known as a self-contradiction) that occurs when an author makes conflicting statements.

Justify Formula™: Premises + Answer choice = Conclusion

The Justify Formula is a useful tool for understanding how Justify the Conclusion questions work. If the answer choice is correct, the application of the Justify Formula will produce the given conclusion. If the answer choice is incorrect, the application of the Justify Formula will fail to produce the given conclusion.

Justify the Conclusion Questions: Justify the Conclusion questions ask you to supply a piece of information that, when added to the premises, proves the conclusion.
Question stem example:
"Which one of the following, if assumed, allows the conclusion above to be properly drawn?"

Least: When "least" appears in a question stem you should treat it exactly the same as "except." Note: this advice holds true only when this word appears in the question stem! If you see the word "least" elsewhere on the LSAT, consider it to have its usual meaning of "in the lowest or smallest degree."

Linearity: Involves the fixed positioning and ordering of variables. In every Linear game, one of the variable sets is chosen as the "base" and is diagrammed in a straight line, either horizontally or vertically, and the remaining variable sets are placed into slots above or next to the base.

Linkage: Linkage involves finding a variable that appears in at least two rules and then combining those two rules. Often that combination will produce an inference of value. Linkage is the easiest and most basic way to make inferences.

List Question: In Logic Games, list questions present a list of variables that can either fill a slot or possibly solve the game. The best technique for attacking List questions is to take a single rule and apply it to each of the five answer choices, one at a time. The first question in a game is often a List Question.

Local: These games questions occur when the question imposes a new condition in addition to the initial rules, such as "If Laura sits in the third chair, which one of the following must be true?" Local questions almost always require you to produce a "mini-setup" next to the question.

Loser: An answer choice which immediately strikes you as incorrect.

Main Point (MP): Main Point questions are a variant of Must Be True questions. As you might expect, a Main Point question asks you to find the primary conclusion made by the author.
Question stem example:
"The main point of the argument is that"

Mapping: These games either do not fix the physical relationships among the variables (Spatial Relations), involve a fixed point and all other variables are placed North, East, South, and West of that point (Directional), or the makers of the test supply a diagram intended to represent the relationship of the variables (Supplied Diagram). There are no numerical elements in a Mapping game.

Mechanistic Approach: This approach requires you to reduce the stimulus to its component parts (a process that occurs naturally as you identify premises and conclusions), and then identify which elements appear in the conclusion but not in the premises. In a nutshell, the rules for this approach condense to: link new elements in the premises and conclusion and ignore elements common to both. The mechanistic approach works for the vast majority of Justify the Conclusion questions.

Method of Reasoning: Method of Reasoning questions ask you to describe, in abstract terms, the way in which the author made his or her argument.
Question stem example:
"Which one of the following describes the technique of reasoning used above?"

Mistaken Cause and Effect: A common error of reasoning that occurs because arguments that draw causal conclusions are inherently flawed because there may be another explanation for the stated relationship. This can occur by assuming a causal relationship on the basis of the sequence of events or when only a correlation exists. This can also occur due to failure to consider an alternate cause for the effect, an alternate cause for both the cause and the effect, or that the events may be reversed.

Mistaken Negation™: Negates both sufficient and necessary conditions, creating a statement that does not have to be true.

Mistaken Reversal™: Switches the elements in the sufficient and necessary conditions, creating a statement that does not have to be true.

Most (in Question Stems): In order to maintain test integrity the test makers need to make sure their credited answer choice is as airtight and defensible as possible. Imagine what would occur if a question stem, let us say a Weaken question, did not include a "most" qualifier: any answer choice that weakened the argument, even if only very slightly, could then be argued to meet the criteria of the question stem. A situation like this would make constructing the test exceedingly difficult because any given problem might have multiple correct answer choices. To eliminate this predicament, the test makers insert "most" into the question stem, and then they can always claim there is one and only one correct answer choice.

Most (in Formal Logic): A majority, and possibly all.

MP: See Main Point.

Must Be True: Must Be True questions ask you to identify the answer choice that is best proven by the information in the stimulus.
Question stem examples:
"If the statements above are true, which one of the following must also be true?"
"Which one of the following can be properly inferred from the passage?"

N: See Necessary Condition.

Necessary Condition (N): An event or circumstance whose occurrence is required in order for a sufficient condition to occur.

Negation: Negating a statement consists of creating the logical opposite of the statement. The logical opposite is the statement that denies the truth of the original statement, and a logical opposite is different than the polar opposite.

New Information: Information not mentioned explicitly in the stimulus of a Logical Reasoning question.

Not All: At least one is not, possibly all are not. Functionally equivalent to "some are not."

Not Block: Indicate that variables cannot be next to one another. Not-blocks only come into play once one of the variables has been placed.

Not Law™: Physically notate where a variable cannot be placed. Not Laws are very useful since it is essential that you establish the events that cannot be true in a game.

Not Necessarily True: The logical opposite of "Must be true." When an answer choice is not proven by the information in the stimulus.

NP: See Numbers and Percentages.

Numbers and Percentages (NP or #%): Numerical situations normally hinge on three elements: an overall total, a number within that total, and a percentage within the total. LSAT problems will often give you one of the elements, but without at least two elements present, you cannot make a definitive judgment about what is occurring with another element. When you are given just percentage information, you cannot make a judgment about numbers. Likewise, when you are given just numerical information you cannot make a judgment about percentages.

Numbers and Percentages Errors: A common error of reasoning that is committed when an author improperly equates a percentage with a definite quantity, or when an author uses quantity information to make a judgment about the percentage represented by that quantity.

Numerical Distribution: Allocates one set of variables among another set of variables. Numerical Distributions occur in every game except Mapping games.

Opposite Answer: Provides an answer that is completely opposite of the stated facts of the stimulus. Opposite Answers are very attractive to students who are reading too quickly or carelessly and quite frequently appear in Strengthen and Weaken questions.

Overloaded: Description of an Unbalanced game in which there are extra candidates for the available spaces.

Parallel Reasoning (in Logical Reasoning): Parallel Reasoning questions ask you to identify the answer choice that contains reasoning most similar in structure to the reasoning presented in the stimulus.
Question stem example:
"Which one of the following arguments is most similar in its pattern of reasoning to the argument above?"

Parallel Reasoning (in Reading Comprehension): These questions are usually broader in scope, asking you to find the scenario most analogous to an action in the passage. There is less of a focus on identifying premises and conclusions than in the Logical Reasoning section.

Partially Defined: There is a minimum and/or maximum number of variables to be selected, but the exact number of variables selected in the game cannot be determined.

Passage Organization (PO): These Reading Comprehension questions ask you to describe a characteristic of the overall structure of the passage. For example, "The second paragraph serves primarily to...," or "Which one of the following best describes the organization of the passage." These questions are similar to the Method of Reasoning questions in the Logical Reasoning section, but are generally broader.

Pattern: A variation on Linear games where the rules equally govern the general action of all variables, as opposed to the specific variable governance found in standard Linear games.

PO: See Passage Organization.

Point at Issue Questions: Point at Issue questions require you to identify a point of contention between two speakers, and thus these questions appear almost exclusively with two-speaker stimuli. Question stem example:
"Larew and Mendota disagree about whether"

Polar Opposite: A statement that is the extreme opposite of another. "Hot" and "cold" are polar opposites.

Premise: A fact, proposition, or statement from which a conclusion is made. Literally, the premises give the reasons why the conclusion should be accepted.

Primary Objectives™: A cohesive strategy for attacking any Logical Reasoning question. By consistently applying the objectives, you give yourself the best opportunity to succeed on each question.

Principle (PR): A broad rule that specifies what actions or judgments are correct in certain situations. These are not a separate question type but are instead an "overlay" that appears in a variety of question types and the presence of the Principle indicator serves to broaden the scope of the question.

Question Stem: Follows the stimulus and poses a question directed at the stimulus. Make sure to read the question stem very carefully. Some stems direct you to focus on certain aspects of the stimulus and if you miss these clues you make the problem much more difficult.

Random: A variable in a Logic Game that does not appear in any of the rules. Because randoms are not referenced in a rule, they are typically weaker players in the game.

Repeat Form: Simply restates the elements of a conditional statement in the original order they appeared. This creates a valid argument.

Resolve the Paradox Questions: Every Resolve the Paradox stimulus contains a discrepancy or seeming contradiction. You must find the answer choice that best explains the situation. Question stem example:

"Which one of the following, if true, would most effectively resolve the apparent paradox above?"

Reverse Answer: Occurs when an answer choice contains familiar elements from the stimulus, but rearranges those elements to create a new, unsupported statement.

Rules: In Logic Games, a set of statements that describe the relationships between the variables.

S: See Sufficient Condition

Scope: The range to which the premises and conclusion encompass certain ideas. An argument with a narrow scope is definite in its statements, whereas a wide scope argument is less definite and allows for a greater range of possibility.

Second Family: Consists of question types that take the answer choices as true and uses them to help the stimulus. Information outside the sphere of the stimulus is allowed in the correct answer choice. Includes the following question types: Assumption, Justify the Conclusion, Strengthen/Support, and Resolve the Paradox.

Sequencing Game: A game type where the rules do not fix the variables in exact positions but instead provide information about the relative order of the variables, as in "J was hired earlier than K."

Sequencing Rule: Establishes the relative ordering of variables. The key to differentiating a sequencing rule from a block rule is that block rules precisely fix the variables in relationship to each other (for example, one space ahead or two spaces in between) and sequencing rules do not.

Shell Game: An idea or concept is raised in the stimulus, and then a very similar idea appears in the answer choice, but the idea is changed just enough to be incorrect but still attractive. This trick is called the Shell Game because it abstractly resembles those street corner gambling games where a person hides a small object underneath one of three shells, and then scrambles them on a flat surface while a bettor tries to guess which shell the object is under.

SN: Abbreviation for Sufficient and Necessary Conditions. May be seen separately in diagramming as "S" and "N." See also Sufficient Condition and Necessary Condition.

Source Argument: A common error of reasoning that attacks the person (or source) instead of the argument they advance. Because the LSAT is concerned solely with argument forms, a speaker can never validly attack the character or motives of a person; instead, a speaker must always attack the argument advanced by a person.

Some: At least one, possibly all.

Some Are Not: At least one is not, possibly all are not. Functionally equivalent to "not all."

Specific Reference (SR): These Reading Comprehension questions provide you with a specific line reference or a reference to an easily found word or phrase within the passage. To attack the questions, refer to the line reference in the question and then begin reading about 5 lines above the reference.

Split-blocks: Indicates that there is a fixed number of spaces between two or more variables.

SR: See Specific Reference.

Stacks: In Logic Games, when two variable sets occur in the same position, one set of variables is diagrammed normally (identified as the base), while the other variable set is placed in slots above the initial slots, essentially "stacking" the variable sets and allowing for the appropriate relationship between variable sets.

Straw Man: A common error of reasoning that occurs when an author attempts to attack an opponent's position by ignoring the actual statements made by the opposing speaker and instead distorting and refashioning the argument, making it weaker in the process.

Stimulus: A short passage containing arguments taken from a variety of topics reflecting a broad range of academic disciplines (including letters to the editor, speeches, advertisements, newspaper articles and editorials, informal discussions and conversations, as well as articles in the humanities, the social sciences, and the natural sciences) that presents all of the necessary information to answer the subsequent question stem.

Strengthen/Support Questions: These questions ask you to select the answer choice that provides support for the author's argument or strengthens it in some way.
Question stem examples:
"Which one of the following, if true, most strengthens the argument?"
"Which one of the following, if true, most strongly supports the statement above?"

Sub-conclusion: A conclusion that is then used as a premise to support another conclusion. This is also known as a secondary or subsidiary conclusion.

Sufficient Condition (S): An event or circumstance whose occurrence indicates that a necessary condition must also occur. The sufficient condition does not make the necessary condition occur; it is simply an indicator.

Super-block: In Logic Games, when two or more block rules can be combined to produce a single diagram. Super-blocks tend to be quite powerful and often control the game.

Supporter: In the Supporter/Defender Assumption Model™, the Supporter Assumptions link together new or rogue elements in the stimulus or fill logical gaps in the argument.

Survey Errors: A common error of reasoning that occurs when a survey uses a biased sample, the survey questions are improperly constructed or the respondents to the survey give inaccurate responses. Surveys, when conducted properly, produce reliable results. However, surveys can be invalidated when any of these errors occur.

Templates: In Logic Games, when certain variables or blocks have a limited number of placement options, the best strategy is often to show the basic possibilities for each option. This powerful technique can sometimes quickly solve the game, and at the least it tends to reveal important information about the relationship between certain variables.

Third Family: Consists of question types that take the answer choices as true and uses them to hurt the stimulus. Information outside the sphere of the stimulus is allowed in the correct answer choice. Includes the following question type: Weaken.

Time Shift Errors: A common error of reasoning that involves assuming that conditions will remain constant over time, and that what was the case in the past will be the case in the present or future.

2-Value System: In Logic Games, a section where all variables must be used and each variable must be placed in exactly one of two groups. Powerful inferences can be drawn from the fact that when a variable is not in one group it must be in the other group (these inferences often involve the contrapositive).

Unbalanced: In a Defined game, when the number of variables to be selected is not equal to the overall number of available spaces. Unbalanced games are either Overloaded or Underfunded.

Uncertain Use of a Term or Concept: A common error of reasoning that occurs when the author uses a term or concept in different ways instead of using each term or concept in a constant, coherent fashion. This error is inherently confusing and undermines the integrity of the argument.

Undefined: When the number of variables to be selected for the game is not fixed, and is only limited by the total number of variables. Undefined games are generally the most difficult type of Grouping game.

Underfunded: Description of an Unbalanced game in which there are not enough candidates for the available spaces. This lack is almost always solved by reusing one or more of the candidates.

Variable Set: The set of people, places, things, or events that are involved in each game. The variables will be involved in an easy to understand activity such as sitting in seats or singing songs. It is very important to always write down and keep track of each variable set.

Variance Test™: Consists of supplying two polar opposite responses to the question posed in the answer choice and then analyzing how the varying responses affect the conclusion in the stimulus. If different responses produce different effects on the conclusion, then the answer choice is correct. If different responses do not produce different effects, then the answer choice is incorrect. The Variance Test can only be used with Evaluate the Argument questions.

Verticality: When a game is diagrammed in a vertical line (or setup), the relationship between the variables arranged vertically indicates adjacency, while the relationship of variables arranged horizontally indicates similarity. This is also true of verticality in blocks.

Weaken Questions: Weaken questions ask you to attack or undermine the author's argument. Question stem example:
> "Which one of the following, if true, most seriously weakens the argument?"

CONTACTING POWERSCORE

Contact Information

PowerScore International Headquarters:

PowerScore Incorporated
37V New Orleans Road
Hilton Head Island, SC 29928

Toll-free information: (800) 545-1750
Fax: (843) 785-8203
Website: www.powerscore.com
Email: lsat@powerscore.com

PowerScore LSAT Publications Information:

For information on the *LSAT Logic Games Bible*, *LSAT Logical Reasoning Bible*, *LSAT Reading Comprehension Bible*, *LSAT Deconstructed Series* or *LSAT Logic Games Ultimate Setups Guide*.

Website: www.powerscore.com/pubs.htm

PowerScore Full-length LSAT Course Information:

Complete preparation for the LSAT. Classes available nationwide.

Website: www.powerscore.com/lsat/lsat.htm
Request Information: www.powerscore.com/contact.htm

PowerScore Virtual LSAT Course Information:

Complete online preparation for the LSAT. Classes available worldwide.

Website: www.powerscore.com/lsat/virtual.htm
Request Information: www.powerscore.com/contact.htm

PowerScore Weekend LSAT Course Information:

Fast and effective LSAT preparation: 16 hour courses, 99th percentile instructors, and real LSAT questions.

Website: www.powerscore.com/lsat/weekend.htm
Request Information: www.powerscore.com/contact.htm

PowerScore LSAT Tutoring Information:

One-on-one meetings with a PowerScore LSAT expert.

Website: www.powerscore.com/lsat/tutoring.htm
Request Information: www.powerscore.com/contact.htm

PowerScore Law School Admissions Counseling Information:

Personalized application and admission assistance.

Website: www.powerscore.com/lsat/admissions.htm
Request Information: www.powerscore.com/contact.htm

INSTRUCTIONS FOR COMPLETING THE BIOGRAPHICAL AREA ARE ON THE BACK COVER OF YOUR TEST BOOKLET.
USE ONLY A NO. 2 OR HB PENCIL TO COMPLETE THIS ANSWER SHEET. DO NOT USE INK.

A

USE A NO. 2 PENCIL ONLY   ● Right Mark   ⊘⊗⊙ Wrong Marks

1 LAST NAME   FIRST NAME   MI

2 SOCIAL SECURITY/ SOCIAL INSURANCE NO.

3 LSAC ACCOUNT NUMBER

4 DATE OF BIRTH — MONTH DAY YEAR
Jan, Feb, Mar, Apr, May, June, July, Aug, Sept, Oct, Nov, Dec

5 RACIAL/ETHNIC DESCRIPTION
1 American Indian/Alaskan Native
2 Asian/Pacific Islander
3 Black/African Amer.
4 Canadian Aboriginal
5 Caucasian/White
6 Chicano/Mex. Amer.
7 Hispanic/Latino
8 Puerto Rican
9 Other

6 GENDER — Male / Female

7 DOMINANT LANGUAGE — English / Other

8 ENGLISH FLUENCY — Yes / No

9 TEST BOOK SERIAL NO.

10 TEST FORM

11 TEST DATE — MONTH DAY YEAR

12 CENTER NUMBER

13 TEST FORM CODE

Law School Admission Test

Mark one and only one answer to each question. Be sure to fill in completely the space for your intended answer choice. If you erase, do so completely. Make no stray marks.

SECTION 1, SECTION 2, SECTION 3, SECTION 4, SECTION 5 — questions 1–30, choices A B C D E

14 PLEASE PRINT ALL INFORMATION
LAST NAME   FIRST
SOCIAL SECURITY/SOCIAL INSURANCE NO.
DATE OF BIRTH
MAILING ADDRESS

NOTE: If you have a new address, you must write LSAC at Box 2000-C, Newtown, PA 18940 or call (215) 968-1001.

FOR LSAC USE ONLY — LR | LW | LCS

Copyright © 2004 BY LAW SCHOOL ADMISSION COUNCIL. ALL RIGHTS RESERVED. PRINTED IN U.S.A.

INSTRUCTIONS FOR COMPLETING THE BIOGRAPHICAL AREA ARE ON THE BACK COVER OF YOUR TEST BOOKLET.
USE ONLY A NO. 2 OR HB PENCIL TO COMPLETE THIS ANSWER SHEET. DO NOT USE INK.

A

USE A NO. 2 PENCIL ONLY   ● Right Mark   ⊘ ⊗ ⊙ Wrong Marks

1 LAST NAME / FIRST NAME / MI

2 SOCIAL SECURITY/ SOCIAL INSURANCE NO.

3 LSAC ACCOUNT NUMBER

4 DATE OF BIRTH

MONTH	DAY	YEAR
○ Jan		
○ Feb		
○ Mar		
○ Apr		
○ May		
○ June		
○ July		
○ Aug		
○ Sept		
○ Oct		
○ Nov		
○ Dec		

5 RACIAL/ETHNIC DESCRIPTION
- ○ 1 American Indian/ Alaskan Native
- ○ 2 Asian/Pacific Islander
- ○ 3 Black/African Amer.
- ○ 4 Canadian Aboriginal
- ○ 5 Caucasian/White
- ○ 6 Chicano/Mex. Amer.
- ○ 7 Hispanic/Latino
- ○ 8 Puerto Rican
- ○ 9 Other

6 GENDER
- ○ Male
- ○ Female

7 DOMINANT LANGUAGE
- ○ English
- ○ Other

8 ENGLISH FLUENCY
- ○ Yes   ○ No

9 TEST BOOK SERIAL NO.

10 TEST FORM

11 TEST DATE
MONTH / DAY / YEAR

12 CENTER NUMBER

13 TEST FORM CODE

Law School Admission Test

Mark one and only one answer to each question. Be sure to fill in completely the space for your intended answer choice. If you erase, do so completely. Make no stray marks.

SECTION 1 — 1–30 (A)(B)(C)(D)(E)

SECTION 2 — 1–30 (A)(B)(C)(D)(E)

SECTION 3 — 1–30 (A)(B)(C)(D)(E)

SECTION 4 — 1–30 (A)(B)(C)(D)(E)

SECTION 5 — 1–30 (A)(B)(C)(D)(E)

14 PLEASE PRINT ALL INFORMATION

LAST NAME / FIRST

SOCIAL SECURITY/SOCIAL INSURANCE NO.

DATE OF BIRTH

MAILING ADDRESS

NOTE: If you have a new address, you must write LSAC at Box 2000-C, Newtown, PA 18940 or call (215) 968-1001.

FOR LSAC USE ONLY		
LR	LW	LCS

Copyright © 2004 BY LAW SCHOOL ADMISSION COUNCIL. ALL RIGHTS RESERVED. PRINTED IN U.S.A.